# Unpartitioned Time

# Unpartitioned Time

*A Daughter's Story*

Malavika Rajkotia

SPEAKING TIGER BOOKS LLP
125A, Ground Floor, Shahpur Jat, near Asiad Village,
New Delhi 110049

First published by Speaking Tiger Books 2024



ISBN: 978-93-5447-949-6
eISBN: 978-93-5447-821-5

10 9 8 7 6 5 4 3 2 1

# Contents

# Prologue

*My husband Rakesh and I walk like children through the forests above Manali. We walk over streams and under waterfalls in Kothi. We stop at an apple orchard and drink cider from a bottle chilled in the icy stream.*

*We walk to Manali. My parents are there, as are my sister Ganeve and her husband Yousuf, with their two sons. My two children rush to us like fat puppies and snuggle up on our laps.*

*This is perfect, I think, as I look at the sun setting behind the distant mountains. I have everything and everyone.*

*Then I feel a chill. This is too much joy. I must be less joyous.*

*I snuggle closer to my children against the chill. We are entitled to be perfectly happy, I think, many people are absolutely happy. The sun drops suddenly behind the mountains. It is now dark, but an orange glow lights the horizon.*

*Still, I fear misfortune—no, it is evil I fear. I want to inhabit the domain of gentle goodness, but I can see that ugliness is everywhere.*

*'Well, it's not easy to be happy,' Jindo would tell me some years later, with the wisdom of his eight decades, 'Frankly,' he'd say, 'you have to be thick-skinned and quite stupid to be entirely happy, and you are neither.'*

*Jindo. My father.*

# PART I

# 1. My Father's Death

I brought in the year 2015 with a glass of red and retired to bed with *The Immortal Hero of Laziness: Oblomov*.

That description is not really true. The nineteenth-century Russian hero was not lazy. Lying down was his normal state.

The cover of the book, showing Oblomov lounging on a richly upholstered chaise, reminded me of my father. As I switched off my bedside light, I thought Papa's lifestyle could be called Jindoistic, a play on his nickname, Jindo. Like Oblomov was managed by the eccentric and truly lazy servant, Zakhar, my father had the diligent and loving chauffeur and majordomo, Daljit Singh. Like Oblomov, my father lived in reclining mode. From a sort of normal life, he began lounging more frequently—lying on a couch, or on a chair with feet up on a table, lying back in the car, and, eventually, paling to a boredom in which he couldn't be bothered to get out of bed.

'What is your ailment?' asked my mother.

'I suffer *araam*.' Indolence, ease, comfort, slowness. '*Araam*' could mean any of these things. And imply many others—like resignation, giving up, letting go. Which one of these did Jindo mean?

At two a.m., there was a knock on my door, and I knew even before my sister entered.

We sat silent on my bed for a short while before going into post-death work mode. Pull out a suitcase; is there any cash in the house? Order a large car for all of us to drive together; my sister, her husband and their two sons, and I with my two children.

It was about four a.m. when we left Delhi for Karnal.

# 2. The Karnal Delhi Road

The diffused light of dawn lit a dull, flat landscape cut by the highway, gleaming under randomly spaced streetlights. Until about thirty years ago, this single-carriageway witnessed an almost daily carnage that left heavy and light motor vehicles, bicyclists, and bullock carts in confused mangles.

Everyone had a personal story of loss on this road. Three of my family were killed in two separate accidents. A splintered windshield glass lodged in a young girl's throat. An aunt and cousin died when their car rammed into a truck to avoid a cyclist.

There was talk of ghostly cyclists and pedestrians, and even supernatural cars seen on foggy winter nights.

To my child's mind, the road was a portal for violent plunges into the unknown. It has been the site of wars for the last 400 years, and further back, it witnessed prehistoric and mythological battles where the victor's narrative could not eliminate the stories of the defeated, who live on as ghosts of alternate possibilities.

Which is why it made perfect sense that before every road journey, we stood in a circle around our grandmother, Bibiji, as she prayed for our safe return.

I sensed my father released to the continuity of the ancient road.

The night drive of our grief was on a clear road. Four a.m. is the hour between day traffic and night truckers. An early butter-yellow winter light evaporated the twilight ghosts.

For over 2,500 years, this road has streamed with traders from Central Asia, scholars from China, adventurers from Europe, sadhus from the Himalayas, and armies coveting Hindustan.

This portion of the road was the battlefield of the story of the eighteen-day Mahabharata war, marking the cusp of the end of the Dwapar Yuga and the rise of the Kali Yuga. Eighteen days of soldiers' cries and trumpeting elephants and neighing horses, each ending with sunsets blackened by smoke from the funeral pyres hanging heavy until impelled by the sounds of wailing women.

From myth, we come to somewhat recorded history in 300 BCE, when Chandragupta Maurya built this road to connect his fast-growing kingdom, spanning the north of the subcontinent from the source of the Ganga to its northwestern limits.

The road was developed by Sher Shah Suri. My father remembered the time when it was called 'Jarnailly Sadak' under the British, and then G.T. Road, its official name, The Grand Trunk Road.

The government of independent India called it Sher Shah Suri Marg, the Sanskrit 'marg' guillotining the English 'road' and the Urdu 'sadak'.

'At least they did not say Sher Shah Suri puth,' I said to my father, 'that's a tongue twister.'

'Thank God they did not say something about feet on the road; then it would be pudd,' my father said with his poker face that was sometimes funnier than the joke. (Pudd means fart in Punjabi).

Now, it is NH1, National Highway 1, a single-carriageway that has grown into a broad four-lane highway with bridges flying over the clogged traffic of villages and towns. Modern India could have named it after Chandragupta Maurya. 'Maurya Marg' has a nice, balanced ring to it that serves what used to be a hidden purpose—eliminating Muslim presence from the historical narrative in the grand plan of connecting (or creating) selected points in history to form a carefully crafted picture of Hindu India.

So flowed the road till the careless, callous Radcliffe Line severed the muscle of a 2,500-year-old continuum, flinging the western portion across a river of blood to be called Pakistan, which my parents still talked of as home.

---

# 3. Riffyujeez

The country watched those partitioned pummelled and humiliated, murdered and tortured and raped to fit on either side of this blood-stained sarhad.

The refugee also became the subject of jokes.

When Neil Armstrong landed on the moon, he arrived at a colony of Punjabis.

'When did you get here?' he asked.

'After Partition.'

In the immediate aftermath, the refugees did not talk much, perhaps for fear of losing or tainting their cherished memories, locked within themselves as precious possessions, only to be taken out sometimes. A photo album of people and places whose pain of exile had bleached them to a sepia tone.

To preserve a memory of their moorings, my family called themselves Rajkotias, literally, from Rajkot, Pakistan. And in the town of Karnal, they built a home that they called Rajkot House. In nearby Jundla, my father tilled the banjar land that had been allotted to them as token compensation for the vast lands and homes they had left in Pakistan.

Jundla and Karnal were on and about the same road that led to Lahore and Rajkot in Pakistan.

This border, a mere seventy years old, cannot partition the wheat and rice-laden breezes that whisper ancient stories and songs, sung in Punjabi laced with Persian and Urdu to the eight-beat dhol rhythm, the spirit of these regions, shaped by millennia-old accounts of valiant battles against hordes arriving over the mountains to reach the richly watered and wealthy plains below them.

---

## 4. My Father on Death

I knew my father was happy to go. He had lain in bed for years, as if to signal death to hurry to him.

'Do you still suffer depression, Papa?' I had asked a few years ago.

'No,' he said, reclining on his side, facing me but seeming to ruminate on something beyond. 'Couldn't be better,' he said, even while I knew he lived in the penumbra between being sleepy while awake and awake while sleeping.

As he dozed, intermittently startled by his own snores, I reached for some books on his bedside table.

One was a collection of poems by Farid that opened as if to the most read page:

*Farida tann sukka pinjar thia,*
*Tallain khundey kaag,*
*Ajai so rabb na bahudiyo,*
*Dekh bandey ke bhaag.*

Farida's flesh has dried to a bony cage,
The crows peck at the soles of his feet,
Even so, he has not experienced the force of God,
What a woeful fate.

I lay close to my father's sleeping form, and sensing me, he smiled and patted my hand, even while his eyes remained shut.

He was undoubtedly done with life, but in contrast to Farid's anguished wait for death, he had developed a prosaic, practical preparedness for it.

It was a plan every morning. A typical conversation with my mother would go like this:

He: 'This is it. Today, I will be on my way. What's your programme?'

She: 'Oh! I was planning to go to a kitty party, but if you are leaving today, I guess I should stay.'

He: 'Oh, no, no. No! Go ahead!' And they would both laugh.

Or it could be:

He: 'We need a bigger generator that works all the air conditioners in the house.'

She: 'We don't really need it.'

He: 'We do. We shouldn't have to worry if we have a house full of guests.'

She: 'We have not had a house full in years!'

He: 'Even so...'

She: 'OK! Let the crop come in...'

He: 'I might be dead by then.'

She: 'I promise, we won't get a generator after you are dead. You won't miss anything.'

And they would both laugh.

Or,

He: 'Is so-and-so still alive?'

She: 'Yes.'

He: 'Get me his number.'

The call is put through, and Papa will say, 'Chal, yaar, let's go.'

Or he could say, 'Oye! You are still here? Don't go without me.'

The only person who did not find this funny was Papa's brother, older by four years. For me, Tayaji, and for Papa, his Bha.

'What's your plan, Bha?' It was clear that Papa did not mean a holiday or a career.

'I have no plan. I intend to be around for a while,' his Bha would say, as always impatient with Papa's self-indulgence. Tayaji survived my father by three years.

═══════

# 5. What Will the Body Wear?

My father lay on his bed, in death as in life, head slightly propped up on billowing pillows. For a fractional moment, I expected he would, as usual, reach out his arms to hold me close and long. But his final stillness asserted itself.

My sister, Ganeve, I, and our four children hugged him for the last time, and then we sat, just looking, to allow for what we saw to soak into our being. Shock will become grief.

Around us, people began streaming in...talk of funeral arrangements. And then the final question, the irony never dwelt upon. What will he wear?

'What colour should his turban be?' we asked our mother.

An old, toothless lady with a knitted scarf on her head commented that it was not seemly to wear a turban to the other world. One must enter the other world with humility, in the natural state, she said. Another lady disagreed, 'The turban is essential; after all, we are Sikhs.'

Mama remembered having recently asked him to wear a turban instead of the usual muslin headcloth he had taken to.

'*Nahi, hun tey ikko vari safa bandh kay javanga.*' (No! I will now wear a turban only the one last time.)

That ended all discussion. He expected to wear a turban and so he must. Through my grief, I chided myself for the particular pleasure in pointedly ignoring the advice of the toothless lady. Ganeve said, 'Let's get his school colour, turquoise blue, firozee.'

His body was bathed by his caregivers. They brought my Papa out, looking perfectly beautiful in a firozee turban and a fine white cotton salwar kurta with a yellow shawl around his shoulders.

Papa's closed lids only lightly covered the twinkling mischief of his eyes, but on his mouth still played a half smile. His right fist was still half closed. That was Mama's joke. She would massage his hand, 'You must learn to open your fist. You say you want to die, but your fist is closed like that of a newborn baby.'

Papa's hands are strong, with broad palms, and his bare feet are slender and long, with a surprisingly delicate arch in a man over six feet tall. Twenty years ago, I had rushed to an emergency ward where he was after a heart attack. From the door, I could see a series of feet on a row of beds and went unerringly to the right pair of unusually beautiful feet.

His luxuriant grey beard enhances a strong, fine-featured face, beautiful in death's repose. My family is very good-looking, and I always felt cheated of this legacy. Ganeve has Mama's high cheekbones, fine, balanced features, and spare body. I often complained that I looked like Papa, with knobs that, too, were singularly unspectacular.

He was offended: 'It's a good thing to look like me, I was the most handsome man in the world.'

He used to tell the story of the stranger who approached him at the Imperial Hotel in Delhi: 'Chalo, Sardarji, Bombay!'

'I might have considered it,' Papa would say, 'had he not said that I would have to cut my hair and shave my beard.'

Once, a guest at a dinner party at my home in Delhi saw Papa's photo in my drawing room. 'Who is this? He looks familiar.'

'My father,' I said, feeling a smile growing inside me as I walked over to look at the picture with him.

'He is magnificently regal. What is his name?'

'Jitinder Singh.'

He shook his head as if he could not quite place him.

'Your friends in Calcutta knew him,' I said. 'Many years ago, he tried a mining business there. It failed, but he earned the name "Duke" for his stylish ways.'

'Duke was your father?' asked the guest.

'Yes,' I said, and he looked at me with respect, admiration, and affection, all at once.

Papa's charm was well known. He was affable with men, but it was women who brightened his eyes. My mother, after the initial sulking, had gotten used to what she then began calling his 'shyama nazar'.

I have seen the most stern and strict sardarni melt into a coy heap with his gallant ways. That always made me laugh, and Papa could never conceal his enjoyment of my laughter.

Over the last several months, he had regular telephone calls from a woman who sold insurance. Papa would listen to her prepared spiel and then tell her, 'I am a very old man and so cannot be insured, but thank you; you spoke well.'

She kept up the routine calls every other week or so. If Mama picked up the phone, she would hand it to him, saying, 'Your friend,' and he would listen and say, 'I am a very old man, and so cannot be insured, but thank you; you spoke well.'

A friend of mine saw Papa for the first time just a year before he died; he was sitting up in bed and smiled and said Sat Sri Akal in his strong, deep voice.

'My God, sir! You are so handsome, how beautiful you are,' she flirted. Papa looked at her in his special way and said, 'I used to be very good-looking.'

'You still are,' she said, and that made him happy for a while.

Papa understood women, and, sensing his understanding, they liked him very much. As a child, his favourite playmate was a girl cousin, and Papa would ask that his long hair be braided into plaits like hers. Bibi was her nickname, and she called him Beeb.

They were friends till his death. She would visit him in Karnal to urge him to walk. 'Come on, Beeb,' she would say, and to humour her, he would allow two helpers to hold him up while he moved his legs in the air to pretend he was walking.

She arrived from Chandigarh for the funeral—and must have started the drive to Karnal the moment she heard. At eighty-five, she is of imposing countenance and has a confidence that comes from a life where beauty and elegant comportment are treated as separate virtues.

## 6. The Funeral

'He wanted you girls to perform the last rites,' my mother said. 'He said you were better than any son. Ganeve, you do the water and ghada ritual, and Chippy, you light the pyre.'

Neither Ganeve nor I had seen a funeral pyre. Traditionally, only men attend cremation rituals. I had been glad for that when Rakesh died at thirty-nine. To walk with the lifeless thing that my husband had left behind seemed futile, and the thought drained me of any residual energy that I was desperate to conserve for my children. With Rakesh, death struck sharp and cruel, turning the atmosphere thick and stagnant with the smell of tragedy around his heavy stillness.

But Papa's eighty-five-year-old form seemed to glow with a flame deep within ice, calling for me to be with him and happy that we were all around him on what is called 'the last journey'.

I placed a steadying hand on his body, lurching with the movement of the hearse. A dead body evokes a respect deeper than to the living: the dead seem to know more.

Papa discussed death as a personal, fond friend waiting for him, and whether he was serious or not was left to the listener to decide; he did not feel bound to seem rational.

Looking at him, a part of me was relieved that Papa had left before my mother. I used to worry that Ganeve and I would not have the wherewithal or patience that is beyond love to look after him the way our mother did.

As he grew older, my sister and I lived with the unspoken question: which of us would move to Karnal to look after him? It would be easy to bring him to Delhi, but we both knew he would be miserable cabined in a Delhi apartment.

He needed vast space around him. A large compound, in which is a large house, in which he lay on a large bed, ruminating on death.

## 7. Living with Death

Rain defines Punjabi life; the equivalent of 'fasting or feasting' here is expressed in rain terms. '*Hadd ya sauka*', flood or drought. I wandered around the house, sensing my father lingering in the physical gap. A gentle rain began, the sound a sign from him to wash away the grief of the house.

A winter rain prepares the soil for wheat planting to begin on the first full moon of January.

We throw puffed corn in a fire five times, chanting:

*Issar aye,*
*Dalidar jaye.*

Let good energy come,
Let stagnation go.

In Karnal, the ritual happened in the outdoor brick tandoor, but the kitchen stove must suffice in my Delhi flat.

As with recovering alcoholics, Papa, but for a few lapses, had not had a drink in the last four decades. But at the end of his life, he enjoyed an occasional glass of red wine, over which he would recount his carousing days, 'A servant was opening a new bottle of Dimple scotch for me and said, "Sardar Sahib, I like this bottle. Give it to me when you are done." I told him to take it in a few hours.'

The day he died, I found a half-full wine glass on his bedside table. Ganeve and I drank from it as from a chalice, the last physical contact with him.

I then sat on the verandah outside my father's bedroom, cupping a glass of steaming, strong, sweet tea that pulled me into my body.

Be in the present moment, says everyone and everything I have read. But how does one disconnect the present from the moments that lead to it? How does one separate one drop from the infinite drops in the ocean, swirling and churning as crests and troughs?

I used to think these things:

'Bibiji, look at the water flowing from the tap. It will go from here to the drain, to a bigger canal, to a river, to a sea, and all the water everywhere is connected.'

'Bibiji, if God made us, who made God?'

'Don't think so much,' Bibiji would say. 'You will go mad.'

Bibiji had good reason to worry about madness. My father had had a bout of something that we would call a generic depression, but I am sure there were finer, sharper definitions if we had asked the doctor to label it. Fearful of his own drug and alcohol hallucinations, he had admitted himself to the Ranchi Mental Asylum. From there, he wrote to my mother:

*I am better. Don't send me the sweater you say you have knitted for me. I will be back soon.*

His letters were like that. Years later, he used to write the same kind to me in boarding school: terse but strangely reassuring.

*Dear Chippy,*

*It is raining. Rain is good for the farm.*

*Your Papa.*

Papa returned from Ranchi functional enough to exist in a stagnant pool of small-town inactivity. But his melancholies would encircle him from time to time, as a snake with its tail in its mouth, allowing for no exit till it decided to slither away, only to return and grip him again with renewed vigour.

We would wait for those moments of respite before the snake returned. The memory of the moments of lightness rendered the next bout of depression even more unbearable for all of us. Though Papa tried to conceal his tumult under a big, benign manner, I could always hear his inner noise.

Over the years, but when I was still quite small, perhaps by his fortieth year, he was done with the external distractions of alcohol and recreational drugs but stayed with prescription medicine until we, his daughters, were properly settled in our own lives. Upon which he set to do what he had always wanted to do: lie down.

There is an apocryphal tale about lying down.

Coming upon an Indian fakir lying on the path of his mighty army, Alexander asked, 'Why are you lying down?'

'It is the best position.'

'But life is about activity,' said Alexander. 'Look at me—blazing victorious over many countries from my home in a distant land, I have arrived.'

'What are you going to do now?' asked the fakir.

'I am going to conquer your country.'

'And then what?'

'I will then conquer the world.'

'And then what?'

'I will become the richest and the most powerful person.'

'And then what?'

'Then I will relax,' said Alexander.

'That is what I am doing now,' said the yogi.

The story resonated with me, seeing Papa's refusal to engage in frenetic activity. He justified it to us as his realisation of a larger universe that did not require very hard work. He would quote the Bible to us, 'Be as the lilies of the valley; they do not toil.'

The one time we did persuade him to do some exercise, he chose the yogic pose of shavasana but got it awfully wrong. A while later, we saw him tottering down the stairs from his bedroom.

'What happened?!' I asked.

'I tried the shavasana,' he said, through a tight, taut, pained face, 'I tightened each muscle too much.'

'Tight! You tightened each muscle, Papa? You are supposed to relax!'

'Who ever heard of a relaxed corpse?' said Papa, 'What about rigor mortis?' You did not argue with that logic.

Another odd bid for exercise by him was to jog, but he was also by then addicted to the rosary that he wanted to tell 108 times a day. He had little else to do and could easily have done both these things at different times, but he did not, and one did not ask why.

Thus, he chose to jog barefoot while telling the beads. Of course, then came the inevitable stress fracture. The doctor said while applying the plaster, consoling in a jocular, companionate fashion, 'It's happened to all of us, Sardarji, one too many and a twisted ankle on an uneven path.'

I looked at Papa and he gestured to not say anything. A drunken totter seemed, somehow, more respectable than crazy barefoot jogging while telling beads.

Papa believed that in God's plan, the dead lived with us in a different dimension. God existed (with the dead) as a free, all-encompassing, undivided, uncontrolled, *something* that need not be seen to know it's there.

I was thirty-six when my thirty-nine-year-old husband, Rakesh, died. Our children were three-and-a-bit and two-and-a-bit years old. We used to sleep with the girl between us on the bed and the boy on a cot next to my side of the bed—the same cot that Papa had got made when I was born.

Rakesh woke me up and said he was not feeling well. I gave him a glass of water and saw that he was not able to reach for it.

'I am calling the doctor,' I said.

He looked at me and nodded. And that was our last exchange. I stood at my balcony, shouting for the servants, and even called out to the house opposite, where the doctor lived.

'Bahadur, Bahadur! *Koi hai*? Doctor, doctor!'

I heard a crash behind me in the room. Rakesh had fallen to the floor. The children were standing on the bed, holding each other and crying.

I called Amma, their nanny, to take them to the next room. I knelt beside Rakesh and tried to shake him; I tried to give mouth-to-mouth resuscitation. I should have pumped the chest, but in my shock, did not think of it.

Bahadur came up and put his hand under Rakesh's nose. 'It's not what you think,' he said. I just looked at him. The doctor who lived next door arrived and, without touching him, said, 'Oho, oho.'

The other doctor, who lived opposite (also called Rakesh and who also died untimely a few years later), said, 'No, no.'

'We will give the adrenaline shot straight to the heart.'

Nothing.

'Can't be true,' Rakesh the doctor said, 'Let's take him to the hospital,' it has some machine (I can't remember which). We carried him in the car, but he was so heavy. It's called dead weight, my mind said, but I refused to think of that and just did as they asked.

We reached the hospital, and they did what they do in the movies when the doctor says, 'Stand back,' and there is a current. I was there. Rakesh the doctor said, 'Go out.'

I said, 'No.'

'Please,' he said. The nurse took me out, and I paced the floor like Papa had done when we were waiting for my sister to be born. But this was anxiety and dread, not anticipation as he felt when pacing as an expectant father and I, a sister. Here, I knew even as I paced that there was no hope.

A few minutes later, the doctors came out, looking serious and sad. I had known he was dead. But somewhere, I still could not believe it.

I had to do something but did not know what to do, so I screamed and crouched on the floor. One scream, that's all. It was odd even to me. I know it was a conscious thing I did because

I did not know what to do. Then, after that one scream, I got up, walked to the car. Rakesh's body was in the back, and I sat in front and I turned and patted Rakesh as if to console him.

We reached the house. They took the body out on a sheet, I think, I can't remember—maybe a mattress? The neighbours had come in by then and taken over.

I was still in a night suit and dressing gown, and Dr. Verma's wife said, 'You need to change. I will come with you.' I took her to my bedroom. The floor by his side of the bed was strewn with syringes. I opened my cupboard and remember thinking: *How odd that Mrs. Verma gets to see my clothes. Never would I have imagined that.*

The bottom shelf had clothes bundled up. That's where I used to put boring Indian wear for solemn ceremonies. I chose the nicest salwar-qameez.

'Do you want to shower?'

'No,' I said. It seemed too much of an effort. Even to change was difficult. I was surprised at how slow and lumbering my body felt.

I walked down and sat by Rakesh's body. I did not know what to do, so I just patted his shoulder as one would a sleeping child.

My sister was not in town.

I called my cousin. Those were the days of the landlines, though the cell phone had arrived, too. 'Hello,' she said. It was five in the morning. I could not speak. I could not say Rakesh is dead. I just could not, and that's when the tears flowed. I still could not say 'dead'. 'I have lost Rakesh,' I said. 'What, Chippy? I am coming.' She later told me that her husband said, 'No, no, he can't be dead. They must have fought.'

'He is dead,' said Kitten. 'Chippy does not cry easily. She won't cry over a fight.'

Friends came. Someone took over. I just sat.

Someone I had not met in years turned up and started organising the ice for the body. We would wait for Rakesh's family to arrive from England, and his sister from America. Rakesh's uncles and aunt, who lived in Delhi, arrived. His grandmother, who lived with us, must have told them.

Then someone said, 'We need to tell your parents.'

'Don't tell them on the phone,' and I gave the number of a neighbour.

I was told that my parents were having morning tea on the verandah and were delighted by the surprise visit from the neighbours. And then they were told.

It was late morning. I got up to see my children's breakfast. Mamta, our cook, was feeding them bread dipped in soft-boiled egg and chocolate milk.

I smiled and sat and had them sit awhile on my lap. I felt a stirring of life through the love for my children.

My parents arrived by afternoon. I was lying down on my bed with the children. My sister, too, arrived.

The room had been cleaned and was fresh and calm; it looked out to a clear blue sky and the treetops in the park outside.

I heard my parents. They had climbed to the second floor. For my father, that was an amazing effort, I remember thinking.

I felt a second surge of life through love as I hugged them and my sister. They were not crying. They could not, just as I could not. Tears are too simple. They just would not fall. They were frozen with my shock. My shock was cold and freezing like the ice on which Rakesh lay. I did not go see him there except when I stood at the door once and looked for a long time.

I went and sat with my parents. I had not slept and just remember thinking, just a few hours ago, this had not happened and I was happy and fighting with him because he had woken up the children and played with them. They had giggled and laughed, and I had got irritated because I would have to get them back to bed. He left to sit with the house guest downstairs, but the children went back to sleep, and I fell asleep with them.

I was thinking all this, and then I said aloud the thought that came to me in my core language, Punjabi, '*Yakeen nahi aa raya, Mama.*' And Mama started crying, and I still did not.

Someone asked for towels because the ice was melting. 'I will get them,' Mama said, 'Just tell me where they are.' And I did.

Then his parents and sister arrived, and in their grief, I remember thinking, my children are safe. Their loss is worse than mine.

And that's my point about the death of a spouse. It is not worse than the death of a child. I had only been with him nine years.

Is it as painful as the death of a sibling? I have spent fifty-eight of my sixty-two years with Ganeve, so, yes, if she predeceases me, I will be shattered, as will she when I go.

But children: I lived for my children, and so, I still believe that the loss of my family-in-law was greater than my own.

I tried to explain Papa's belief in the dead being among us to my three-year-old daughter and two-year-old son after their father died. 'He is here with us,' I said as we snuggled together under our razai on a winter night. 'See my hand, touch it,' I said, loving their chubby hands in mine.

'Now see, I put it under our razai. Just because you don't see, it does not mean it's not there.'

The 'it' that never dies but only changes form; the unseen remainder 'shesha', the serpent seat upon which reclines Vishnu, ruminating upon the world he owns, head propped up by one hand, the other resting upon one raised knee. Just like Papa's frequent posture.

Is there an all-explanatory entity? And does it have a form, or is it formless? Is it external or internal? Is it an all-pervasive energy that encompasses everything that we know and do not know yet? Or is it something apart from everything we know? Or is it one thing among everything we do not yet know? Or is it everything that is actually one whole that collapses into a core silence that cannot be described and so is called nothing and that nothing is everything? Shunya: the core nothingness around, or within, which is everything.

―――――

# 8. After the Funeral

The pyre had smouldered for two days. A priest scrabbled among the ashes, looking for a bone that he held up triumphantly, 'This is sukh ram, the sign that he has attained nirvana.' But I thought that a bit much.

We went to Gurudwara Kiratpur Sahib to immerse the ashes.

It is a white marble building along which flows the Sutlej. On that day, the river mirrored the clouds, blue-black shot with the yellow sparkle of a mild sun, trickling as a promise of eventual healing.

*There must be something more than this life,* I thought; but a woman's cries as she emptied a bag of bone and ash into the river made me feel guilty for my momentary comfort. *That is a mother's wail,* I thought. *When will she find peace?*

As I emptied my silk bag containing my father into the water, I did not say what the bhaiji had told us to. I did not say, 'Laoh, Papa, be on your way.' Through a fresh flow of tears at this final physical letting go, I could only say the Sikh greeting of parting but also meeting, 'Sat Sri Akal,' the almighty is truth, and the truth is almighty.

'Sat Sri Akal,' I said and watched the river folding the bones within its waves and carrying my father very fast as if it knew where he wanted to go. From Kiratpur to meet the Beas near Amritsar and the Chenab, and flow into Pakistan, and thence onwards into the Arabian Sea, into which had also flowed his beloved Persian poets.

The bhaiji's voice carried the words, sung in Raga Ramkali, from the gurudwara to the river:

*The wind merges into the wind, the light into the light,*
*The earth and dust unite, the weepers gather to acknowledge this,*
*Who has died, oh! Who has died?*
*Meditate to be learned about the universe,*
*No one knows the next step; even those who weep will go the same way,*
*Bound by fear and love, their worldly dreams blind them,*
*This, too, is the god's creation,*
*And the creator orders that beings come and go,*
*Thus, there is no dying and death,*
*Whoever knows this is satisfied,*
*O Nanak, teach me that there is no death.*

The certainty of death is the melding with 'that'. The truth of 'that', mystics tell us, cannot be described. The path to 'it' leads to a jungle of mystery and legend, the epics and mythology and philosophy and science and yoga and meditation and meditative living.

The journey has many distractions, each promising to be the purpose of life and allurements that question the need for purpose. There is no way of knowing when one has arrived at 'it', which, all said and done, is but a perception, easily distorted by the perceiver's idea of who she is.

The journey begins with the dismantling of self; ancient Indian philosophers called it nyeti. I am not my history, my family, my property, nor my education, friends, career, earnings. I am not even my tangible self, my body or any part of it; I am not even my beliefs, or even my idea of self, I am none of these: I am what remains.

This meditation is important, say the wise, even while warning against self-absorption, which creates houmay (ego), bloating the self to a deadly tumour, feeding on stupidity, and thoughtless and selfish acts that destroy humanity even within the self.

*Kar sadhu anjuli pun vadda hai,*
*Kar dandavat pun vadda hai,*
*Sakat har ras sadh na janey tin antar houmay kanda hai,*
*Jeo jeo challey chubhey dukh pavey,*
*Jamkal sahar sir danda hai.*

The prayer of hands extended humbly is great,
There is greatness in prostration of humility.
Those who do not know this are afflicted by the thorn of the ego,
The thorn hurts the afflicted person,
That hammering on the head is the worst punishment in the world.

The call of 'who am I?' is answered by this painful thorn that knows its fragility against the True Seeker, burning through artifice to reach a deep recess that connects to similar pools within everything and everyone else.

Wading into the pool of introspection, the first thought in the shallows is that we are identified by culture and a lineage that one can be proud of (or not), but that is only a context for the 'I', which is actually part of the 'it' of the universe.

The bold shed their artificial 'I' to strike out to unknown depths and onwards, to the point from where the return is as exhausting as getting to that point...till, perhaps, the realisation of the point where the answer is not 'found' but reverberates as a sense that cannot be dressed in words.

What remains after shedding it all, everything I know, or can see, or believe, or perceive, all that I am part of? I am my own consciousness that is part of a larger consciousness, *Aham Brahmasmi*: I am two birds, the one that eats and works and nests, and the other, deeper, self that watches the eating and working and nesting.

The Guru Granth Sahib uses the same analogy.

*Shalok, Third Mehl (Guru's contribution)*: 'How rare is the dervish, the Saintly renunciate, who understands renunciation! Cursed is the life, and cursed are the clothes of one who wanders around, begging, from door to door. But if he abandons hope and anxiety, and as Gurmukh receives the Name as his charity, then Nanak washes his feet and is a sacrifice to him.

'O Nanak, the tree has one fruit, but two birds are perched upon it. They are not seen coming or going; these birds have no wings. One enjoys so many pleasures, while the other, through the Word of the Shabad, remains in nirvana. Imbued with the subtle essence of the fruit of the Lord's Name, O Nanak, the soul bears the True Insignia of God's Grace.'

*Pauri (the conceptual staircase)*: 'He Himself is the field, and He Himself is the farmer. He Himself grows and grinds the corn. He Himself cooks it, He Himself puts the food in the dishes, and He Himself sits down to eat. He Himself is the water, He Himself gives the toothpick, and He Himself offers the mouthwash. He Himself calls and seats the congregation, and He Himself bids them goodbye. One whom the Lord Himself blesses with His Mercy—the Lord causes him to walk according to His Will.'

Easy to say all of the above to comfort myself, but I could

not forget the woman's wail. I wondered, worried, and ached over when she would feel better. For tragedy is not in death but in its timing.

## 9. Non-Settling

My father's introspection was water churning with the strife of two vastly different lives: before 1947, and after.

Before the actual lying down, my father had led a sort of normal life. He used to drive, run some errands, and visit our schools to charm the teachers and sit through our plays but, all through, there was no doubt that his chosen leitmotif was laidback. Till he just...lay down.

The same attitude pervaded his method of farming. Bapuji, my maternal grandfather, asked my mother, 'So, Bibaji, (daughter) Sardar Sahib (he always called his son-in-law thus) goes to the farm every day?'

'Bapuji, please ask whether he goes there at all.'

'Oh,' said Bapuji, 'what is needed is management. The British managed to rule sitting far away; he does not really need to be there himself.'

My mother later told me, 'Bapuji has loved your father ever since he heard him quote from the Guru Granth Sahib to describe his life; '*Kai kot baithey hi khai,*' many beings just sit and eat, in contrast to others, '*Kai kot galaahi thak pai,*' many beings work themselves to exhaustion.'

An aunt would make fun of my father's lethargic visits to the farm.

'He wears his brown cords and boots up to his knees and Daljit Singh drives him to the farm.

"Choudhry Sahib," he will ask the manager, "everything is all right?"

"Jee, Sahib," Choudhry will reply.

"Chalo, Daljit Singh, let's go back."

He might as well have gone barefoot,' my aunt said.

We tried to explain my father's eccentricities as the effect of Partition that perhaps exacerbated his inner wound, the one we all have: the wound from the time the universe shattered from the whole into thousands of billions of pieces of matter, yearning to heal by uniting again.

Papa and I did not really have too many deep, flowing talks that revealed such insights. I learned the most while listening to him talk to others.

He worried about the staff. *'Dil lag gaya?'* he would ask, and when they nodded and smiled, you could see that he felt happy. He was very protective of them in an old, feudal manner. 'Don't talk to my staff like that,' he told a visiting sardar, who was rude to the bearer who dropped some tea on him.

I saw him tough only once: he sacked a farm worker who had lied about his leave and did not return for the crucial time of harvest. When the worker did return, I saw him sitting on his haunches in the driveway where Papa was strolling, as was his wont.

'He is crying,' I told Papa, wanting him to take him back. 'He is a rogue and he will find another place very soon, don't worry about him,' said Papa, and that was that.

Papa's politics would be central-liberal, I suppose. He feared the communists for obvious reasons, having said which, my nana, also from the same class and background, embraced communism. My nana gifted me a subscription to the Punjabi newsletter *Gadar* to practice reading the script. Papa stopped the subscription because he worried about its influence on me.

This was the only time I saw him worried or trying to influence my reading.

He preferred the Americans to the Russians even while telling me about their racist society. I knew about white supremacists and the Ku Klux Klan and the importance of Brown vs. Board of Education just in my early teens.

Many times, I learned not so much from discussions but from stories, narrated to me but as if speaking aloud to himself. They were his thoughts, ruminations that I listened into.

Bibiji had an American tenant for a house she built in Delhi with a windfall received from a change in succession laws that benefited her as a female heir of a deceased relative. Kelsen was his name. He visited us in Karnal. He thought Ganeve was the most beautiful child he had seen. Ganeve, who did not understand English, still got that and insisted Kelsen be given more cake.

Papa spoke of corruption to Kelsen, and Kelsen solemnly stated that there is a lot of corruption in America, too, and we felt quite better about our country.

'We are much better off here, are we not, Papa?' I asked. 'Yes, I think so; we are lucky, I guess.' That was always said with a tinge of sadness because our state of being was not attributed to any talent but just luck. So easy not to have been lucky.

We got our electric coffee percolator samovar from Kelsen when he left and I used it in Delhi till just a few years ago. I have never found one that looks so beautiful. The coffee would bubble and spread its presence in the entire room and the sound and the smell were very comforting.

*

After Partition, my father's family tried to reattach their context to a chunk of rocky, barren land (*Pahari banjar*, as described in the revenue records) in village Jundla, District Karnal.

He lived on the farm in the early days with what I would call Jindoistic anonymity: resigned. It is as it is, so be it. There is acceptance, and hence, no desperate need to scurry around and fight and politic to be socially relevant.

This was perhaps his transition moment beyond provenance and identities: comfortable in the belief that we are all going the same way and that everything only changes its form. The teachings of the Guru Granth Sahib nourished our household. There are eighty-four lakh joons, Bibiji used to say, and we could be reborn as any one of them: a plant, a tree, a stone, or a grain of dust in a mountain or plain or desert or by a stream; or a drop of water in it, or just a leaf, or an animal. The Buddha and the Jain Tirthankaras had explored the same idea and concluded that the chance of being reborn as a human is as rare as the chance of a turtle getting lassoed by a free-floating rope in the ocean.

All is one spirit that rests in well-mannered quiet to be sensed as the breeze, rippling water, or swaying trees, or when caressing our faces. It is elegant and subtle, but it is all-encompassing of the seen bound by the unseen.

*Tithey khand mandal varbhand,*
*Jey ko kathey ta mant na ant,*
*Tithey loh loh aakar,*
*Jiv jiv hukam tivey tiv kaar,*
*Vekhey vigsay kar veechar,*

All of creation and the solar systems are part of the embodiment
    of truth,
Whatever you can say, there is always more; it is that which cannot
    be said that is infinite;
There are many patterns of which we are a part;
This pattern of creation acts according to its inner order,
See it, experience it, think about it,
To see, one needs prayer and humility.

There was always prayer in our house. Ganeve and I learned Gurmukhi for a 500-rupee reward from our grandmother, so we would be able to read the big book.

I would recite aloud while Bibiji accompanied me, under her breath.

'I don't understand it,' I said to her.

'*Rutt lai*—just learn it by rote.' The sense will emerge when the song settles in your heart.

'Do you understand?' I asked one night, lying next to her.

'A lot more than I used to; you just have to keep saying it and it makes itself understood.'

'Hmm,' as I snuggled in to sleep next to that perfumed, soft body of strong belief.

Her belief in life and faith that must prevail over injustices and unspeakable horrors in the name of religion.

*

My father's belief prevailed over the fear of death: it was the inevitable next step and that was that.

'Do you have any attachments, Papa?' I asked.

'None. But I do like the two of you. Don't really want to leave you, but there is no choice there.'

I once asked Papa if things would have been different if I had a brother. No, no, no, he said, virtuously. Forget it, said Mama, of course it would have been different.

His favourite story about an attachment that fought death was of Tamerlane or Chenghiz Khan, I can't quite remember which.

'He ordered certain favourite things to be arranged around his bed, so he could gaze at them till the last drop of life evaporated from him,' Papa told me.

'Does one really go away?' I asked. 'Perhaps the dead can see all the beautiful things in the world.'

'I don't know,' Jindo said with that slight smile that had become typical of his last years, 'Let's see.'

Jindo's stories were an integral part of him. They were of various colours, haunted by deeper stories that had a feel of magic and mystery.

He was good for my sister and I. His inactivity allowed us to stream into a new channel because he gave us only a sense of something without burdening us with his meaning of it. Too much history is as bad as none at all.

Rather than an energetic climbing over, he passively slipped under barricades of socialisation, so that we could step over him into the actively forming new world. He was not that alarmed by it, unlike others of his generation, because he was a man before his time, of a sort who would always be before his time: of the age of Aquarius.

By all accounts, he had begun his life with energetic humour that changed to active rebellion spurred by drink and drugs, which broke him from definition and he wandered, unhinged, grasping at psychiatrists and medicine to hold him from hurtling into the unknown...to return to his family.

'He is crazy,' said Mama, 'he liked the electric shocks at Ranchi.' But I knew that our father wanted to be sane for the love of us.

I also understood that his hurtling mental travels liberated him from all perceivable limitations of nation, state, religion, community, projecting him into many galaxies, beyond them, to all of creation and beyond, to that which is something, if anything; beyond words that are always limiting and fraught with the danger of narrow perspectives; he wandered in that inconceivable zone for a while, till he returned to us. And then, in the last few years of his life, he floated back to those realms without a name, but this time, he wandered without a drug or drink or doctor to settle into satisfied silence. It was not happiness, because that would be too active; it was a quiet resignation lived with self-deprecating, dry, gentle humour. It seemed quite satisfactory to him, though we wished it was different, but did not know in what way. The vast majority he was different to seemed so ordinary.

Yet, in one of his last conversations with me, he said, 'What have I really done all my life?'

Sensing that we had reached his final days, I held him tightly and said, 'You are our link with the here before and, truly, you are also our link to the hereafter, and the link is worthy and strong; we love you, Papa, as oxygen in my blood, till I don't know whether what I feel is my love for you or yours for us.'

My Papa smiled and snuggled deep into his razai, feeling complete and cosy with the slender, wiry bodies of his three grandsons sprawled across his great, lean frame. A few days later, he was dead.

After he died, I dreamt of my father walking in a gentle, green meadow to settle in his typical sideways recline on the soft bank of a stream.

I believe that upon his death my father had the following conversation:

'*Par tu keeta kee*,' (But what did you do?) God asked.

Papa said, 'Don't ask me, I don't care, I hurt no one, I helped my servants and many relatives. I kept my daughters happy and I lived with elegance while confronting difficult truths. I never forgot you. Thank you for my wife and her patient soul and thank you for the love of my daughters. I would not have survived without them. And now, stop troubling me; I want to rest.'

And God would have smiled and said, 'Let him in, make his takht under a shady tree in an orchard through which flows a sharp, cold, clear river, fresh from the snows. This is a favourite child. Pampered and spoilt and, though irreverent, is reverence itself. Thank God, we will now have some decent conversation.'

# 10. Bhog

The day of the final prayers was clear, the sun flowed easy to thaw the January cold and lit Jindo's photo to the truth of his gentle, irreverent smile. *He always knew something,* I thought as I looked at the picture.

The ceremony was well attended. I watched my relatives working their aged bodies to kneel before the book.

My father had never bothered with this. One of the last times I saw him in a gurudwara, he had chosen to avoid the massive effort of getting up from the floor by bowing low rather than kneeling. Rather than sitting on the ground, which would require effortful getting up, he had sat on a low step in the doorway, resting his elbow on the higher one, his long legs stretched out but carefully away from the book.

The bhaiji sang:

*Farida dariyave kandey bagla baitha kale karey,*
*Kale karendey hanj no achintey baaj paye,*
*Baaj paye tis rabb dey kelaan visariya,*
*Jo mann chitt na chetey mann so gali rabb kiyan.*

The swan plays by the waterside,
Playing with joyful abandon;
Not sensing the hawk that will swoop to kill;
The hawk swoops to kill its creative play; that, too, is an act of God,
The mind that does not dwell on the hawk is surprised by death.

The kirtan was as my family liked it; we were purists, no instrument should crash on the perfect meld of voice in metre with the tabla. It is about the song; no priestly commentary. Our grandmother's instruction to the bhai used to be, 'Don't give us a lecture, don't beguile us with pretty tunes, sing the true note in the raga as prescribed in the book.'

A goodly smell of sooji roasted and cooked in desi ghee arose from the pershad degh. I cupped my hands to receive the silky kada, warm on my palm that felt the same as when I received it as a child in such congregations.

# 11. Ardas

We stood up for the ardas, the resounding enunciation of the formation of the Sikh identity. The bhaiji called:

*Ek Onkar: Waheguru ji ki Fateh*
*Sree Bhagauti ji Sahaa-e,*
*Vaar Sree Bhagauti ji ki Paat'shaahee D'assveen,*
*Pritham Bhagat'ee simar kaae Guru Nanak laeen' D'hiaa-ae,*
*Phir Angad, Guru t'ae Amar Das-Ram Das aae hoeen' sahaa-aen*
*Arjan Hargobind no simro Sree Har Raae,*
*Sree Har Kishan d'hiaa-ee-aae jis dit'haae sabhe dukhe jaa-aae,*
*Tegh Bahadur simri-aae ghar naau nid'he aavaae d'haa-e,*
*Sabh thaa-een' ho-e sahaa-e.*
*Dassvaen' Paat-Shah Sree Guru Gobind Singh Sahib ji sabh thaa-*
    *een' ho-e sahaa-e,*
*Dassaan' Paat'shaahee-aan' d'ee jot Sri Guru Granth Sahib ji d'ae*
    *paat'h d'eed'aar daa d'heaan dhar kae bolo ji, Waheguru.*
*Panjaan' piaareaan', chauhaan' Sahibzad-eaan', chaalee mukt-eaan',*
    *Hat'hee-aan', jappee-aan', tappee-aan', jinhaa' Naam jap-eaa, vand*

*chhakeaa, d'aeg chalaa-ee, tegh vaahee, daekh kae andit'h keetaa, Tinhaan Piaareaan', sache-aare-aan dee kamaaee daa dhe-aan d'har kae Khalsa ji bolo ji Waheguru.*

*Jinhaan' singhaan' singhaniaan' nae dharam haet sees deettae, baand baand kataa-ae, Khopariaan' luhaa-ee-aan', charkharee-aan' tae charhae, aare-aan' naal chiraa-ae ga-ae, Gurduaare-aan' dee saevaa la-ee kurbaaniaan' keetee-aan', dharam naheen' haareaa, Sikhee kaesaan' svaasaan' naal nibhaa-ee, tinhaan' dee kamaa-ee dah theaan dhar kae Khalsa-ji bolo ji Waheguru.*

*Panjaan' Takhtaan', sarbatt Gurdvaareaan' dah theaan dhar kae bolo ji Waheguru.*

*Prathmae Sarbatt Khalsa ji ki Ardas hae ji, Sarbatt Khalsa ji ko Waheguru, Waheguru, Waheguru, chitt aavae, chitt aavan kaa sadkaa sarab sukh hovae;*

*Jahaan' Jahaan' Khalsa ji Sahib, ta'haan' ta'haan' rachheaa riaa-it, Daeg taeg Fateh, bihrd kee paaej, Panth kee jeet, Sir'ee Sahib ji sahaa-ae, Khalsae ji kae bol baalae, bolo ji Waheguru.*

*Sikhaan' noon' Sikhee daan, Kesh daan, Reht daan, bibaek daan, visaah daan, bharosaa daan, daanaan' sir daan, Naam daan, sree Amritsar ji dah ishnaan, Chukiaan', Jhandae, Bungae jugo jugg At'aall, dharam kaa jaaekaar.*

*Bolo ji, Waheguru.*

*Waheguru ji ka Khalsa, Waheguru ji ki Fateh.*

Victory to the one almighty,
Illumined and represented by the spirit of Bhagwati,
Here is an account of the spirit through ten Badshahs,
The first who saw this spirit was Guru Nanak,
Then came Angad, Guru Amar Das and Ram Das assisted the spirit,
Remember Arjun, Hargobind and Har Rai,
Think of Shree Har Krishan, darshan of whom ended all sorrow,
Think of the ninth Guru Tegh Bahadur,
Be with us everywhere and help us,
The tenth Guru Gobind Singh Sahib be with us everywhere all the time, please,

The spirit of the tenth guru in this Granth Sahib that is our guru,
    view it, people, and think upon it and say, Waheguru,
The five beloved, four sahibzadas, forty martyrs, the fighters who
    fought with their hands and prayed with their souls and did
    tapasya in their wars: They shared their food and ate together,
    they started a large langar with a degh (cooking utensil), even
    while fighting with a tegh (sword), they accepted what they saw,
    those beloved and true,
Who worked like that in the name of Sikhi, remember them all
    and say, all of you, say with me: Waheguru.
Those Singhs and Singhnis who gave their heads for their faith,
    got their limbs cut off, got their scalps skinned, were put on the
    rack, were hacked and sliced with knives, who sacrificed for the
    gurudwaras, were good Sikhs in dress and breath; remember their
    deeds, oh Khalsa ji,
And let's say it together, say with me: 'Waheguru.'
Bow to the five takhts and all the gurudwaras,
O almighty one, protect the Khalsa and give it a strong heart and
    make it victorious in every spiritual and material battle,
Give me Sikhi, represented in kesh, sharing, discernment, wisdom,
    charity, Guru's Name, bathing in the sarovar decorated with
    bungas and standards and flags and drums that roll the name of
    Dharam and the gurus.
Hail the Khalsa in the name of the almighty; victory to the almighty.

A new stanza had been added after 1947—in the Punjab, this
date signified Partition more than it did independence:

*Sree Nankanaa Sahib tae hor Gurdvaareaan', Gur'dhaamaan' dae
    jinhaan' thon Panth noon' vichhor-eaa geaa haee Khullhae darshan
    dee-daara tae sevaa san-mbhaal daa daan Khalsa ji noon bakhsho.*

May we have darshan of Sri Nankana Sahib and all those gurudwaras
    from which we have been torn away.

Ganeve and I stood with our mother to greet the people filing
out of the Darbar Sahib towards the dining tent.

I saw Angoori, the cleaning lady of the house for so many years. Angoori with the belly, big laughter that Papa loved and laughed with, and her son, Joginder, who he became very fond of; Joginder, who would sing while swabbing the floors and lie flat on the ground to ensure that the mop reached the furthest dark corners under the sofas. Papa worried for a while that the boy may have taken to drink, but was happy to be proven wrong.

Angoori and Joginder stood outside the dining tent. 'What's happening?' I asked.

'No one is serving us.'

I felt a surge upward from my belly and tightened my mouth to stop the acid. 'Come and sit here,' I said, guiding them to a table.

'No, no, no,' they said.

'But of course, I am so angry that these people have let you stand here on the side.'

And I sat with them and we wept a bit together.

## 12. Sikhi

Nanak's first words after his spiritual epiphany were about humanity transcending religion and caste: *'Na koi Hindu na Musalman.'* He came to be known as *'Baba Nanak Shah Fakir, Hindu ka guru, Musalman ka pir'*.

Nanak's method of teaching was practical.

Bibiji used to tell us sakhis at night as we drifted to sleep:

*One day, Guruji saw a congregation at the Magh Mela of people offering water to the rising sun. 'What are you doing?' he asked.*

*'We are making offerings to our pitras,' said they.*

*'How far are your ancestors?' asked Nanak.*

*'In the land of the Gods—forty-nine-and-half crore kos away.'*

*Guruji then began throwing water in the opposite direction.*

*'What are you doing?' asked the worshippers.*

*'I have a small farm about 250 kos from here; if your water will reach your fathers in the other world, I am sure my offering will reach my farm that is at least in this world.'*

Another story:

*At Mecca, Nanak fell asleep in a mosque with his feet towards the Kaaba. An enraged maulvi shook him awake. 'O, maulvi, turn my feet away and place them where there is no God.' The maulvi turned his feet away from the Kaaba only to find that the Kaaba followed.*

'Did the maulvi place Guruji's feet back so the Kaaba could return to its original position?' I remember asking my grandmother.

'The point is that it is all kudrat,' replied Bibiji.

The essence of his teaching, called the Mool Mantra, is the opening line of the Sri Guru Granth Sahib.

Says Nanak:

*Ek Onkar*
*Sat Nam*
*Karta Purakh*
*Nirbahu*
*Nirvair*
*Akal murat*
*Ajooni Saibhang*
*Gur prasad*
*Japp.*

One God
The truth
The maker

Without fear
Without hatred
Beyond time
Many forms
This is the Guru's lesson
Meditate on it.

Many years later, my eclectic reading took me to Lao Tzu's *Tao Te Ching* and I found something that resonated, 'The named is the mother of all things and yet, once named, becomes less than what it really is. The truth, thus, is the balance of what cannot be named with what is named.'

Bibiji would tell me of Nanak's travels to Baghdad, Afghanistan, Ladakh; he could reach a faraway place just by meditating on it. Nanak's travelling companions, who would close their eyes when he asked them to, (*Beam me up, Scottie*?!) were the Hindu Bala and Muslim Mardana, who accompanied Nanak's song on the rebab. 'It is the karamat of the mystic,' she would say.

'There is no karamat, life itself is karamat,' said my practical mother, though never before her mother-in-law, 'To call Nanak's travels a karamat undermines the fatigue and intensity of those arduous journeys.'

Nanak witnessed Babur's invasion in 1525. His armies did not spare Muslims either, in the sacking of Saidpur. In that period, England had signed the Magna Carta and Europe had entered the Renaissance period. Da Vinci would paint the Mona Lisa around this time, Michelangelo presented a sculpture of a naked David and painted a kind, bearded God, creating a naked Adam and Eve. The Americas were ruled by the Aztecs, Columbus had landed in North America just two decades earlier, mistaking it for India. An Abyssinian kingdom thrived in Africa.

The Prophet Muhammad had died 800 years earlier, and

Islam was spreading rapidly with the energy of a new religion. The Ottomans had defeated the Venetians, and the Arabs began their imperialistic policy, using Islam as a tool. Yet, the Sufis had emerged 400 years after the Prophet to protest the politicisation of Islam as oppressive and reinforce its liberal tenets.

The Sufi movement reached Punjab through Turkey, Persia, and Afghanistan. Sheikh Farid had sung in Punjab 300 years before Nanak, and later Bulleh Shah sang:

*Chall oye Bulliya,*
*Authey challiye,*
*Jithey loki anney,*
*Na koi meri jaat pehchaney,*
*Nai koi mainu manney.*

Come; O Bulliya,
Let's go to that place,
Where people are blind,
They don't see my caste,
And don't know me.

Nanak was part of the beginning of the Hindu Bhakti reform movement in the North. In the South, it had begun about 700 years earlier. Bhakti, derived from the Sanskrit bhaj, apart from the obvious meaning of devotion, also means to share, partake, participate, and belong. Thus, Nanak insisted, *Naam japo, kirit karo, vand chako.* (Meditate on the almighty Rabb, work, and share.)

The Sufi and the Bhakti movements dissented from ritual and caste divides to focus on inner spirituality rather than outer symbols. So, to those who mindlessly circled trays of diyas and incense around an image, Nanak sang of the celestial arati:

*Gagan mein thaal,*
*Rav chand deepak bane,*
*Taarka mandal janak moti,*

*Dhoop malay aan lao,*
*Pawan chavro kare,*
*Sagal ban raai phulant jyoti*
*Kaisi aarti hoye,*
*Bhavkhandana teri aarti,*
*Anhat sabad bajant bheri kaisi,*
*Kaisi aarti hoye, bhavkhandana teri aarti.*

The sky is the prayer-platter, the sun and the moon are the lamps, the stars and the constellations are the pearls and jewels. The sandal-laden air that comes from the mountain is the incense, air is the fan, the entire flora of the earth are the flowers... Oh, what an aarti it is! O destroyer of fear!

At Hazur Sahib in Nanded, this verse is sung as the head priest circles the book with a thali of diyas. 'How odd,' my mother would say, 'to do what Nanak said not to do!'

Nanak's dissent against constructed religiosity was mirrored in other facets of Punjabi society. Punjab has always celebrated dissent.

There is the story of Abdulla Bhatti, locally called 'Dulla Bhatti Wallah'. In 1599, he was publicly hanged by Akbar at Lahore for leading a peasant movement against the empire. His last words, recorded by a contemporary Sufi poet, were that a Punjabi would rather die than sell his land.

Bhatti Wallah is remembered every full moon in January, celebrated as the festival of Lohri. My mother has a memory of a tonga ride with her father past many Lohri evening fires and children singing 'Dulla'.

*Dulla Bhatti Wallah,*
*Oye!*
*Dulley nay dhee viyahi,*
*Oye!*
*Khand shakkar payee,*
*Kudi da salu pata.*

Dulla Bhatti Wallah,
He married off a daughter (of the village),
With jaggery and sugar,
The girl's dupatta had been torn (loss of honour).

Concerned that the hanging of Dulla Bhatti would foment greater rebellion, Akbar adopted a policy of appeasement towards the increasingly popular Sikh guru, Amar Das, the third after Nanak.

On his way to the North, Akbar stopped at Amritsar and ate langar sitting in a pangat (line) with the sangat (congregation). He presented fifty-one gold mohurs and granted tax relief to peasants because their crops had failed that year due to a bad monsoon. Sikh fortunes rose dramatically under Akbar's patronage.

The emperor presented the Guru's daughter, Bibi Bhani, with a piece of land. On this land is a lake with a story—a story that my grandmother used to tell me:

*A king asked his three daughters who they loved best. Two said they loved their father as their benefactor and the third said she loved her father, but not as much as she loved God. The king abandoned this third daughter to her God by marrying her off to a leper. Accepting her fate, the princess pushed her husband's cart to wherever God willed. By evening, they reached a lake. Leaving her husband under a beri tree, the princess went to the village nearby to beg for food.*

*The leper drowsed in the dappled shade of the beri, watching the lake shimmering in the sun, its blue-grey water rippling with the breeze. He noticed something.*

*Crows dived into the pond to emerge as white swans.*

*The leper crawled to the edge of the lake and stretched his legs into the cool shallows lined with a velvet soil squelch. He exulted in the sharp sting of the leprous rot awakening as alive flesh.*

*He plunged his head into the water and felt a new face. He was about to swim into the deep but held back. 'Not yet,' he must have thought, 'I need to convince my wife that I am the same man who married her.' And when she arrived, they saw together how the healing waters dried the sores on his left hand, which he had kept out of the water.*

The allegory is easy: swimming in the pools of introspection has a transformative power to turn the thick, material body into consciousness.

The beri under which she had left her husband is called Dukh Bhanjini: God's shade helps lighten sorrow. It is in the centre of this sarovar that the Sikh guru built a temple that came to be called Harmandir Sahib.

I, too, experienced something significant in these waters. I was born with clubbed feet. My inability to walk, even after two major surgeries, was diagnosed as psychosomatic; due to abnormal fear and anxiety. I could toddle along if someone held my hand, but I would not venture out by myself.

Mama and Papa decided to take me to Harmandir Sahib to bathe in the sarovar. I was already three years old and so have a memory of the time. I remember my mother carrying me down the steps to the water's edge. The silence frightened me. I remember holding an iron chain attached to the bottom step just above the water. I remember a tentative enjoyment overcoming my fear. I remember a fearsome Nihang warning Mama that I must not piss there.

'Don't do susu,' my mother said, and I remember I giggled.

Then I remember returning to Karnal on a train called the Flying Express that was simply called 'Flying'. The next morning, I stood as usual, holding the edge of the dining table for support, and then something came over me and I let go and walked free to the window to look at a bird nesting in the low branches of a tree.

I remember the commotion following my instinctive, unthinking, first steps.

'*Tur payee tur payee tur payee!*' (She is walking, she is walking!) shouted everyone. The servants came out from the kitchen and Bhola Singh, the cook, said he would get the ingredients ready for Bibiji to make kada pershad.

I believe I walked because my child's mind understood intuitively that something important was going to happen. I had entered the lake and I, always a good child, anxious to please, wanted to cooperate for the desired result.

Many years later, when we discussed my sarovar experience, Papa recounted the time he had swum to the middle of the sarovar, till a Nihang admonished him for kicking the water. It was disrespectful: 'beyadabi'. I know of no one else who has tried to swim in the waters of Harmandir Sahib. Jindo's relationship with all things solemn and serious was that of a naughty child who knew he was beloved.

After Guru Ram Das, the guru gaddi became hereditary. 'How can spirituality be hereditary,' Papa would scoff. Guru Arjan Dev started the construction of the Harmandir Sahib Gurudwara, the foundation stone of which was laid by a Muslim fakir, Mian Mir. A separate identity was forming:

*Na ham Hindu na Musalman*
*Allah Ram ke pind paran.*

We are neither Hindus nor Muslim,
We are the body and breath that are one; call it Allah or Ram.

Many have attributed this line to poet-saint Kabir.

The bloody episodes in Sikh history began with the martyrdom of Guru Arjan Dev by order of Jehangir as punishment for having received the emperor's rebel son, Khusrau. Arjan Dev's son and successor, Har Govind, set up a Sikh army and took to wearing two swords, one for miri (temporal) and the other as piri (spiritual).

'This is very difficult,' Papa once said, 'One can't be both a spiritual and temporal leader; that is when the problems begin.'

Har Govind was succeeded by his grandson, Guru Har Rai. Once, his retainers clashed with the emperor's guards and the guru was ordered to be arrested. The bailiff arrived to find the family preparing for their daughter's wedding. Since the guru was away, the Mughal soldiers ate the mithai and plundered his property. They did not get far, because the Sikh soldiers followed swiftly to punish the imperial army, which may have included forcing them to throw up what they had eaten. The imagery survives to the day. When a fundamentalist cousin objected to some celebration of Bhindranwale's death, he said, 'Just wait till the mithai is beaten out of you.'

Shah Jehan's son, Dara Shikoh, was a man of letters and philosophy who enjoyed the company of learned and saintly men of all religions, Guru Har Rai among them. When he lost the battle of succession to Aurangzeb, he sheltered with Guru Har Rai.

Thus, after Guru Har Rai's death, the Sikhs were important enough for Aurangzeb to invite the next Sikh guru, Guru Har Kishan, to Delhi. Guru Har Kishan died of smallpox in Delhi while still waiting for an audience with the Badshah. His last words were 'Baba Bakale' (the baba of a place called Bakala), which were taken to mean that he had named as his successor someone from Bakala. Many Sikhs from Bakala claimed to be that successor.

At the time, the ship of a Sikh trader named Makhan Shah was caught in a heavy storm off the coast of Gujarat. He prayed to Guru Nanak, promising 500 gold mohurs to his successor if he survived. The ship floated safely into harbour and Makhan Shah arrived at Bakala to make good his promise.

Baba also means grandfather. Guru Har Kishan's granduncle, Tegh Bahadur, lived at Bakala. Makhan Shah reached Tegh Bahadur's house. He was led to a small underground room where a man sat, meditating in candlelight.

Makhan Shah offered two gold mohurs.

Tegh Bahadur's eyes flew open and he said, 'What happened to the 500 you promised, Makhan Shah? I even hurt my shoulder, pushing your ship into harbour.'

Makhan Shah ran up the stairs to shout from the roof top, '*Gur ladho rey oy*!' (Oy! I have found the guru). The detail that I loved was how Bibiji described Makhan Shah's vigorous celebration. 'He took off his shirt and swung it over his head like a victory flag,' she told me.

Thus was discovered the ninth Guru, Tegh Bahadur. He settled at Patna where his son was born: the tenth Guru, Gobind Singh. When Gobind was only about nine years old, a group of Kashmiri Brahmins visited Patna, seeking Sikh protection from forced conversion to Islam by the armies and mullahs under Mughal rule.

Guru Sahib Tegh Bahadur accepted their case and asked them to send word to Delhi that they would convert to Islam if the emperor could persuade Guru Tegh Bahadur to do so.

The Guru was summoned to Delhi and charged with contempt of Islam in his teachings. The Guru read the passages about Islam in the Guru Granth Sahib to the emperor.

*O Baba, the Lord Allah is Inaccessible and Infinite,*

*He is Allah, the Unknowable, the Inaccessible, the All-powerful and Merciful Creator,*

*In the Dark Age of Kali Yuga, the Atharva Veda became prominent; Allah became the Name of God,*

*The Primal Lord God is called Allah. The Shaykh's turn has now come to recognise that.*

Finding nothing offensive in the book, the emperor asked the guru, on pain of death, to display his spiritual power with a karamat. The guru refused, saying that the miracle would be what survived his death.

Both knew that it was no longer about Allah and the Guru Granth Sahib but about the Imperial Court against the growing power of the Sikhs. In 1675, Guru Tegh Bahadur was beheaded at night at Chandni Chowk, within sight of the Red Fort. The place of the beheading became the Sis Ganj Gurudwara.

The Guru's body would have been laid out for public display but for a disciple called Lakhi Shah Vanjara, who stole it immediately after the execution and cremated it by setting fire to his own house nearby. That became the site of the Gurudwara Rakab Ganj.

The severed head was taken by one Bhai Jaita Singh to Anandpur Sahib and cremated by Guru Gobind Singh on the banks of the Sutlej. That has become Gurudwara Sis Mahal Sahib, at what is known as Gurudwara Kiratpur Sahib, where we took Papa's ashes.

Guru Gobind Singh then embarked on his lifetime's battle against Emperor Aurangzeb. In his autobiographical poem *Bachittar Natak*, the Guru describes the sacrifice of his father, '*Sis diya par sirar na diya.*' (He gave his head but not sirar). The word 'sirar' has a range of meanings. With a Persian etymological root, it means 'secret'; with only a slightly different emphasis, 'sharar', it means 'spark'. In the popular interpretation, it has come to mean 'integrity'.

A typical Sikh art calendar of the ten gurus makes prominent the first and last. Nanak is the wandering ascetic with the flowing beard and half-closed eyes of a mystic. And the tenth guru, Gobind, a tall, fine figure in soldierly attire, with a sword and sometimes a falcon on his wrist, sometimes, sitting on a low diwan, telling beads, with books sometimes, but always the sword.

Guru Gobind Singh harnessed the community with the power of symbols to create the Sikhs we now know as warriors; the free verse of Nanak in praise of God was tightened by the tenth Guru to a drum roll rhythm to say the same thing:

*Na rupam,*
*Na rekham,*
*Na rangam, na ragam,*
*Na namam na thaman:*
*Mahajyot jagam.*

It is without form,
Or line,
Or colour, or sound,
Or name, or anything like it,
It is the universal life.

I remember an early-dawn awareness of Bibiji's voice, saying this prayer and returning to deep sleep, lulled by the rhythm of it.

Guru Gobind spent his years fighting the Mughal armies and lost four sons and his mother in battle. Aurangzeb died in 1707; the guru, in 1708.

An ascetic named Madho Das Bairagi was blessed by Guru Gobind Singh and renamed Banda Bahadur to unite the Sikhs after him. The Guru left him his gold-tipped arrows as a sign of his support. Banda Bahadur thus rebuilt the Sikh army in the name of the tenth guru and fought several battles, till he was captured and executed along with many other Sikh soldiers, who are remembered as martyrs. After him, the Sikh army reconvened with renewed ferocity to assume the role of custodian and protector of the Punjab from Afghan raiders.

Decades later, in 1739, Nadir Shah, harried by the Sikh guerrilla warfare tactics, asked, 'Who are these mischief makers?'

'These are a group of fakirs who visit their Guru's tank (at Amritsar) twice a year and, after bathing in it, disappear,' replied Zakariya, Governor of Lahore.

'Where do they live?' asked Nadir Shah.

'Their houses are their saddles; they can go for long periods without food and rest. They are known to sleep on horseback. We have put prizes on their heads, but their numbers keep increasing. They are never despondent, but are always singing the songs of their pirs...A drop of nectar from their Guru transmutes a coward into a lion—so wonderful is its effect.'

---

# 13. Sardars

My father's family trace their Sikh origin to Bhagat Singh, Choudhry of Ruriala village in the Gujranwala district. He converted to Sikhism in 1759, about fifty years after the death of Guru Gobind Singh. Sikhi was gathering a fast-growing community with its non-ritual philosophy, albeit with a ritualistic pageantry. The holy book wrapped in silk and brocade presides over a durbar, under a canopy of brocade guarded by a sewak with a silver-handled chaur. Even the humblest homes keep the holy book encased in the finest material they can afford.

Sikhism suited the Punjab. Already moulded by the Sufis and saints of the Bhakti movement, Sikhism melded Hindu and Muslim tenets into a creed that had shades of both, even while being clearly apart.

It is with this new religion that our ancestor, Bhagat Singh, made a strategic alliance by marrying his daughter, Devi, to the powerful Sikh warrior and chief, Gujjar Singh Bhangi.

I like to think that Devi was a great beauty. Waris Shah's

'Heer' epitomises the ideal Punjabi woman: her complexion the colour of sharaab, which is also the effect of beholding her; her kohl-darkened eyes like the nargis flower; her lips are surkh, through which glisten a necklace of chamba pearls; her nose is as sharp as Hazrat Ali's sword; her chin is like the vilayati apple. She has proud, exuberant breasts, and her thighs are slender and her arms are firm and rounded like a belna; her navel is a deep, cool trough of perfumed water. Her hair is like the snake that guards a treasure; her height is just right as the most beautiful plant in a garden: not too short but not that tall either. Her slender hands fan out like chinar leaves. She shines like a drawn sword, but can hurt like one, too.

The baraat must have been handsome; only men, mostly warriors, wearing splendid silks and luxurious beards and colourful turbans. All of them would have a sword in their cummerbund and they must have galloped to the eight-beat keherwa on the dhol.

Devi and Gujjar Singh would have circled the Guru Granth Sahib, each of them holding one end of a silk or brocade pallaa. Devi, face covered by a thick veil of phulkari embroidered by the women in her village, needs to be guided by her brothers as she circles The Book with her groom. In a bid for women's empowerment, the modern ceremony has removed the veil and she must walk by herself instead of on her brother's arm.

Gujjar Singh Bhangi's turban must have had a kalgi. Surely a brocade achkan with jewelled buttons. Devi's ghaghra, I imagine, a deep rose; on her wrists, an ivory choora inlaid with red on which, tied with a thread, is the gold leaf tasselled kaleeran (for the kali, or wrist), gifts from her friends and sisters.

What would Devi's thoughts have been? Husbands are always a gamble. The poetic, passionate philosophy of the physical and spiritual was all very well, but the prevailing social reality was an overbearing male patriarchy. The perpetual worry of every bride—*Does my husband's handsome maleness allow for him to treat me tenderly without embarrassing him?*—still persists. *I am not a jooru ka ghulam,* her husband will defensively announce to his male friends, *I am not subservient to any woman.* Even to treat her as an equal would be considered subservience because a man was supposed to be the protector of honour and family possessions that included women.

My father was quite different. 'Take off your gold bangles when we go for our evening walks,' he would tell my mother.

'Arrey, I have a big, tall sardar walking by my side; why should I fear anything?'

'I am not that type of a sardar.'

In Kasauli, once, they were scared by a sound at night.

'Go and see,' he told Darshan.

'I am not crazy, you go,' she said to him.

'I am not crazy either,' he said.

By the year of Devi's marriage in 1759, the three power centres in Punjab were the Afghans, the Marathas and the Sikhs. Ahmed Shah Abdali had invaded Punjab four times and retained control of Lahore.

In 1760, Devi's new husband, Gujjar Singh, joined a Sarbat Khalsa meeting at Amritsar and marched onwards, led by Jassa Singh Ahluwalia, to take Lahore back from the Afghans. The Sikhs were welcomed by the Lahoris, but even while they were celebrating, Abdali was preparing to march on them again.

Sensing the danger of this larger, stronger army, Jassa Singh Ahluwalia allowed his soldiers to take their women and children to the plains and then return to duty.

Abdali learned of the movement of Sikh families and sped up his attack to cover 240 km in two days in pursuit of their retreat.

The Sikh soldiers and horsemen gathered their families into

a circular fortress and engaged the Afghans in hand-to-hand combat. The Afghan killing spree stopped only when the night fell, and they were too tired to kill any more.

This was 5 February 1762, and became known as the Vadda Ghallughara, where about 50,000 Sikhs were slaughtered, in contrast to the Chhota Ghallughara of 1746, where 7,000 Sikhs were killed by the Afghans.

Ghallu is from ghol. The ghol is to fight so fiercely that you merge with the enemy. Death in such a battle meant being honoured as shaheed. As children, we used to have ghol competitions of intense wrestling with no rules until achieving the end goal of sitting flat and fat on the opponent.

Abdali returned to Lahore with cartloads of Sikh heads and hundreds of prisoners in chains. From Lahore, he went on to Amritsar and, using gunpowder, blew up the Harmandir Sahib.

By May 1762, the Sikhs were ready to avenge the Vadda Ghallughara. They cleaned the tank and rebuilt their gurudwara to celebrate Diwali.

Abdali again attacked, but the Sikhs forced his retreat. He then returned for the last time in 1764, accompanied by the poet Noor Muhammad Qazi, who wrote an eye-witness account in his *Jungnama*:

'They [the Sikhs] come stealthily like thieves and attack us like wolves.'

Abdali was inching his way back to Amritsar and the same Afghan troops that had covered 240 km in two days for the Vadda Ghallughara now took four days to cover sixty kilometres. They reached Amritsar, fought the Sikhs in the narrow galis, and reached the Golden Temple to find thirty Sikhs guarding the shrine. 'Not a grain of fear among them,' says Noor Muhammad.

It is battles such as these that taught the Punjabi to celebrate the moments of tenuous peace between invasions.

*Khaada pitta lahey da,*
*Baqi Ahmed Shahi da.*

Quickly eat and drink what you can; it alone is yours; what remains
belongs to Ahmed Shah (Abdali).

Summer would soon arrive and so Abdali turned around to ride
back into the mountains, but the Sikh bands stayed on his heels.
'What! In my reign, my own palanquin trembles for fear of these
infidels,' Abdali roared, so says Nur Muhammad.

'If you wish to learn the art of war, come face-to-face with
them in battle,' says the poet. 'Their bodies are like rocks and
in physical grandeur, every one of them is equal to more than
fifty...if they retreat, do not think they flee...it is a battle strategy.'

In 1765, during Baisakhi, the Harmandir Sahib was built
again, and the pool cleaned and refilled. The langar was resumed
on an even grander scale.

On 16 April 1765, just six years after his wedding, Gujjar
Singh fulfilled the promise his father-in-law, my ancestor Bhagat
Singh, must have seen in him. He, along with his uncle, Lehna
Singh, and a cousin, Sobha Singh, captured Lahore from the
Afghans and divided the city among themselves.

To Gujjar's share came the area from Shalimar Bagh in
Lahore and the jungle on the eastern part till Amritsar. He
constructed an attractive settlement with a mud fortress, new
wells, and a mosque. The area is the site of the present-day
railway station of Lahore and bears his name as 'Qila Gujjar
Singh'. He died at Lahore in 1788.

The second generation of the triumvirate rulers of Lahore
was unpopular and the Sikhs united under Ranjit Singh, marched
into Lahore, and crowned him Maharaja in 1802.

Maharaja Ranjit Singh kept the Afghans at bay, took the
Kohinoor from the Afghan ruler Shah Zaman, and earned the
title Sher-e-Punjab.

He was intuitively a secular man with a cosmopolitan sensibility. One of the many European travellers who visited his court, Hugel, describes Maharaja Ranjit Singh as a phenomenally ugly man; smallpox had not so much pitted the skin on his face as made a mottled mask over it. It had also blinded him in one eye while the other roved inquisitively and restlessly all around the room as if with a life of its own. Ranjit Singh was a secular ruler. He joked about his blind eye as God's way of ensuring that he would look upon all religions with his one good eye.

His body was short and ungainly, 'but as soon as he mounts his horse, and with his black shield at his back, puts him on his mettle, his whole form seems animated by the spirit within and assumes a certain grace of which nobody could believe it susceptible...' says Hugel, 'The passion of Ranjit Singh for horses has passed into a proverb in the East...their bridles, saddles are bejewelled.'

For the common man, Ranjit Singh was a benign king who never passed a death sentence except for one instance when his French general mistook the Maharaja's order to get rid of a troublesome chief literally; the Maharaja treated it as a genuine misunderstanding.

European visitors were struck by the informality of Ranjit Singh's Court. He was essentially a comrade in arms with his men. His days were spent outdoors, riding or hunting with his soldiers or sitting cross-legged on his special chair, watching his horses and army manoeuvres. While indoors, he liked sitting on the carpeted floor rather than his gold-plated, medium-sized throne.

His avoidance of extravagant displays contrasted with his complete lack of frugality and abstemiousness. His excesses of wine and women became legendary to describe the quintessential sardar.

He had several wives and maintained a harem. He entertained lavishly, and his favourite courtesan was a Muslim dancing girl called Kaulan. He enjoyed things of beauty; his tents were lined with Kashmiri shawls and carpets, and courtiers and royals illuminated his darbar with their glowing jewels, pashminas, silks, and brocades, which were but a foil to the lethal, specially soldered swords that were worn as part of the dress code.

As if to be a deliberate foil to his darbaris, Ranjit Singh's dress style shone with understated elegance. He wore plain salwar kurtas, pashmina in winter, and fine cotton in summer. His only adornment was the Kohinoor baazuband.

At this time, the English Regency style of high, stiff neckties was being transformed slowly by the influential socialite Beau Brummell, with his still enduring fashion statement of male clothing in navy and charcoal grey over clean linen underwear after a daily bath that the English, it seems, were not inclined to generally.

*

Then there's the story of the Kamala Sardars related to my family through complicated marriage networks. Their ancestor, too, had been a general in Ranjit Singh's army.

'What an odd name,' I said to Bibiji. Kamala means mad.

'There is a story,' she said. Their ancestor, the general commandant with Maharaja Ranjit Singh, laid siege to a fort that held out fast and long enough for the Sikh army to begin losing morale in the heat and with fast depleting provisions. To prevent retreat, the Sardar general ordered all the cavalry horses to be destroyed.

'Did the general destroy his own horse as well?' I asked.

'Must have done,' Bibiji made a reasonable guess, 'to show solidarity with his soldiers.'

Anyhow, the siege succeeded, and they took the fort. Maharaja Ranjit Singh received his tired, bedraggled soldiers walking back in victory with a sorrowful, 'Where are my beloved horses?' When he heard the story, he moaned, 'Oye, kamlia,' (Oh, you madman!) The descendants thus bore the name Kamala as a badge of honour. Their bloodline also carried an equestrian passion that exponentially depleted the fortunes of each successive generation.

Two Kamala brothers, Shyam Singh and Jagat Singh, brought this legacy of crazy passion for horses into independent India.

Shyam Singh Kamala jockeyed his own horses and continued as an active rider even into his eighties. I remember him as a small, wiry man with a graceful energy that could mount, tame and live on horseback. His grey beard enhanced an unlined, narrow face with high cheekbones and long eyes with an upward slant. His standard attire was a white turban, kurta, and churidar pyjama tucked into calf-length riding boots.

His son, Prithpal Singh Kamala, was the last scion of equine obsession driven to final impecunious circumstance. He took a job with an uncle of mine to look after his stables, particularly the prized stud called 'Sant'.

I would often find Prithpal sitting cross-legged on a chair, reading the Punjabi newspaper to Sant.

'I will teach you how to ride,' Prithpal told me on one such visit and lifted me on to the magnificent sire of racehorses.

Smelling my pathetic fear, Sant neighed impatiently and threw me off, cantering away from my stupid mediocrity. My pain at falling off a high horse was not in the least alleviated by Prithpal, who, even while gallantly helping me up, could barely conceal his disappointment at my lack of sardarni mettle, a disgrace to a long line of riding sardars.

My uncle came charging out of the house and attacked

Prithpal for letting his beloved niece (who was young and yet to be married, was his concern) ride a racehorse. He, too, seemed divided between concern for me and the nervous health of his prize horse handling a hopelessly incompetent rider.

But where was Sant? He had bolted to the end of the driveway, where he stood, pawing the ground in a royal, hyper-anxious frenzy. Just then, Prithpal's fifteen-year-old son vaulted with practised ease onto Sant's back. Sensing empathetic control of the reins, Sant broke into a smooth gallop, celebrating a new relationship with the young boy.

The father watched with the same awe as my uncle and I. 'He has never ridden before. I did not want to teach him because horses have ruined us,' Prithpal said.

'It's in their blood,' said my uncle. 'By God! I know what blood means now. The horses have had their revenge by ruining them but cannot resist the blood that talks to them.'

Ranjit's empire of fifty years disintegrated fast after his death on 27 June 1839, culminating in the British annexation of the Punjab after two well-documented Anglo-Sikh wars. Despite his proclaimed Sikh faith, four queens, including the mother of the heir, Khadak Singh, seven servant girls, and Kaulan, became sati with Ranjit Singh.

Ranjit Singh's son, the prince 'Khadak' (he who can shake and shock) Singh, was a weak simpleton. The ditty about him that passed down to us was:

*Khadak Singh key khadakney sey khadakti hain khidkian,*
*Nahi, ji—*
*Khidkion key khadakney sey khadakta hai Khadak Singh.*

When Khadak Singh shakes them, the windows rattle.
No, no—
Khadak Singh rattles at the rattling of the windows!

Khadak Singh was murdered one year later. His son Nau Nihal Singh died in mysterious circumstances soon after the funeral. The palace intrigue killed many successors.

Wrote Shah Muhammad:

*Payee khadakdi nitt talwar mian,*
*Gaddi valian nu naheen bahin dende,*
*Hore kaun kiss dey panihaar mian,*
*Shah Muhammada hoi hunn maut sasti,*
*Khali nahi jaana koi vaar Mian.*

Friends, every day the swords rattled,
They would let nobody sit on the gaddi,
Who is whose friend, whom Mian will trust to drink water from?
Says Shah Muhammad, death was cheap.
No attack went empty, Mian.

Ranjit Singh's second son Sher Singh ruled for less than a year. He was shot by Ajit Singh Sandhanwalia while showing the new maharaja a new gun he had acquired. The maharaja's young son Partap Singh, who was playing close by, was hacked to pieces by a Sandhanwalia aide, Lehna Singh.

Soon after the crime, the killers and conspirators met the Prime Minister, Dhyan Singh, in an open field and asked who should be the next maharaja.

'Daleep Singh (the third son of Ranjit Singh), of course,' said the Prime Minister, at which the Sandhanwalia conspirators said, 'He is to become king and you his vizier, and what do we get for our trouble?' They shot and killed the Prime Minister as he rode away.

The Sandhanwalias then entered Lahore Fort and shut the gates. The Prime Minister's son, Heera Singh, rallied the army under its French generals and won back the fort within the hour. Before lighting his father's funeral pyre, Heera Singh put the head of one of the conspirators on the lap of his step-mother, who had chosen to burn with her husband as sati.

A military council proclaimed five-year-old Daleep Singh as emperor and his mother, Rani Jindan, the Queen Regent, but demanded the unfair return of the wealth to keep in check its powerful and dangerously restless army.

*Patti jhoordi ei Rani Jind Kauran,*
*Kithey kadda main kalgian nitt todey,*
*Mere saamney koia ney veer mera,*
*Jaindi tabiaa lah hazaar ghodey,*
*Koi hovey jo inna da garab todey.*

The queen is angry and frustrated,
Where do I get jewels every day for them?
There is no brother who comes forward for me,
No one with a thousand horses,
Who will break their pride.

To isolate the queen, the sardars murdered her brother, Jawahar Singh, who had come to visit her.

She is said to have uttered, '*Jatti hovan tey karan Punjab randi.*' (If I am a true Jatti, I will render Punjab a whore.)

## 14. Sardar Mann Singh

In all this while, of my ancestor Bhagat Singh's two sons, the elder, Sewa Singh, died in battle leaving no heir, and the younger, Deva Singh, took over the ancestral village of Ruriala. His son, Sardar Mann Singh, fought the first Anglo-Sikh war as adjutant of the cavalry in 1845.

By this time, the East India Company, which had been kept

at bay all these years by Maharaja Ranjit Singh, was circling in. The Queen Regent, Rani Jindan, planned to invite them to attack, thinking that they would then protect her rule.

*Arzi likhi firangi nu kunj goshey:*
*Pehli paar da mulk tu mall sada,*
*Soi ladangey hone bekhabar jehadey...*

She wrote the Firangis an appeal,
Come and occupy our land,
The army will fight without knowing the truth...

The Sikhs lost the battle as per Jindan's secret plan with a few of her generals and the British. Generals Lal Singh and Tej Singh deserted their troops on Jindan's orders. Even thus abandoned by their commanders, each Sikh officer led his platoon to fierce battle, causing heavy losses to the British.

Lord Hugh Gough, Field-Marshal, wrote, 'Policy precluded me publicly recording my sentiments on the splendid gallantry of our fallen foe, or to record the acts of heroism displayed, not only individually, but almost collectively, by the Sikh sardars and the army; and I declare were it not from a deep conviction that my country's good required the sacrifice, I could have wept to have witnessed the fearful slaughter of so devoted a men.'

Till the actual victory by deceit, the British were petrified:

*Shah Muhammada Singhaan ney gorian dey,*
*Wangh nimbuan lahu nichode ditti,*
*Shah Muhammada ikk sarkar bajho,*
*Faujaan jitt key ant nu hariaan nee.*

Says Shah Muhammad, the Singhs fought the whites,
And squeezed blood from them like juice from lemons,
Says Shah Muhammad, because the leaders left,
The armies lost even after winning.

Jindo used to recite this verse with particular pride, and the irony of his doing so while lying in languid repose was not lost on me, or him for that matter.

Bitter at the treachery of the Sikh leaders, Mann Singh became a mercenary soldier recruited by the British to command a troop of fifty horses in Lahore. The East India Company appointed his elder brother, Jodh Singh Adalati, at Amritsar.

Mann Singh sat out the second Anglo-Sikh war, which was supposed to avenge the previous defeat by treachery. The Punjab was formally annexed in 1849, and a weeping Sikh soldier surrendered his arms to the British with the words, 'Ranjeet Singh *ajj mariya hai.*' (Ranjit Singh has died only today.)

Sardar Mann Singh returned to active military service with the English during the 1857 revolt. He would have been more than fifty years old by then. He served throughout the siege and capture of Delhi. 'He assisted in the capture of the King of Delhi and the capture of the three princes who were executed,' wrote the historian Ibbotson.

I first heard about Mann Singh as our ancestor on a trip to the Red Fort with our father when I was about twelve years old. A guide took us to a magnificent gate and told us, 'It is called Khooni Darwaza. It is here that Bahadur Shah Zafar's three sons were killed by Sardar Mann Singh, and their heads presented to him on a platter.'

'That is your direct ancestry,' said my father, quickly followed with the assurance that the tale of the platter was the guide's embellishment. Mann Singh had promised Badshah Zafar safe passage back to the Red Fort from Humayun's tomb, where he was hiding. In gratitude, the emperor gave him his ring and the Begum her earrings.

'"Gave?" Or did he take?' I asked.

My father admitted with embarrassment that 'take' was

likely, but they could also have been gifts from a grateful Badshah for taking him on the safe passage.

I was haunted by this story till I read William Dalrymple's *The Last Mughal*. Mann Singh, says Dalrymple, accompanied Colonel Hodson, who had been charged with bringing out the emperor from his shelter at Humayun's tomb. It is Hodson who shot the princes and took their jewellery.

Later, Dalrymple mentions a sardar who turned his back on two princes in his charge, saying he did not see them and thus let them escape.

I have adopted this additional story as reasonable and in keeping with what I believe is the essence of Mann Singh's descendants; my father, uncle, grandfather, and great-grandfather were kind and generous and would not easily give up this expression of themselves to a fascist authority.

There is a picture of Colonel Hodson and his regiment in William Dalrymple's book. Mann Singh stands relaxed, not very tall, beard flowing over his chest to a slightly protruding stomach. His position in the hierarchy is clear: in a formal photo, he stands on the far left while the British officers are sitting. The picture shows him as not particularly happy or proud. He could have made a different choice, but that would have been a different story.

These were the events of 1857. In 1859, Ivan Goncharov, in Russia, published the novel *Oblomov*.

Mann Singh retired from active military service in 1877 and was appointed manager of the Darbar Sahib by the leaders of the Sikh community. In 1879, he was made an Honorary Magistrate. He died in 1892 at about age eighty-one.

Mann Singh's eldest son, Jawahir Singh, succeeded him as a Provincial Darbari, Zaildar and Honorary Magistrate in Gujranwala. Jawahir Singh died in 1907 and was succeeded by his eldest son, my great-grandfather, Sardar Rajwant Singh.

This is the story of a typical Jatt Sikh family, a breed who thinks that they have a divine right to sport a flamboyant, heroic style embellished with vast amounts of alcohol.

A relative who swash-buckled with the name 'Prince' was drinking with my father once, 'Have another, Jindo, yaar, we are Jatt Sikhs, made lions by Guru Sahib.'

'Did you know that none of the gurus were Jatts?' Jindo asked Prince.

There was a silence, and then, from the disillusioned Prince, 'Lehh! What's the point of all the drama then!'

## 15. Papaji Vaddey

We called Rajwant Singh 'Papaji Vaddey'—elder father. Papaji Vaddey was a tall, spare man, impeccably dressed in white turban, black sherwani, fine muslin white kurta, and churidar pyjama, finished with always polished black shoes. He carried a slim cane. My memory of his white-bearded dignity is balanced by my glimpses of him, turbanless in his bedroom, a bald head with a few grey hairs bravely tied into a top knot.

Papaji is said to have begun drinking at fourteen years of age, but I remember him as a careful, every-evening-two-Patiala-peg man, which he would mix with various churans as health experiments. He led an exemplary family life of duty tempered by distance but undoubted affection for all, except for my father, who irritated him. He was very fond of me.

He, along with his younger brother, Babaji, left Ruriala in 1915 for an estate outside Gujranwala that his wife named Rajkot. Raj, short for Rajwant and Kot as in house. The colonial-style bungalow at Rajkot was set in acres of citrus orchards that became famous in the Lahore Mandi for its juicy red maltas.

World War I was in full swing, and it was the beginning of the anti-British Gadar movement in Punjab. Papaji was Honorary Magistrate (colloquial Punjabi, 'Haneiry') for his area. Papaji's wife, called Beybeyji, was a large, plain-featured lady with a formidable countenance and good humour. 'When I travel with my husband on his ikka, people must wonder why he has to carry the dhobis pund (bundle) with him.'

Beybeyji installed the first telephone in the region. She entertained the Governor's wife to garden parties at Rajkot. She was influential enough to have the Governor transfer an English bureaucrat who had kept her waiting too long for an appointment to discuss agricultural reform in her area.

That Beybeyji and Papaji had a robust marriage is apparent from the fact that the birth of their two younger sons, Charanjit and Jasbir, coincided with that of their two grandsons, my uncle, Amarjit, and my father, Jitinder, born to their eldest son, Raghbir, my grandfather, and Persin Kaur, my grandmother, whom I called Bibiji.

## 16. Bibiji

Her name was Persin Kaur; she was a Mann, a far larger, wealthier and more influential family than the Rajkotias.

She was a traditional beauty; complexion of golden wheat, a sharp nose, and angular face framed by perfect circles of black hair that other women enviously dismissed as artifice. But the curls defiantly survived a difficult life of five decades of widowhood, loss of home, and acute financial hardship.

Bibiji was dismissive of all men except her brothers and sons. She did not adhere to purdah, choosing instead to present a strange man with a side profile of haughty disdain.

She was imperiously impatient; a famous family example was when she decided to do the right thing as a mother-in-law and attend and assist in the birth of her grandchild. She waited a full week around the due date and then returned to Karnal, accusing her daughter-in-law, my aunt, of tardiness in birthing.

Bibiji did not speak English but read the English newspaper. She spent the day with Gurmukhi. She read spiritual texts and a Sikh political 'rasala' (small book) called *Nirguniyara*.

She was proud of Punjab and her Sikhi, which is why I remember her deep shock when she saw a Sikh beggar. She gave him money but was visibly embarrassed at the giving, as was he, at the receiving. I confess, though, that it was the only time I, too, saw a Sikh beggar.

We slept in Bibiji's room. We were scared of the dark and so Bibiji taught us a night mantra that we would say at the end of kirtan Sohaila, the night prayer.

*Goun ja karke Shankar vattey Brahma darey phaans,*
*Sanp, chor, sheen, dain,*
*Charo jan vimash.*

Shiv and Brahma circle me in protection;
Snake, thief, lion, witch,
I am protected from all four.

We had to say it four times without blinking and then clap three times loudly, heralding lights out, and then snuggle in to sleep. Bibiji was also scared of the dark, I realise now, because she had the added ritual of shining a torch under the bed before going to sleep.

She was also a very nervous passenger in a car, and while

it irritated me then, I realised that after my husband's sudden death I, too, had become a difficult car passenger and suffered fear of flying for a long while. The latter fear I have managed to overcome because the cost of not being able to travel was just too high, but I am still a dreaded car passenger and have a very difficult relationship with the person driving. I think it comes from processing sudden loss. Like a rug being pulled from under you. Bibiji was widowed at the same age as me, about thirty-six.

My father was seven when his father died, and Tayaji was twelve. Photos of my grandfather, Raghbir Singh, are all over our house. A pleasant-looking man, just a bit shorter than his imposing wife. Unlike most sons of landowners, he was a hardworking, earnest man who worked even larger tracts of land than he owned by leasing. He maintained a small, independent residence on the estate with a separate car, chauffeur, and personal staff. When he died in about 1940, he left a substantial bank account of his separate earnings.

I don't know about my dada, Sardar Raghbir Singh's education, but he clearly was modern in his thinking. He had the foresight to send his older son, Amarjit, into a new English boarding school at Dehradun that became the famous Doon School. My Tayaji was the first number 17 in Doon School and the first number 8 in Welham Boys' School, a prep school for Doon School.

He gifted my father a German Brownie camera on his seventh birthday. The memory of the gift would melt my father's face into a layer of softness even deeper than the one with which he looked at us: the look of a small boy receiving an exciting gift from a father he adored. My father developed a passion for photography. He brought his father's Rolleicord camera with him to India as his only prized possession.

Dadaji Raghbir Singh died of a burst appendicitis in about 1940. Papaji Vaddey lost his wife a few years later and never married again. His sense of loss can only be assessed from the discontinued parties and disconnected telephone.

Among my father's memories was the one of two women who came to condole on his father's death. Lying in his special place under a garden hedge, he saw them laughing as they dismounted from the tonga. He heard one say, 'I don't know how to condole,' and then start a loud wail as she neared the house.

## 17. Sardar Jitinder becomes Jindo

After his father's death, Papa left for his mother's village in Mananwala, accompanied by his young maternal uncle, Sardar Jaswant. 'Don't cry, Jitti, we will look after you,' he remembers his uncle saying.

Jaswant, according to my father, had both attributes that make a good man: kindness and generosity. That he was also very handsome made him a particular hero.

Mananwala was an old-fashioned village with havelis built of small bricks, and commodes placed over pit latrines. My father attended the village school there. My mother was from the same village.

'I told the village schoolmaster that I would give him one rupee if he ranked me first in class,' my father said.

He told me of the day when, feeling lonely and bereft, he put his head on Bibiji's lap and wept. 'Why is he crying?' asked his uncle Jaswant.

'He wants to study in Doon School with Amarjit, but I can't afford it and in any case, I don't want to send him away too,' she said.

'I will send him to Chief's College Lahore. It is a good boarding school and close enough to you.'

'Jitti, come here, yaar, we love you; you are our jindo.' And so my father became Jindo, piece of my heart.

Jaswant had a daughter who died when she was four years old. Jaswant died soon after. Jindo told me in all seriousness that his uncle had looked so handsome on his wedding day that someone had cast a 'nazar' (evil eye) on him.

In 1979, I was a direct witness to his bond with this uncle, whose piece of heart he had been. It was when we visited the Harmandir Sahib. We were up at three a.m. to watch the procession of the Guru Granth Sahib, borne on a silver palki, carried into the sanctum sanctorum. My father came forward as a bearer of the palki and as it was set down, I saw him caress an engraving on its side. In Gurmukhi, after Ek Onkar, it records that the palki was donated in memory of Sardar Jaswant Singh Mann.

## 18. Some More About Papa

Papa believed that Jaswant was reborn as Prince Charles of the House of Windsor. You did not argue when he was in this mood; you just admired the insouciance with which these outrageous statements were made. So close and familiar did he believe himself to the Europeans that he once wrote to the Pope, asking for the name of his tailor, so he could advise on the dress code for the Vatican. Years later, I wrote Papa a card from the Vatican post office, 'Am here to locate the tailor; will let you know when I have news.' To my extreme regret, it never reached Karnal.

Jindo saw more death than is fair for a fifteen-year-old in a good world. First, his father, then his paternal grandmother, then his young cousin, who he loved because she was his beloved uncle Jaswant's daughter, and then Uncle Jaswant, his father figure.

He also saw a murder and an attempted suicide at Rajkot. He would tell me that story, 'I heard a shot from the servants' quarters and Bibiji sent me to enquire.'

'How old were you then?' I asked.

'About eight years.'

The quarters were a good distance away for a small boy. By the time he got there, the servant had shot his wife but could not shoot himself because he forgot to reload the gun. Then he tried to hang himself and when he could not manage that either, he swallowed many sleeping pills that he vomited because he downed them with too much alcohol.

Jindo saw the dead woman and watched the servant messing around with his suicide attempts before running back to the house to tell Bibiji. He told me he had stumbled and fallen many times on his way to her. The servant was arrested and eventually hanged.

The incident affected Jindo deeply. 'Nothing, no crime is so bad that the criminal be killed for it. The State has no right to take away what it has not given.'

By 1945 or so, Jindo had his own first close encounter with death. He was diagnosed with tuberculosis.

Two similar near-death encounters in later life gave him a kinship familiarity with it. He claimed victory over anything by joking about it:

'*Sundari,*' he told his nanny, '*jab mar jayegi to chithi dal dena.*' (When you die, send me a letter.)

And Sundari, laughing, would hug him: '*Jiyo, jiyo, Jind-ji. Main zaroor chithi bhej dangi.*' (Yes, yes, Jind-ji, I will surely write to you.)

Papa spoke often of Sundari.

Guru Nanak describes day and night as the male and female nurses playing with us in their care.

*Pavan guru pani pita mata dhart mahat,*
*Divas raat dui dai daya,*
*Kheley sagal jagat.*

The wind is our guru; water, our father; mother is the earth,
The day and night are both man and woman nurses to us,
So, the world plays as a family.

## 19. Education at Aitchison College

The British set up four schools for feudal families across the country. Popularly known as Chief's Colleges, the curriculum, though taught in English, was designed to maintain the status quo. The one at Lahore was called Aitchison College, named after the Governor of Punjab.

My father excelled in agriculture studies, history, and literature, particularly Persian. 'I was good at studies,' he told us. 'I always came second.'

'Wow,' we would say, 'Among how many boys were you always second, Papa?'

'Thirteen,' he said.

The entire school had forty boys on a 150-acre campus. They had private ensuite bedrooms with a study, and the bathrooms had a backdoor to allow for their personal valets. The valets even carried the boys' books to class.

'What type of scholars are those who cannot even carry their books?' scoffed my mother.

My father's valet, Joga, set up a Ponzi credit line to keep his Sahib safe from financial embarrassment and the need to ask for extra money from home.

This became the pattern of our lifestyle later, which a cousin described as 'living "before" our means, rather than "beyond"'. Papa would always spend in advance the notional income of the crop that was yet to arrive at the mandi. That he invariably also lived beyond his means is another matter.

Bibiji arranged to rent a house in Lahore for her visits to Jindo in Aitchison. Munshi Makand Lal, given the task of looking for accommodation, was overheard telling the wide-eyed servant audience at Rajkot that there was indeed a very big sardar called 'To-Let Singh' who owned the maximum number of properties in Lahore.

In school, my father was lucky that he got away with some serious misdemeanours, which were treated as mere escapades. One was cheating. Good students were only those who were effortlessly so, since studying and jobs were not a top priority for the boys. The thought of cheating at cricket shook the boys' moral value to the core, but not so at their exams. Boys would write their question on a sheet of paper and throw it on the floor. Another boy would pick it up, write the answer, and throw it back for the dull querist.

My father's biggest academic hurdle was geography. At one exam, not bothered with the subterfuge of paper on the floor and so on, he sauntered over to his friend Anup Singh's desk.

'Anup,' he asked, 'is Calcutta the jute port of India, or Bombay?'

'Calcutta, Jindo,' said Anup.

'What a silly question, Papa,' we said, even while admiring his elegant daring.

'The examiner goggled as I walked back to complete my

answer sheet,' Papa said, 'and when I submitted my paper, he asked, "So, Jitinder, do you think you will be a success in life?"'

'I don't know, sir.'

'I think you will be a great success.'

Education was generally not the strong suit of the Jatt sardars. An example: After a valiant struggle, Papaji Vaddey's youngest son managed to reach college. Confident of at least the passing grade, he asked his father to advance him some money for a party in Lahore. When the results were out, Papaji, still reading the newspaper, held out his hand for the money he had given earlier.

Our family and their ilk intuitively drifted to the army and police for no reason, it seemed to me, other than to alleviate rural ennui. Identity was defined by the land they inherited and there was no effort to achieve political relevance or adapting to the modern world by joining a workforce that was becoming an increasingly affluent, English-speaking, class of professionals and businessmen.

One exception to this norm was Sardar Datar Singh, a rich landlord of an entrepreneurial and scientific bent of mind. He earned a knighthood for the first dairy project in Punjab. The local Superintendent of Police in Rajkot, a man of wit and humour, sent the news of Datar Singh's knighthood by telegram to Papaji Vaddey.

*Sur ho gaya Datar,*
*Gauan char-char.*

Datar has become Sir,
By grazing his cows.

Papaji Vaddey's younger brother, Babaji, joined the police force. He was superintendent in Dehradun in the mid-1930s, during the height of the Quit India protests. Babaji was informed of a protest in the city. Upon seeing that it was peaceful, he did not interfere till Sardar Patel telephoned, requesting an arrest.

So, Babaji contributed to the freedom cause with Patel's arrest.

Of my father's classmates, an extraordinary exception to the general Bertie Wooster-type characters was Akbar Bugti. My father and Akbar smoked the school dining room by blocking the chimney with the carcass of an eagle. To my always active imagination, it was a portend to the Punjabis smoked out of their homes just a couple of years later in 1947.

'Who shot the eagle?' I asked.

'Akbar,' said my father. Typical that he could not bring himself to lie about even something I would never have known otherwise.

Decades later, Akbar Bugti led the rebel Baluch cause against Pakistan and, in 2006, was killed in a bomb blast in his cave hide-out.

## 20. Illnesses and Superstitions

Close to the end of World War II, freedom was imminent and talk of Partition treated as mere paranoid rumour.

In about 1945, my father was diagnosed with tuberculosis and sent to the sanatorium at Kasauli. He does not remember how often, if at all, his mother came to see him. His uncles stayed away and his favourite among them, Jaswant, was dead by then.

An effect of the sanatorium was Papa's anxious nursing of our childhood illnesses. He understood fevers. He would ask us to breathe on his hand and we could tell from his face whether our temperature was high. We felt safe, but he lived with the dread of losing a child.

Once, when I asked about death, he folded his hands and

said he did not want to talk about it because I must plan to die only after him.

In about 1974, my mother dreamt of her dead mother visiting her in a tonga. 'Bibiji, take me with you,' my mother said.

'No, no, Beeba, you have work to do,' my grandmother responded in my mother's dream, and gave my mother a box of mithai.

'I knew then that I was going to go through a bad time, but I would be all right,' my mother told me.

Soon after this dream, Papa started complaining of weakness. This was first wrongly diagnosed as tuberculosis, the treatment of which caused immense damage, till it was finally identified as an enlarged heart.

In boarding school, I did not realise just how unwell he was. Mama would write the usual letters in her careful round hand about the puddings she had learned to make. 'Papa is all right, but needs to rest a bit,' she wrote.

Thinking that Papa was going through a bout of laziness where he could not even write his usual two-line letter, I was not alarmed by his silence.

He recovered enough to attend my school sports day.

I had left my father at home at the beginning of term as a black-bearded fifty-year-old; now I saw him completely grey, propped up with a walking stick.

At that first sight, I felt a physical stunning till my blood moved enough for me to put my arms around him and hug him close.

It took him about three years to recover his balance, but my sister does not remember the pre-grey-beard Papa.

His third illness was a heart attack at about age sixty-two. I was married and in Delhi at the time. My husband answered Mama's call at one-thirty a.m., that she was bringing Papa to a

Delhi hospital. I reached the emergency ward and saw a row of hospital beds and reached for the bed with the most beautiful feet that I knew were his.

Later, my mother told me that through his attack, he had asked that they drive in his new car, followed by the ambulance. The car was sold as inauspicious soon after the illness. It had arrived on a Saturday, and since then, we do not buy any metal on that day.

We have a small legacy of superstitions. My father did not wash his hair on a Thursday because his tuberculosis was diagnosed after a hair wash on that day. There had been two accidents on the G.T. Road, killing two close relatives over two successive winters, and both times, the milk of our cows sweetened and condensed over the farm fire had been brought to the house and laid on the dining table. After that, no milk cake was cooked on the farm.

In his seventies, Papa began feeling acute pain that he suffered for a full year before it was diagnosed as tuberculosis of the spine.

He received the doctor's orders of complete bedrest with palpable relief.

It is after this episode that he did not leave his bed. When the doctor said he could, he did not; when they said he should, he would not; and when they said he must, he refused.

Beneath such specific episodes of illness was the perpetual disease of his mind, precariously sailing on its turbulent inner waters.

One of the early drugs prescribed for his depression was a commonly used entertainment drug called Dexedrine, which, combined with alcohol, brought on a grandiosity that was fun only for us children.

My mother did not talk much about living with Papa's mental health until about the last year before his death. Ganeve and I watched in silent shock her tears, releasing her anger, hatred, sorrow along with painful love: all that she had pent up over years of supporting him without calling attention to herself. I, too, had a glimpse of how deep the mental health issue was when, on one of my visits to Karnal, a year or so before he died, I asked Papa why he really went to Ranchi. He told me in all seriousness that the Russians had indeed been chasing him. I was frightened and I quickly changed the subject.

In 'A Beautiful Mind,' the economist Nash was asked whether he really believed the Russians were after him. His answer was that the idea was as real to him as the other ideas that came to him.

## 21. 1947

'We will hold to the lies and pretend this is true, for that is the only justification for the damage we have caused.' (Anonymous saying.)

The summer of 1947 was as usual. Bibiji left for Srinagar with her normal accoutrements of staff, trunks of clothes, and some jewellery. Papa was discharged from the Kasauli Sanatorium and joined his mother and a joyful reunion with his loyal playmate and uncle, Chacha Jasbir.

He told me of an exuberant walk up Shankaracharya Hill to exercise his newly healed lungs. Life seemed perfect with good health and youthful optimism set in the scenic perfection of the valley.

On their descent, they met a man panting uphill. 'Sardarji, how much further do I have to walk?' he asked.

'As much as you have walked up, that much more,' said

Jasbir even though the top was round the bend. After a frozen moment, the man ran downhill, cursing his wife, while Jasbir and Jindo laughed.

Papa would often laugh by himself, thinking of the time spent with Jasbir.

Another story was how, at Murree, they got their Sikh chauffeur to loosen his beard and hair and sit under a tree in the lotus position. They made enough money from simple people who respectfully genuflected with small offerings of money that bought them a decent drink and dinner.

An era is best described by its humour and I am ashamed of these stories, but Papa's innate honesty would have approved of me writing them. He, in any case, found them funny till the very end.

The following months took their cruel revenge on the naughty young sardars. Papa's joy of freedom from the sanatorium ended with the Partition of Punjab as the price of India's freedom from the British.

1947 tore and shredded people from the land that they had cultivated over centuries, grown into, and evolved and entwined with to form a cultural foliage that breathed and sweated a knowing beyond religion.

There is no one explanation for Partition. Separate factors gathered to an overwhelming wave that submerged all before it.

Why did the idealism of freedom not encompass freedom from communal hatred and violence? The answer may help process this poisonous legacy out of us.

August 1947 was not a ghallughara. It was not a defeat in battle and loss of territory after an old-fashioned conquest. The dead of 1947 are not martyrs for a cause. They are victims of a genocide.

To say that August 1947 was an eruption of a violent and

perverse instinct that lurks as a virus in the deepest recesses of the human mind is to excuse the masterminds who manipulated those recesses for horrific results.

What happened in 1947 was a cheap, synthetic, cynical, plastic, rayon nationalism, injected into the blood of a robust, uncomplicated, yet complex people. Who were the enemies? The leaders who betrayed them, or the kafilas moving across fresh borders drawn across a land's ancient history of continuous, organic growth? One old woman said of Partition: kings have come and gone, governments have changed; this is the first time that people have been changed to suit governments.

So grew the autoimmune disease of communalism, where the patient actively dehumanises himself. He fires badly-constructed weapons of nationalism that, with each shot, kill something within him. The heat tortures his own spirit, then burns and kills its humane values.

The dismembering happened under the watch of uniforms that could not conceal communal identity. New karmic bonds were forged, of blood and revenge. The blood bonds of 1947 are held by our leaders to encash for power by manipulating fear and communal divides; each transaction creates another bond that increases the power of the bond holder by exponentially diminishing the value of human life.

None of the national leaders of the time understood the Punjabi ethos, contained in the rounded inflections of its language: the *ghaghgha, bhabhbha* (phonetic for Punjabi letters G and B) that tie you close to the soil, and the smell of its subterranean waters. It is beyond religion.

Punjab knows the secular from within. Punjabiyat melded Sikhism, Islam, and Hinduism with Sufi and Bhakti songs rich in Persian Punjabi verse and the poetry of its mystics. It has dealt with invaders, Islamic and the ones before and after that. They fought and moved on and settled together, for in the end, we are all going the same way.

*Ram gayo, Ravan gayo, jako bhau parvar,*
*Kaho Nanak thir kuch nahi supney jeeo sansar.*

Ram, Ravan, the biggest families, all will leave,
Nanak, this is but a dream.

Events hurtled to Partition, and it seemed no one could stop it, or that no one wanted to.

Once again, as in the Anglo-Sikh wars, the Punjabis were betrayed by the guile of many who said they formed a nation, and no one asked why Punjab was not being treated as part of it. The Punjabis were betrayed by a nation whose borders they had protected. A recruitment chart of the British Indian Army shows that 28 per cent of the Indian Army was recruited from Punjab, 18 per cent from Madras, 13.8 per cent from United Provinces, 6.8 per cent from Bengal, 5.1 per cent from Bombay, and the remaining, in dwindling smaller points, from the rest of the country.

As to the Sikhs, whether they fought for the British in World War II as my nana Major Sahib had done, or did good works for the freedom struggle with the Congress, or lost their lives as members of the Gadar Party formed in 1913, much before Gandhi arrived in India, or via the communist left that was strong in Punjab, as my nana did, too, they all served loyally as a community the cause of a nation. That new nation then drew a dagger across the Punjabis, who left their souls in the places from where their bodies were removed.

In 1947, as if a precursor to the callousness that became endemic in free India, the country celebrated its freedom while Punjab lay wounded, hurting, lost, bewildered, pilloried, and raped.

The story is the same for Bengal; but that is for someone else to tell.

Perhaps my family could have adopted Islam and stayed on. I had asked my father once why they did not convert and stay on in Pakistan. After all, I reasoned, my Warraich clan had originally come with Ghazni, and who is to know what is really in the heart. In any case, I said, Sikhism is not that unlike Islam; like them, we have a book and no idols; our book also mentions Allah. Papa said, nothing matters but my comfort with myself. That's my religion. That's all it is.

'That should make it easy to convert,' I said, 'for survival.'

'Even so, an essential part of Sikhi and the reason why it was created was to have the courage to stand up to any despotic power. To convert from fear would not be correct, just as Muslims and Hindus should not have to covert from fear.'

Papa had always liked the opening verse of the Quran, 'In the name of the one benevolent and compassionate.' And yet, Sikhi is also Hindu because, though we have no idols, we celebrate the stories of Ram, Krishna, and Durga. We worship the book as if it is an idol. As far as my mother is concerned, this is a criticism. I would agree, but for my weakness for the magnificent pageantry around it.

And so, they left their homes, and something else that was larger than wealth, something that they could not articulate, had not been given time to think through.

The Hindus and Muslims and Sikhs of Punjab moved as a mass across the new border, torn from the past, forced into the future, too shocked to hope that the replanting of life would be of value.

'Apathetic...tired...hungry...hopeless...a woman in a bullock cart feeding a baby at her breast...another picks the lice off the matted hair of a girl.' The better types among them [who] have

[the] energy to think "eagerly ask whether there is some vacant land anywhere they can settle". Land, land is the one thing occupying their minds. These people obviously had their roots deep in the soil.' (*The Holocaust of Indian Partition: An Inquest*, by Madhav Godbole.)

With the Partition, the colour of the old Punjabi writers and poets faded to sepia and the water in their stories dried. Their work smelt of flesh and careless, callous semen, thrown in violent fury and desperation, rotting its many humane possibilities in an earth stinking with blood.

The intensity of Manto's stories brands the memory into the bones of the reader, changing her forever. They are difficult to re-read. I, of the generation born in 1962, break into miserable, scared sweat when I think of the short story, 'Khol Do', of the girl who was raped even by her protectors till she was delivered to her father as a barely breathing corpse. 'Khol do,' says the doctor for the windows, and the girl moves to open the knot of her salwar for yet another rape.

Then there's the story of the exchange of lunatics between Pakistan and India: the mad Bishan Singh who lay down in his village right in the middle of no-man's-land.

Amrita Pritam invoked the spirit of Waris Shah, who had lived when my ancestor was marrying his daughter Devi to Gujjar Singh Bhangi in 1762.

*Ajj akhan Waris Shah nu ki tun kabran vichchon bol,*
*Te ajj kitab-e-ishq da koi agla varka phol.*
*Ik roi si heer Punjab di, tun likh likh maare vain,*
*Ajj lakhan dheean rondian tainu Waris Shah nu kahen.*
*Uth dardmandaan dia dardiaa, uth takk apnaa Punjab,*
*Ajj bele lashan bichhian te lahu di bhari Chenab,*
*Kise ne panjan panian vichch ditti zahar rala,*
*Te unhan panian dharat nun ditta pani la.*

I ask Waris Shah to speak from the grave,
And open a new page of love,
When one Heer cried, you wrote a tome,
Who remembers you when a million Heers weep?
Get up, you compassionate recounter of pain; look at your Punjab.
The Chenab flows with blood.
Get up and look at your Punjab in pain,
Someone has poisoned the five rivers,
Someone has poisoned the waters you had sung about.

My mother cannot recite this poem without choking. A newspaper photo of a line of carts would tense her face and stop her for a split second.

For Punjabis, the fear arose again in the seventies with the rise in the Khalistan separatist movement and again, when blood was spilt in 1984. Mrs Gandhi was assassinated by her Sikh bodyguards, resulting in anti-Sikh riots orchestrated by Congress leaders who, once again, betrayed the Sikhs.

Now, the Sikhs became suspect in the new land that they bravely had made their own, prospered in, and made prosperous. I have a memory of an unarmed Sikh man being shot dead by the police on the highway near Tallania. I also remember feeling scared when a motorcycle with a Sikh man riding it came close to us till we saw that he was someone we knew.

My sister acted in a film called 'Amu' set in the 1984 riots. She lost her husband and son in the script, and her broken heart wailed through her throat, too deep for tears to reach. I watched in frozen shock: it was not only a film.

The same reality repeated in many parts of the world; the reality of children dying in Syria, refugees being refused entry to newer parts of the earth that all of us have claim to.

All this is my reality. I know why my father lay down.

Sufis, saints, prophets have died, saying that they live

among fools. Don't you see something so obvious? Identity is not the core; nothing so impermanent can be the core; there is permanence only in the nothingness that is the core of the whirling change. Focus on that centre. It is a peaceful shunya, zero. Mystics of all religions have experienced it, and all scriptures say it in different ways.

My father's ashes were delivered by the Sutlej to connect with the love of what he had been compelled to leave: Pakistan.

## 22. The Days of Partition

When the Partition was announced, no one knew what it would mean. Even Jinnah retained a house in Bombay, perhaps thinking he would be able to divide his time between the two countries.

Both sides of my family made arrangements to be away from their own homes only for a short time until they returned when things settled. Bibiji, till her dying day, kept the keys to her cupboards in Rajkot that she had left 'only for that summer'.

When the riots began and it became clear that a nation was dying, Bibiji decided to go with Jindo and Jasbir to Rajkot to collect any belongings of value that they could. Even then, they did not believe they were not safe.

As they disembarked at Lahore, the Muslim Station Master recognised them and his eyes widened with fear for them—and himself, since he knew he was going to help them. Bound by loyalty and feeling pain for the beauty of the innocence of two sixteen-year-old sardars he had seen grow up and the beautiful widow Persin Kaur, he rushed to gather them into his office as a hen her beloved chicks.

'You cannot go to Rajkot, you cannot go,' said he, shocked

at the foolhardiness of this. 'How could Sardar Bahadur Sahib have allowed this? And Sardarni Sahib, you are here? How do I say the word of what they do to women?'

The Station Master found three seats in a compartment on the first train out of Pakistan. Jasbir accepted Jindo as his leader, even though he was older and the chacha. Jindo had a rare quality of mental agility and physical presence that is called 'purrsnallty' in Punjab.

Jindo scanned around for protection, and, sighting a young British officer on the railway platform looking to embark upon their train, he called out, 'Officer, would you please sit with us?'

The officer, even while responding warmly to Jindo's clear English, warned, 'I can't use my service revolver if there is violence.'

'I understand, sir, but your presence may deter a mob anyhow.'

The officer entered their compartment and agreed to sit at the window in clear sight of any mob.

Then Jindo looked for a gun. A Sikh in their compartment had one and Jindo asked him for it, but he refused.

'No one would part with a gun at a time like this,' Jindo commented when telling me this story.

'Force it from him,' Jindo told Jasbir, who immediately wrestled the gun from the furious Sikh, ready for a serious fight till Jindo said, 'My chacha is the best marksman in the Punjab. He needs the gun for all of us; even I am not going to take it from him.'

The Sikh sat back, nervous and fuming at the humiliating defeat from a stripling boy.

And the train slid out of Lahore, carrying a silent collective. Silence: where are the words for leaving the greatest place in the world? *Jis Lahore Nai Dekhya O Jamyai Nai*—one who has not seen Lahore has seen nothing; music, food, laughter, brave, bold and generous hospitality. Silence for leaving and fear for whether they will reach.

Thus passed an hour in heavy silence till the train crossed the Wagah Border. The past is already behind, and there has to be relief of arrival to a new life, whatever it may be. Even babies, thus far silenced by the muffling grief of departure they sensed, began wailing after they crossed the border. There was life to be lived; food, attention, relief, fear, anxiety. At that moment, no adult stopped a baby from crying because their own tears told the same story.

Descending onto the platform at Amritsar, Jindo felt the exhaustion of what was almost an anti-climax. The English officer grabbed Jindo's arm affectionately and said, 'Will you join the Indian Army?'

'I don't know, sir.'

'You should; you will make a great officer. Good luck.'

All passengers on the next train out of Pakistan were killed by a kafila of Muslims, claiming to avenge some other killing of Muslims by Hindu and Sikh mobs.

How far do you go to look for the aggressor? How many were victims elsewhere? All fighting like cornered animals, for they knew not what.

This is my father's story till Partition.

Now for my mother's.

## 23. Mama

Gurdarshan Kaur, known as Darshan, was born in a prominent Mann family of village Mananwala, which was also Bibiji's village.

Darshan's ancestor, Budh Singh, a general in Ranjit Singh's army, was rewarded for military service with a jagir of as much land as he could cover on his horse in a day. 'Good thing Sardarji did not go around in circles,' said an irreverent friend.

When the general died, his youngest wife was pregnant, and her child, if male, would have been an equal heir to the property. This young, pregnant woman was compelled to commit sati. 'Where are the good Sikh teachings in this?' I asked my mother. She had no answer.

The sati chose to dress in all her jewellery that she scattered along the way to the pyre so that the greedy family would not at least get that. She cursed the family that whoever built a brick house would have no surviving heir. One of them did, and his only son died. How far down a lineage must descendants expiate the sins of their ancestors? Don't please ask the obvious next question; that brick houses were bound to be built eventually and so on. This is a story I tell you.

Now, all prayer ceremonies in my mother's family remember the sati and regret and remorse is expressed and one share of the kada pershad is still kept aside in her name.

Bibiji was also part of the Mann baradari in the same village. My mother's household had a close relationship with Bibiji's family, and my parents could be called cousins, though several times removed, by a complicated network of relationships.

For Bibiji, my father's marriage had become urgent because he had evinced an interest in a nurse from Coorg. Thus, it came about that Bibiji reached out to her own family to ask for my mother's hand in marriage for my father.

My mother's family lived in the Lehndi Patti side of Mananwala. Lehndi Patti literally means the descending disc of the sun. Bibiji's home was in the Chardi Patti (rising sun) side. After Partition, those of the Chardi Patti liked to say that the placement of their houses reflected a superior rank.

After his father died, my father spent a lot of time with Bibiji at his maternal home in Mananwala.

My mother said, 'A child should not be brought up in his maternal home; is always aware that he does not belong there. Your Papa was aware that his maternal family was wealthier than that of his father and so he has always had a complex about rich people. He had an inferiority complex and was always insecure because the home that he spent so much time in was not his own.'

I understood what she meant. Whenever we would visit a fancy house, Papa would return slightly morose, and then say, 'This is not too bad, is it?' and I, who loved our home, would be affronted. 'How can you even ask, Papa?'

Thus, this sense of inadequacy in a material context made my father worry that we should not feel inferior to his older brother's children, who were obviously prosperous because of Tayaji's independent salary in the Army and Tayiji's valuable real estate in Delhi.

In contrast, my father's only income was his half-share from Rajkot Farm. Unlike my Tayiji, who had brought real estate as dowry, my mother brought nothing. My maternal grandfather was fierce about no dowry. He had broken a previous engagement because the boy's family demanded land and jewellery.

My mother's family, though not well-off at all compared to the Rajkotias, had an elegant, understated integrity that, to me, is the hallmark of a fine upbringing. This quality, matched with her father's modest means, made my mother an ideal daughter-in-law.

I remember overhearing my mother and Tayiji chatting on a summer afternoon in the cool, darkened drawing room at Rajkot House. 'If I had your kind of money, I would have them all dancing on the palms of my hands,' my mother said.

'You are wrong,' said Tayiji. 'It's my money that works against me. He is careful that my financial strength does not affect his authority as husband.'

My mother, without problems of wealth, accepted her lowest position in the family hierarchy and worked with quiet industry to be a good daughter-in-law and wife. But it is as a mother that she excelled. It was her fierce focus on making us independent that was unique for those times. It was the intensity of a woman who has felt stung by dependency.

That she felt the humiliation was what made her unique: most women married to wealthy men did not question their financial disempowerment.

*

My mother's uniqueness was born from the power dynamics of the overwhelmingly matricentric home that she had been brought up in. Her grandmother, Beybeyji, was a maverick who had not allowed her husband's body to be cremated till her four sons had transferred some land to her name to ensure her financial independence.

My mother's father was an extraordinarily handsome man. Tall, lean, with beautiful, aquiline features. He rose to the rank of Major in the British Indian Army and was called Major Sahib. He fought in World War I and was recruited during World War II as in-charge of prisoners of war. He had a short tenure as aide-de-camp to King George VI and lived in the barracks at Hampton Court. At official receptions, he was a bizarre sight: a teetotaller sardar, sipping from a delicate China cup.

His obsession with punctuality was legendary. My father used to make fun of my mother's household as ruled by a bell—a bell to announce mealtimes to the army of cousins; a bell not only to announce the time to shit, but also a chime for when the job must finish.

My father enjoyed scatological humour, but there is surely some truth to it, given my mother's obsession with bowel movements as she aged. Their quality influences her temperament, ranging from savage snark about her failure to cleanse and great, visible contentment when she did well.

Major Sahib was industrious like my paternal grandfather had been. Even in pre-Partition India, he chose to farm his acres himself rather than being the customary absentee landlord. His own traditionally landlording father sniggered at his son's politics of humility and industry, which he unfairly equated with being humourless. Under Gandhi's influence, Major Sahib gave up the title of Sardar Bahadur and took to wearing white khadi kurta salwars with a white turban. The only occasion he gave way to some vanity was the wedding of his younger son in 1970. I did not know of his titles till I read the wedding card, and I did not know how decorated a soldier he had been till I saw the number of medals he wore on his threaded brocade choga which I saw only that one time. He looked grand and handsome, and I was intensely proud to be his first grandchild.

My nana's younger brother, Bhupinder Singh, was a lawyer and a politician, particularly popular for his energetic opposition to Prohibition, advocated by puritanical nationalists. Nehru was fond of him, but deprecated his drinking habit, thus revealing his own lack of understanding and slight contempt for the Punjabi.

Bhupinder Singh married a fashionable sardarni from Calcutta. Her contrast to the rest of the family was noticeable even to my child's eye. She spoke Hindi all her life and her saris were an exotic contrast to the salwar-qameez ubiquitous in Punjab.

My grandmother, Jaswant Kaur, was very amiable, and I experienced her as being far more relaxedly maternal than my mother. She brought up and loved Bhupinder Singh's younger son as her own, who always felt closer to us than his own siblings.

Beybeyji's third son did nothing much and was my father's favourite for precisely that reason.

Of Beybeyji's three daughters, Gurbachan Kaur never married. She was a great influence on my mother and, hence, on Ganeve and I. She had blue eyes that I did not know were sightless till I was about eight years old. She became blind at fourteen through a suicide bid with a quinine overdose. The cause of her desperate grief remains a murky secret of the immediate family. All I do know is that she always said that her only two brothers were Major Sahib and Bhupinder Singh. She never acknowledged the third.

Her father decided to secure his blind daughter with land, upon which she set up the 'Budh Shakti Ashram' in Mananwala to educate and provide vocational training to destitute girls. After Partition, the ashram travelled to India as 'Mata Gujri Ashram', and I knew her as 'Ashram Waley Bibiji'.

*

My mother described her fervent nationalistic pre-Partition childhood. Her young cousin Bhupinder Singh's eldest son was named Hind Ravi. He quickly learned to earn generous tips from visiting sardars by saying, 'Jai Hind.' Forty years later, he led the Republic Day parade as Commandant General.

Just before Partition, my nana, Major Sahib, had set up 'aman' committees for communal harmony, and hope stayed till the last few days, when the sound of drums and guns and rising smoke closed around the village and all hope of peace. *'Niklo, niklo,'* (Leave, leave), he is said to have called out in the village lanes, rushing home to draw plans for evacuating the Hindus and Sikhs. He was the last to leave.

Not anglicised like the Rajkotias and not given to holidaying in the hills, my maternal family packed their luggage on bullock carts that took them to the main road, from where they embarked on a bus for India. In the melee, Mama was seated on a gadda without anyone from her family until they were united in the bus. My mother still remembers the panic of separation.

The village was waterlogged after a heavy monsoon. An old woman with joints frozen in the August rain asked a young Muslim man to carry her onto the bus. He refused and hurried past. Major Sahib had the 'wajood' (stature) to slap that man in those communal fraught times and ordered that he help the old woman. The man obeyed. Major Sahib's moral presence was strong enough to touch the inner darkness that we all have because we are too weak or too lazy with the effort of constant rightness.

Darshan still weeps when she thinks of her father, walking through the village lined with Muslims bidding farewell and giving rotis, which he accepted in a khadi scarf.

'Like a beggar,' she cries.

They climbed on to the bus and shared the rotis with the passengers. Just enough for one round of hunger.

My mother is still choked with the memory of other people on the bus, opening their tiffins to tortuously fragrant clouds of achar and roti that they, in their turn, did not share.

'You will have to wait, kudiye,' said Darshan's mother, 'we will eat when we get to Amritsar. Have patience. Pray. Now you know why I tell you not to waste food; do you realise its value? Pray that you are never hungry again. Pray that we will be all right.'

A refugee camp on the way served a stale dal that gave Darshan dysentery. She remembers retching on her mother's lap, asking, 'Bibiji, will I die?'

The family reached Bhagowal, District Gurdaspur, where Major Sahib's sister was married. All told, there were ten cousins, their parents, and many servants who had taken refuge there.

I asked my mother, 'Did you ever feel jealous that you had lost a home while this batch of first cousins lived in luxury?'

'My bua tried to make sure that we did not feel too miserable. We were all in the age group of ten or thereabouts. It was like a mela playing in the orchard. Every occasion was made special by Buaji. My brother, Asram Pal, was very funny. "Bhain, let's not take our books to India," he had said while packing in Mananwala.'

But they had a teacher in Bhagowal.

'But sometimes you must have felt something,' I prodded.

'Well, the Bhagowal cousins had begun resenting the lack of space. Someone once told one of them, "You have become weak." And the cousin replied, "That's because I have to share my food with refugees."'

Major Sahib had had to give up six dogs. He asked an Indian Army officer to take charge of them along with some antique guns and valuable carpets. Months after Partition, he waited in vain for the friend to volunteer return of his 'amanat' (items given in trust). Finally, he had to visit him, embarrassed, both for himself and his friend. He did not get his things back.

The dogs whined and pressed close to my grandfather. 'It hurt to let the dogs go,' he told me.

'Why could you not have brought them with you?' I asked.

'We had no food for ourselves, how would I feed six dogs? Maybe my friend thought he had earned my valuables for keeping my dogs. They were well-looked after, I have to say.'

Major Sahib sent his servants to various refugee camps with the assurance that he would send for them when he settled again. Which he did when he reached his allotted land in village Tallania.

The majordomo was Ram Pershad, and the housekeeper was a woman we called Dadi, eavesdropper and carrier of village stories, yet never disliked because she was of ceaseless, robust cheer.

Darshan's family celebrated Independence, while Jindo's family, though far better off, felt no joy. Darshan loved the fast-modernising, independent India. 'They all sit around, counting the servants they had,' she said about Jindo and his family, 'but we are far more comfortable here. They may say their life of the past was grand, but it was like living in a *dhatthha khoo*.' (Dry, broken well.)

But I know Darshan has not forgotten. One day, she saw in my home a glass lamp that I had bought from Hyderabad. 'Bapuji had bought lamps like this for our newly renovated home in Mananwala just a few months before Partition.'

## 24. Village Tallania, District Fatehgarh Sahib

Last night, I dreamt of aged walls, desolate without a roof. I am drawn within to a pool of haunted stillness. I know I am in village Tallania, and my father's voice in my dream confirms it, 'These are monuments of interest. One was built when you were a child and is now buried under the street outside the house.'

It sounded garbled the next morning, yet it made sense to me. There is, in fact, a gurudwara outside my maternal grandfather's house that served as a mosque before Partition.

The ancient wall of my dream is perhaps the one in the Fatehgarh Sahib Gurudwara that is a straight walk over fields green with paddy, copper with wheat, or yellow with mustard.

It is here that Guru Gobind Singh's two younger sons were bricked alive by the Nawab of Sirhind. Tiny shields and swords forged and crafted for the size of the little sahibzadas were found here.

My nani would say of me, 'What a *karma valli kudi* that

she does not feel the discomfort of village life!' But I loved its lively contrast to the lurking emptiness beneath listless activity that existed on bad days in Karnal. Here was political gossip, Parliament debates discussed as if we were there, jokes, loud laughter, and warm, honest, simple food.

My nana had a vision of the commune style of farming, and the extended family contributed according to their capacity, trusting Major Sahib's fair divisions of crop shares and titles to acres of wild shrub that he had bought near Meerut for the price of kaudis (a metaphor for very cheap, a defunct currency of Mughal times).

Much like his future son-in-law, my father, was doing at Jundla, my nana lived in a tent, breaking and levelling the land to build temporary sheds for himself and the farm labour. A village grew around it, and it fell to his honour to name it. In memory of Gandhi, he called it Ram Raj.

Eventually, he built a simple pucca house, made luxurious by the tall trees and green fields that I looked out to while eating quantities of milk condensed with jaggery over a slow fire. The sweet was called palang tod (breaking bed): my early teen imagination conflicted between the bed being broken by sexual vigour or by fat.

My nana had the largest house in Tallania. It had belonged to the Muslim landlord, who had left with his entourage. The village centre was a circular chaupal with a peepul tree, a small gurdwara that had been a mosque, and my nana's house. There was an outer circle of houses, connected to the inner circle with little lanes.

The entrance to my nana's house in the centre was marked by an arch high enough for an elephant to pass under in its days of pre-Partition glory. Centuries had bleached the wooden gate to pale wood, bound by thick, broad, iron decorations of a leaf pattern. There was a huge iron bolt that needed two men to shut. The arch was supported by thick walls on either side, within each of which was recessed a room for the munshi's residence and office.

My mother would tell me how they had cheered up when their aunt promised them that the house allotted to them at Tallania was the grandest in the village, which it undoubtedly was. When they entered the courtyard that the grand gate opened onto, they wept. It was desolate, treeless, and bare, even of a blade of grass. On the far side was parked a tonga and a horse tethered to its feeding trough. Beside it was a well. Further back were barrack-style mud constructions for workers' quarters and several latrine cubicles. A wooden door to each cubicle opened onto a mud mound to squat on for your business.

The absence of Western-style toilets was a marked difference between Rajkot House Karnal and my nana's house in Tallania. But I was not uncomfortable because a healthy digestion did not make me linger. Soon, modern plumbing flushed the mud latrines into distant memory. The one bathing room in my nana's house was the size of a very large bedroom, with a chair to put your clothes on and a cupboard for basic soaps and oils. A large brass tap poured water into a shining brass bucket. The water pumped from the well was always just right. Cold but not icy in summer and tolerably warm in winter.

There was an inner courtyard surrounded by the rooms and kitchen. It had a handpump in the corner and a slender naali from it along the edges of the courtyard puncturing the boundary wall, through which it opened onto the road outside. As children, we were allowed to piss into the naali rather than having to go out to the latrines in the outer courtyard.

The rooms opening into each other were lined with stacks of steel trunks, functioning as wardrobes for clothes and bedding, fine wear, and shawls. To me, it seemed as if my young maasi was perpetually packing or unpacking. The floors of the house were mud and I remember the gobar lep, a thin mixture of dung and mud believed to have antiseptic properties, carefully spread on top.

The bones of the house were exquisitely sparse. In my mind's eye, I dressed that house in grand, maximalist style, but then it would not be the house of those lean, straightforward, honest folk that were my mother's parents and her siblings.

The electricity supply was sporadic with longer periods of absence. 'Bijli' became a separate being, received with joy on her infrequent and surprise visits. My mother told me of Bijli's very first arrival: 'On that day, everyone gathered to say an ardas early evening, and then we called "Waheguru ji ka Khalsa, Waheguru ji ki Fateh," as Beybeyji switched on the light.'

'Thank God it worked just then,' I said.

The only telephone in the entire village was installed in the verandah overlooking the inner courtyard. The only times I saw a charming affectation of pre-Partition times was when the gurudwara granthi, who also worked with my grandfather, answered the telephone as 'Major Sahib's secretary'.

The steady rhythm of a pendulum clock measured time in the verandah; the hours marked by a musical chime that I miss and am still looking to replicate in my house in Delhi.

The oldest inhabitants of the village were the baazigars (village artists and dancers). I wandered into their homes to eat bajra-roti and achar, and heard their music that later became popular across the world as bhangra rap.

I had already learned from life in Tallania that fun was also messy; flies and sweaty mithai. Hot days were fun with cold drinks and the joyous contentment of the end-of-day bath in temperate water. We slept on the roof under mosquito nets through which we saw clear, plentiful stars, shared by those of this very village who were now in Pakistan.

In Tallania, I learned to smell Punjabi. We described our salwar kurtas and dupattas not as purple or light pink or red or orange or yellow but jamuni, pyazi, lal sooha, santri, basanti. In summer, we drank milk with ice and sugar. We plucked jamuns and falsa and sat under the trees for hours. Evenings were special with home-made mango ice cream, the taste of which was only the final pleasure that began with gathering fresh mangoes, helping the cooks churn the sugar and milk in a steel cylinder turning in a wooden pail packed with ice and rock salt. The sound of the turning handle heralded the contentment of tasting the generous scoops of creamy, cold, sweet ladled into special green glass tumblers.

In winter, we ate sattoo (pulse flour) and fresh, soft gur (jaggery) as we basked in the sunny courtyards.

Our meals, without distracting 'table' conversation, were of mutton curry with onions and chillies, and rotis daubed with desi ghee. White butter melted in creamy dals. Breakfast was dalia with white butter and gur. Boiled eggs were eaten with roti and achar. There was no bread. We drank ganna juice flavoured with lemon and black salt at eleven a.m. Everything and our bodies smelled of earth soaked in fresh, clear water. We played with dolls stitched by our cousin, Baby. We dressed them in bits of cloth discarded by the local tailor.

At night, my aunt, Mamiji Ranjit (Mamaji Asram Pal's wife), would tell us stories of movies, describing each scene with luxurious leisure. I still remember the story of the film 'Aankhen', which opens with Mala Sinha, who, *gulabi salwar-qameez wich badi sweet lag rahi shi*. (Looked very sweet in a pink salwar-qameez.)

The safety of village life allowed me an independence that I was not used to in Karnal. My cousin Baby and I could go without adult supervision to the annual village fair outside the Gurudwara Fatehgarh Sahib to remember the martyrdom of the little sahibzaadas. The gurudwara was small and charming and we could walk into the langar asking for food and chatting to the bhaiji about what we wanted to eat. Evenings were cosy where the villagers could gather to listen to the kirtan and chat among themselves in a low, comfortable rhythm that I found very soothing as I lay with my head in my nani's lap.

At the time, Ganeve was too young to be an interesting playmate. One day, I deigned to engage with her in a game of hide-and-seek but then changed my mind and left her hiding under the bed, while I ran to Baby's house and on to the fair. Ganeve, I am told, called out to me several times to seek her, till she fell asleep with disappointed excitement. When she woke to realise my betrayal, she wept her heart out. This, I still remember and regret. Baby's oldest sister consoled Ganeve with a card game.

It says something of my mother that she did not scold my cruelty, and I was quickly ashamed of it for precisely that reason.

Mama was, however, given to moral intensities that I sometimes found cumbersome. She did not understand, for example, that I had asked for a few paise to buy kachi lassi, and, finding the shop had run out, bought sweets instead. She treated that as fraud and I had to go without home-made ice cream that evening, the pain and humiliation of which I still remember.

Soon, Ganeve was old enough to join us at the fair to buy cardboard pipes and cotton candy and chaat and plastic toys of fluorescent pink and green, and gold. I took Ganeve on her first Ferris Wheel ride. Two men turned the wheel by pedalling the bars in a quickening rhythm. Ganeve, much to my embarrassment, wailed through the event. A group of boys watching us began laughing at her. I felt morally bound to defend my sister. She was mine alone to be mean to, but for the world, we were united.

As the wheel took us to the ground, I began scolding them. 'You should be ashamed,' I said, and the wheel went up. The next time it went down, I had time to say, 'A little girl cries,' and the wheel swung up, and the next time down, I said, 'and you show your ugly, yellow teeth.' This was typical Punjabi snark of 'showing teeth' rather than dignifying it as a smile. The 'yellow' was my own addition, learned from the wolf's big, yellow teeth that he showed to Red Riding Hood.

The boys followed us on the fairgrounds and over the fields as we walked home later in the evening. There were at least five of them, and I had a discomfiting sense of their presence, but that's all. The times were kinder and gentler, and heinous things happened, but somehow, it felt safer.

Tallania has a unique syncretic history. Near the gurudwara is the Rauza Sharif. Its story is that a dying pir could not go to Hajj but had a vision of Mecca and so the Kaaba came to him instead.

The other story of the mosque is that the Nawab of Malerkotla condemned the dastardly killings of the younger sahibzadas and believed that the Rauza Sharif must redeem the land as a continuing symbol of purity and peace. The effect of the nawab's courageous dissent lasts till this day and Malerkotla did not suffer communal riots during Partition.

But the Rauza Sharif at Tallania is now often barricaded during Sikh religious festivals. My father attended the mela on one of his rare Tallania visits. We went to the Rauza Sharif. The police would not let him through, but agreed to send for the pir, who emerged from a smaller door within the large gate—a tall man with a grey beard and green choga and skullcap, telling a tasbi (prayer beads).

My father spoke to him in Persianised Punjabi and I remember the pir's face opening to a warm smile as he led us in. The others crowding behind us were not allowed to follow.

I remember the peace of the place. There were old trees and a big pool of water over which resounded the calm, deep power of the call of the azaan. Maybe this was the water of my dream. We wandered in the dappled shade of an ancient mango orchard.

About an hour later, we stepped out into blazing light and gaudy festive colours: dust kicked by horses and tongas, car horns and rickshaw bells, tooting cardboard trumpets and tuneless flutes, over which flowed the sound of a melodious reed pipe and children's laughter.

The pir of Rauza Sharif attended my nana's death ceremony in his green choga and skullcap. He knelt to the book and sat with us through the kirtan, and shared the langar afterwards.

## 25. Teja Singh Choorkhana

At Tallania, the Mata Gujri Ashram was set up by my Ashram Waley Buaji. It is a simple barrack-style construction of verandahs enclosing small, bare rooms, cheered only by the views of tree-bordered fields.

I took life at the ashram as fun child's play. Only in hindsight did I realise its intense political activism. Buaji's achievement as a blind woman in conservative late-19th to mid-20th-century Punjab defies any simple description or adjectives. She broke through rigid Sikh practice and connected not only to others but beyond to a place without patriarchy.

She was not religious but spiritual. There was no darbar sahib at the ashram. The only small Guru Granth Sahib kept in a cupboard was gifted by Bibiji to me and I keep it still, propped on the small wooden stand that she gave me along with it: the sort used for the Quran. I read it sometimes, to meditate on the spirit that inspired her.

There are many stories of Bibiji's ashram at Tallania. The girl rescued from under a bridge by Teja Singh Swatantar, a 'bhari kaamrade', meaning a heavyweight communist. She came with him to the ashram, crying and shivering and shaking and tired and scared and hungry. 'We have to change her name to hide her identity,' said Bibiji. They called her Jeevan, life. She never knew if her family reached Pakistan.

The days of my annual visits to Tallania were spent playing with the ashram girls, who enjoyed the break in their routine. Hide and seek, pakdan-pakdai, gulli-danda, geetian with a small ball, hopscotch, oonch mange neech.

The only male presence at the ashram was Teja Singh Choorkhana, a fierce-looking old sardar, who spoke little but let me jump on his back while he lay face down on a manjee in the shade of the neem tree.

I learned his story much later when I read Ashram Waley Buaji's biography *Bhuley Visray Log* (The Forgotten People). It was written by a tailor named Shiv Nath, whom Bibiji had met at a sahitya conference in Sirhind, the old-day Literature Festival.

A photo in the book shows Choorkhana standing next to Pandit Nehru, his rough clothes and plain, strong features an incongruous contrast to Nehru's manicured, aquiline beauty. Why were they side by side? How important could the ashram caretaker be?

In the 1930s, he was recruited by the Gadar Party from village Choorkhana. His fearless and reliable work impressed many senior revolutionaries, among whom was Dafeydar Lachman Singh, later hanged by the British for treason. By association,

Choorkhana came under the police scanner and the law required his daily presence at the police station as a 'dus numbri', feared offender.

The Pathan thaneydar asked Choorkhana, 'Sardar, if your head hits a brick wall, will the wall break or your head?'

'Khan, my head may break, but if I have struck the wall with the might of my heart, the wall will surely break, too.'

The Khan hugged him. 'Carry on the good work,' he said, 'but it will help if you marry, because I can then tell the authorities that Choorkhana has matured and settled into family life.'

A fellow revolutionary's sister married Choorkhana in a stark ceremony without silk or feast and not even a granthi to read the rites. Choorkhana read the lavan (wedding verse in Guru Granth Sahib) himself, as he and his bride circled the book. The marriage, however, did not throw the police off his trail, and soon after, Choorkhana, along with some other Gadris, was tried by a Lahore court on uncertain charges. Of all the accused, seven were acquitted, thirteen sentenced to life imprisonment, and Choorkhana and two others were sentenced to be hanged.

Lodged at Central Jail in solitary confinement, he refused to meet his old parents or his young wife and newborn child because he wanted no 'rona-dhona' (show of tears).

Came the day scheduled for his death; Choorkhana waited. Late evening, a havaldar informed him that his death sentence had been commuted to life at Kala Pani, the Andamans.

Preparing to leave for the Andamans, Choorkhana finally met his family on the condition that no one would cry. His brother brought some money that Choorkhana refused, asking that it be used to 'look after the Singhni' (wife, literally translates to lioness).

At the Andamans, the detenus realised that their solitary confinement could be alleviated by visits to the dispensary. These revolutionaries, with muscular names such as Baba Mohan Singh 'Dakna', Nidhan Singh 'Chugha', Master Chatar Singh, Bhai Paramanand 'Jhansi', would feign illness regularly to gather for conversation and an invigorating fight with jail officers. In one such fight, Dakna kicked an officer on the stomach to send him flying back to land, sitting, on a faraway chair. Decades later, the memory of the officer's surprised look could still break Choorkhana's grim, rough face into a rare smile.

After about a year, Choorkhana and a few others were released for reasons they did not know. The left-behind Ghadris made them promise, 'Don't forget. Talk about us.'

The civil disobedience wave was high and still rising when Choorkhana returned to his village. The Akalis had begun a movement to liberate the gurudwaras in Punjab from mahants (priests). Congress leaders like Saifuddin Kitchlew asked Choorkhana to expose the Akali agenda of distraction from the cause of national freedom.

News arrived that many prisoners of the Andamans had been moved to Madras, and Choorkhana was ordered to trace them in the new jails. He first visited Gandhi at Ahmedabad. 'He (Gandhi) did not really know what I was doing or what I wanted but he gave me a rukka (note) for a man in Trichinopoly that, in the times, was dangerous for free movement because of "marshallah" (martial law).'

In Madras, Choorkhana, accompanied by some Gadris, met Baba Jwala, who lay on the cell floor along with another sardar, Choor Singh. 'Why are you lying here?' Choorkhana asked.

'Ask this jailor haramzada why he whipped us.'

It was because they had refused yet another meal of rice and sambar. The jailor was angry because he knew the meaning of haramzada even though he could not understand the rest of the Punjabi.

Choorkhana left dry rations with the jailor, who seemed more pathetic than bad, given that his only request was that Choorkhana tell the inmates not to be so rude.

In the Rajahmundry jail, many Sikh inmates gathered to talk to Choorkhana. The police asked, 'How do they all know you?'

'They don't, but they smell home in us.'

The Rajahmundry jailor took them to meet Baba Pirthee, who would not face his visitor because he had sworn not to set eyes on the 'kanjar' (pimp) jailor who was standing with them. The matter for most of the inmates was of rations: they yearned for dal roti. At all the jails, Choorkhana arranged dry rations of dal and wheat to save the restive Gadri sardars from a sentence of rice and sambhar.

Language was also an issue. In Cannanore, Paramanand Jhansi, Gurmukh Singh, and Kesar Singh were allowed to meet Choorkhana and his band of Gadris on the condition that they not speak Punjabi. That they knew no other language did not concern the jailor. The Gadris conversed by barking like dogs.

In Vellore, Choorkhana's accidental reference to Gandhi while talking to the prisoners alerted the listening guards. 'Have you come from the Mahatma?' they asked as they tore open his belongings to check for anything. Fortunately, the note from Gandhi could not be found because Choorkhana had lost it.

The police put the Gadris on the first train, watching till it was out of their sight to make sure that the sardars did not jump off and sneak back into the city.

Choorkhana returned home to find his wife in a state of catatonic depression. After medical aid, once she was functional, he left for Amritsar again to help with the langar for a meeting organised by Lala Lajpat Rai.

He was arrested and jailed at Amritsar along with Saifuddin Kitchlew and Shaikh Shahabuddin, who were under trial in a bombing case. 'We were very happy to see each other,' said Choorkhana. 'This is where I learned about revolution and politics. Every day, there were lectures, and I became something from something else.'

One day, Choorkhana, sitting in the jail courtyard, thinking perhaps of what he had become from what else, heard a voice call to him, 'Jatheydar.'

He looked up to see, across the wall of the adjoining cells, 'a sardar of youthful beauty'.

'I wanted to meet you many times but the problem was of these various warrants. I am glad I have met you finally. Give me your blessings.'

'Oye, what blessings, bachoo,' said Choorkhana. Then Choorkhana, the one who would not cry and I never saw smile, that Choorkhana, reached for Bhagat Singh's hand and kissed it.

'Bhagat Singh had a magic to him,' Choorkhana told Shiv Nath. 'When I kissed his hand, he raised it to shout, "Inqilab! Inqilab!" I can never forget his young face, raising slogans at the heavens.'

After a long silence, writes Shiv Nath, Choorkhana then said, 'It is only that energy that can be called youth, not these young men with cigarettes stuck through trimmed beards.'

'I understand about cigarettes, but as to beards, even Bhagat Singh was clean shaven at the time,' said Shiv Nath.

'That was because his work was khufiya, secret. He had to disguise himself by shaving his beard.'

What struck me was that a Sikh 'beard' was to not have one.

My father told me that Bhagat Singh is said to have kissed the noose that was to hang him. All Sikhs sentenced to death would say the prayer of *Chandi Di Vaar* while walking to the gallows, Papa had told me. Though I know now that Bhagat Singh was an atheist and is unlikely to have had *Chandi Di Vaar* read out to him.

My grandmother used to recite this prayer along with Jaap Sahib at three a.m.

I learned the rhythm of words as a marching beat.

*Chakur chehun ar burn jati ar pati nehun jeh,*
*Roop rang ar rekh bhaikh kohoo keh na sakur keh,*
*Achal moorat anbho parkas ametoje kehjai.*

He who is without mark or sign,
He who is without caste or line,
He who is without colour or form,
and without any distinctive norm,
He who is without limit and motion,
All effulgence, non-descript Ocean.

In 1945, Choorkhana was arrested and thrown into Lahore Jail again. There he met 'kaamrades' Kishori Lal, Gulab Singh and Malik Kundan Lal, who tried to persuade him to join the communists. 'But I resisted, saying I trusted Nehru, who would achieve 'sudhaar' (reform).

In the 1946 election, Nehru persuaded Choorkhana to stand from Sheikhupura, but Choorkhana told Shiv Nath that even the election fund did not reach him because many Congress workers spread rumours that he would give the money to the communists. 'The idea was to block all popular progressives. I was shaken and disillusioned, and that is when Bibiji sent word that she needed me at Mananwala to work at the ashram she had set up. After securing his wife financially by selling some land, Choorkhana reached Mananwala, where he lived at the ashram till Partition and, after that, the Budh Shakti Ashram at Tallania.

At Tallania, Ashram Waley Buaji also set up the first all-women college called Mata Gujri College. Choorkhana tells the story of Bibiji's visit to Calcutta to gather funds for the college. 'After her speech, the devotees wanted their 'chadava' (money offering to the Gurudwara) to be given to her, but then Master

Tara Singh stood up to say that Bibiji was a communist and atheist and the money would not be used for Sikhi, and so the chadava was eventually given to Master Tara Singh.'

Buaji Ashram Waley eventually lost control of the college to religion and the Akalis.

Around the mid-seventies, she was diagnosed with cancer of the stomach. Her last words, according to Shiv Nath, were to tell the bhaiji not to pray so loudly: 'Why not whisper, or, even better, why not keep quiet?'

Choorkhana died about a month after she did.

It is these stories that became the strength of my mother, who, one day, pissed off with the overwhelming machismo of the Punjab sewadars at the Golden Temple during its Bhindranwale presence, said loud enough for them to hear, '*Unna di soti maro ainney dey sir.*' (Beat them on the head with their own sticks.)

# PART II

# 26. Karnal

After Partition, my father's family settled in Karnal, where the soil, it is believed, has soaked the blood of the heroes of the *Mahabharata*.

'Covered in blood, the earth was beautiful...as if covered by large numbers of shakragopa insects during the monsoon; as a young lady dressed in a white garment dyed with saffron, the colourful flesh and blood decorated in gold; earrings and ornaments...dislodged; golden necklaces and armour... elephants covered with blood...like mobile mountains...pierced with gold-tufted arrows, beautiful mountain tops, lit with torches; wondrous red and gold smeared with sandalwood, drenched with blood.

'...in horrifying pain, with their temples and frontal lobes shattered, the elephants shrieked and fell down...in many different kinds of ways, their severed arms covered in gold quivered powerfully...like the bodies of serpents'.

The villagers at the allotted farm in Jundla told Jindo that the nearby khai was purified by that blood.

'A terrible and large river with currents of blood, fierce in form, was created there and began to flow. The severed heads were like rocks. The hair constituted weeds and moss... full of large numbers of bones...flesh, mud and mire...terrible currents of blood...the river...extended Yama's kingdom'. (*The Mahabharata*, Bibek Debroy.)

Karnal, the villagers said, is named after Karan. This

enthralled me: 'Maybe some war happened here, Papa.' The story may be rooted in some incident, war, maybe just a skirmish, but something; the classic story of a family feud over land and lineage.

Jindo was scornful of those who could not see the difference between literature, mythology, and history. Bibiji scolded him for laughing aloud at some Sikh clergyman visiting Rajkot House, who claimed, 'We knew that the 'kalgi' (jewel for the turban) we saw at the British National Museum belonged to the Guru Sahib because each Sikh in the delegation felt his heart beat faster when he stood close to it.' Ignoring Bibiji's scowl, he winked at me, and I hid my grin behind my storybook about Greek gods.

Such humour only helped alleviate heavy time, as at a dreary railway station. We were all going somewhere, but my father was getting anxious about the train's delay. Maybe Jindo's heart lifted as he grew closer to the end; nearly there, just a few more moments. But through most of his life, he had not really settled.

His difficulty in settling, I understood from the story he told me of meeting a Maratha Regiment officer at a cocktail party at his brother's house in Delhi.

'Where do you live, Sardar Sahib?' asked the officer.

'Karnal.'

'Ah! It was founded by Karan,' the officer said. 'My mother used to read to me a novel called *Mrityunjaya*. Whatever there is to know about Karan is there, but it is in Marathi. I will find out about a Hindi translation.'

'I don't read Hindi, Janab,' said my father. I only know Urdu, Persian, Gurmukhi, and, of course, English.'

'You should learn Hindi; it is your Sanskrit roots.'

'Our Punjabi draws a lot from Persian,' said my father

'Really? Yes, of course, I understand. Yours is the region that the invader Muslims came upon repeatedly.' He made the region sound like a whore.

'You are now settled in Hindustan,' said the officer. Jindo's heart throbbed at the way he said the words 'settling' and 'Hindu'.

'Well, we are originally from what you would call Pakistan,' said my father.

'It IS Pakistan. They are enemies,' said the officer and Jindo shrugged while he swallowed something inexplicable and unpronounceable—a discomfort, a pain, a humiliation. He should be somewhere else, a place of his own where he was proud, not having to justify his lineage to a Maratha Hindu.

'I will find out about *Mrityunjaya*,' Jindo said, wandering off to refill his drink many times before he felt he could talk to someone else. It is I who eventually read and loved the novel.

'Papa,' I told him, '*Mritunjaya* is interesting. Karan, too, suffered a sense of alienation. Do you know his story?'

'Vaguely. Sundari, my ayah, used to tell me stories from the *Mahabharata*.'

And so, I told him: Karan's life was spent in seeking provenance for identity. The waters beside which he prayed to the rising and setting sun are called Karantal. Karan's acts of charity were legendary; no seeker of alms was turned away.

Born to the unmarried Princess Kunti from Surya Devta, she cast him away in a basket on the river Drashtavati. He was found and adopted by a childless charioteer and his wife. They called the baby Vasusena.

Later, Kunti married Pandu, elder son of the ruler at Hastinapur. In the meanwhile, hearing his inner warrior blood, Vasusena sought to be trained in arms by Dronacharya, guru to the princes, but he was turned away as a son of a lower caste. Vasusena then sought the great Brahmin warrior Parshurama, who had vowed to kill all Kshatriyas to avenge his mother, who had been disrespected by one. Vasusena told Parshurama he was a Brahmin and so was accepted as a student. Parshurama grew to love Vasusena dearly, until he discovered his lie. Parshurama banished Vasusena from the ashram with the curse that the knowledge he had obtained by false means would desert him when he needed it the most. Bewildered by how easily love can turn because of caste, Vasusena returned to Hastinapur.

The Kaurava prince, Duryodhana, recognising Vasusena's talent at an archery competition among warriors where he defeated Arjuna, anointed him as ruler of Anga. He was already engaged in political rivalry against his Pandava cousins and was gathering allies for the inevitable great battle.

'Match all this for dislocation, Papa. You were never alone. Your entire family was with you. Everyone knows where you were from. You just moved from one place to another but your identity was never questioned. You can't match this great story of dislocation, Papa,' I said.

'Carry on,' said Jindo.

Let's come to the point where, close to the war, Krishna tries to lure Vasusena away from the Kauravas by finally telling him his true story; that he is the oldest brother of the Pandavas. Vasusena's heart is not heavy any longer because it is burnt away by longing for something. He is left with the stillness of no heart, which is also the realisation of being a small drop in the river of events that he had been thrown into.

I imagine Vasusena's camp at Karnal. It would be beside one of the lakes formed by the Yamuna as she meanders after her unreserved, passionate cascade down the high Himalayas. The colour of the landscape is many shades of green and blue with slivers of brown along the banks. In summer, the jungle is sun-bleached to a thin canopy, sprinkled with the fine dust of the burning loo, rising from the deserts of Rajasthan. It will be washed only in July, when the black, grey, and silver clouds thunder down streams, renewing the forest to its lush thickness. In winter, the sun warms to a bright light, and the night smells of wood fires. In all seasons, the morning and evening skies drip soft pink, turning to flaming orange and a golden blaze. It is serene with birdsong; kingfishers pierce the water's transparent skin for their piscine food.

One such morning, beside the lake, Vasusena prepares for war in meditative stillness. Indra appears, disguised as a beggar. He asks for Vasusena's armour and earrings. 'This is my protection and the armour is embedded in my flesh,' says Vasusena. The beggar remains standing with outstretched arms. Resigned to loss and death, but resolved to not break his vow of charity, Vasusena hacks at the armour on his skin with his sword and cuts off the earrings.

That is when Vasusena became Karan: the one who tore his own flesh with his hands.

The beggar sprinkles healing water on Karan's bleeding flesh. Karan asks Indra his offence to have suffered deceit by a devta. 'To protect Arjuna, my son,' says Indra.

If injustice is also destiny, what's the point in God?

'Do you believe?' I asked Papa.

'I do,' he said, assuredly, and I felt better. If he believed, it must be true, and my own doubts were of no consequence. Jindo's Western education compelled him to think of time as linear, but his religious upbringing gave him the instinctive understanding of time as cyclical, enfolding within it an entirety where all was ever-present, even as infinite. It cannot be understood with the limited perception of a physical being; the obvious has to be transcended with a mystical inner sight.

Karan fought with the passion of the damned till he was killed by Arjuna when he was unarmed and had forgotten the skills that Parshurama had taught him.

He lay on the battlefield, radiant in the evening light, sensing his father's presence in the rays that caressed his wounds. 'What is the point of glory and fame when you are dead?' asked Shalya, Karan's charioteer.

'I will have an honourable death and will receive one-sixth of the good karma of the people I protect. Those who think of me and remember me and try and understand me will understand the fineness and sharpness and beauty of dharma and a life of opportunity to earn good karma, even in misery,' I imagine him saying in reply.

Three thousand years after the *Mahabharata* is said to have been written, of a battle said to have been fought in these parts, Karnal became the refuge of families displaced by the Partition.

## 27. Karnal, Post Partition

As Karnal grew out of myth into recorded time, it seemed to retain the barrenness of the mythological war-zone, as if waiting for new heroes to give it a renewed purpose. The original occupants of the land around Karnal were Muslim aristocrats who had left for Pakistan. Among them was Liaquat Ali, who became its first Prime Minister. There were in the Karnal region two old Sikh families of Shamgarh and Sikri, whom we called 'oorikey', literally 'from here,' but the layered meaning is the families that retained wealth, unlike the refugees.

Apart from these families of note, there were many Rajput Hindu farmers. 'Same as you, no?' said a bureaucrat at the land rehabilitation office in Karnal, 'these people here are Jats and you are Jats as well.'

'They are Haryanvi Jat, we are Jatt Sikh; it's very different,' said my father.

The smirk of the bureaucrat said, 'The days when I have to suffer the superior airs of a childish feudal dickhead are gone,' but he could not muster the courage to say anything.

My father dealt with his pain of being treated as a political non-person by withdrawing into inactivity and a silence that barely covered the discordant notes of his inner world.

So absorbed was he in thinking his life through that Jindo began to find that the most interesting, but also the most empathetic person who understood him, was himself. His cocoon of self-sufficiency was often mistaken for snobbery, or plain madness. Sometimes, you could see him gesticulate with his hands as if making a point to an inner being that he was arguing with. That his personal revolt was inconsequential to society and difficult for family was not relevant; the point was that it was authentic.

When they gathered in Karnal as refugees, my father experienced a closeness of family that was never repeated after they fanned out to their allotted lands.

The allotments began coming through, and, slowly, each of the chachas prepared to leave for their farms. Pritpal in Lucknow. Charanjit and Jasbir close by, in Panipat.

Papaji and my grandmother, as the widow of his eldest son, and her sons, Jindo and Amarjit, received their land about forty kilometres west of Karnal, near village Jundla. It was a tract of banjar sandy soil overgrown with keekar shrubs.

I found in an old gazetteer among Papa's books, a description of Karnal in 1907 as a cantonment settlement: 'Karnal consists of plain country. The water shed runs close under the city; the soil, where not rendered barren by swamp, is stiff and fertile. The source of the Sarusti is close by. This most sacred river in Northern India after the Ganges does not flow from the mountains but begins in a large depression in the North of the Mustafabad pargana of Jagadhri.' The officer notes with an interesting literary flourish, 'Like the Brahmins who trade on its sanctity, [the Sarusti] lives on the contributions of its neighbours (feeder streams).'

He then describes the dense jungle around. 'You may shoot deer at dawn, partridge and hare in the morning, duck and sniper in the hotter hours and pick up a peacock on the way home. The nardak was a favourite hunting spot for the old emperors. Lions were sometimes seen within thirty-five kilometres of Karnal, while tigers were numerous in its immediate vicinity, one having carried off, just a few days earlier, a fakir at the imperial bridge where the Grand Trunk Road crosses the old canal. The vegetation is dhak, keekar, khajur. Mango groves abound. The old canal has a fine selection of trees on its banks, many of them rare. The finest fruit gardens in Northern India are here, and the mangoes surpass even those of Saharanpur.'

Karnal in the gazetteer is charming with mango orchards along a Mughal canal. In my Karnal, the canal is dry and the town has decayed into unplanned, inaesthetic modernity.

Greenery and canal notwithstanding, the officer notes as curious the regularity with which drought and famine occurred in this area. 'The famines were terrible—not a blade of grass to be seen. What little there was, was eaten by locusts; cattle died, the price of grain rose to 8 seers per rupee; jails were filled with loan defaulters and many rich landlords, too, died of hunger.'

The general description of the area around Jundla, where my father would eventually get his farm, is where 'rain can never be too plentiful at the right time and unseasonal rain, even a little bit, brings pestilence, or washes off pollen and kills or freezes young plants'.

Bibiji used to say of Karnal, 'When we were in Rajkot (it was always Rajkot, never Pakistan), we were told that our crop would be more expensive because there was a famine in Karnal. We thought of it as a faraway hell, and here we are now.'

Tubewells helped avert famine, but hail or rain at the wrong time still killed our crops, constraining our father to take heavier loans to maintain the table. But for me, a bad crop year laced the sweet juice of a plump fruit with the sourness of guilt.

Rain and crop were central drawing-room talk. Our happiness was in the context of weather. I remember a feeling of deep happiness in winter afternoons in the verandah that were cold enough for us to need a 'dabda' (iron vessel) with a coal fire to warm us as we ate gur and peanuts. We were all together, warm, eating, and smiling. Happiness on summer evenings smelled and tasted of home-made mango ice cream and Rooh Afza.

But for me, the year gathered meaning around the end of June. That was what life was about. Bibiji would begin holding out her handkerchief to check the direction of the wind. The westerly 'pacchho' was hot, dry, and frustrating with disappointment, and the white clouds did not help. We knew them as 'kumhar baadal' (potter clouds), the sort that suited the potter because they would not damage his unbaked pots even while giving respite from the blinding sun.

Then began the cool easterly. '*Pura vag gaya,*' (the easterly wind flows), she would announce to us, and we would all be excited.

I can smell the rain on the easterly wind even before it sheds its bounty. I can smell it even before I see the monsoon clouds, dark as Krishna's skin and heavy with joyous promise.

'*Monsoon ayeee, ji monsoon ayeee,*' we would chant.

Bibiji would say: '*Aan diyo, aan diyo.*' (Let it come, don't jinx it.)

And Papa would say, *'Hanji, main nai kuchh kainda.'* (Yes, yes, I won't say anything.)

The crop talk was along the lines of, 'We are growing basmati. It is very low-yield, but a successful crop commands a good price.' A crop the colour of deep green would bring Jindo leaping home to tell us, 'First class; *kaali bamm.*' As black as a bomb was the description of that deep, deep green of a healthy crop; so green it looked black.

A monsoon happiness is like no other, just as Raga Malhar is like no other. We were happy in a way that can only be in the monsoon; it is a feeling borne by the musical play of the universe. The sound of the rhythm of the rain, the clash of the clouds, the smell of the cool breeze, laden and languorous with the embrace of moist earth.

There is a perfume made of this smell. 'It is ittarigil,' Jindo told me. We also had a school prayer, 'We thank thee, Lord, for the goodly smell of wet earth.'

———

## 28. Rajkot Farm

Any small town is oppressive, as a halfway, unformed life that does not have the glamour of a city or the beauty of a pastoral life.

I imagine Jindo, at sixteen, going to reconnaissance their newly allotted land. A stretch of uncultivated, virgin land, thick with groves of keekar, teeming with deer. The land is chalky white stretches, dandruff in thin patches of green hair. There, he set up 'Rajkot Farm'.

I remember the drive to the farm in later years when Jindo could afford a car. 'Roll up your windows,' we were told, as our tiny Standard Herald Fiat and later the Ambassador car, rocked and swayed while the sun-bleached dust surged and swirled thick around us, blinding the glass as if describing the situation of those who had lost their bearings. No one chatted during the drive—it was always a shock.

Till 1947, my father must have existed without any questions. He was with family in its extended form and had not spent time thinking about his cultural roots till they were cut from him. After which, all repotting attempts were pervaded with a sense of foreboding, cultivated by past losses. That to allow this sense of uncertainty in a people under a new, noble Constitution is a violation of their right to security of tenure is not dwelt upon by the bumbling ineptitude of our leaders. I wondered what my father must have thought as he viewed his land; minuscule compared to the vast tracts of fertile, green crops and orchards that they had left, in what in a day had become the enemy, Pakistan.

The only thing that had become familiar to my father was the weight of his heart that he learned to live with, like a mule with its burden. Many find distance from home liberating from context, but my father knew his limitations. He knew no life without land.

Most of our family who remember my father as inert seem to have forgotten his diligent work with government offices for allocations of barren land that he then broke and tilled with a hired tractor. He lived at the farm in a makeshift tent.

I imagine a shout from among the workers levelling a small pahari known among the villagers as tibba. They had unearthed shards of pottery. Could the pottery be a sign of this area being part of the ancient Harappa and Mohenjodaro civilisation?

The careful, self-taught student of history within my father needed that the pottery be gathered and sent to the Archaeological

Society of India, but the desperation of the refugee prevailed, and he simply ordered that the land be levelled. Who to even tell of his find? Bibiji would be angry: 'What a foolish distraction when all is lost, and we are trying to rebuild.' Papaji Vaddey would call him a bloody fool for even talking about it, and Bha would have no time for it either. Later, in the light of a fire, my father may have poured himself a whiskey while he looked at the pottery that the workers had gathered and placed under a keekar tree. Recently, excavations in Rakhigarhi, about forty kilometres from our farm, have revealed that this region is, in fact, part of that civilisation.

Early mornings, I imagine my father emerging from the tent to meet a clear day. 'I would clap my hands and startled deer would run out of the keekar forest,' he told me of those days. A shikari like Jasbir would have chased them with his bullet, but my father enjoyed looking at their fleet run.

In the day, my father may have walked through the village and no one would notice him, unlike the time about a year ago when they would have said, 'Sat Sri Akal, Sardarji,' and he would have known their names and talked to them and many would have been playmates.

He remembered two of his uncles in their old world had beaten a worker for not standing up when they passed. 'Beaten till their own arms hurt,' my father told me the story with shame, as if the telling would relieve him of the guilt he felt.

He may have climbed on a bus to Karnal and someone would have got up to give him a seat, because he had that air. He would have looked out to the fields, remembering his own in Pakistan with the blurred vision of held-back tears.

In the early years, my father was energetic enough. The depression came later, and even then, he recovered enough to manage the farm till finally he gave up its management to Darshan.

Then he lay in bed, telling the red beads of a tasbi that someone had gifted him from Mecca, and reading history books.

—————

# 29. Papaji Vaddey's Jindo

The house allotted to them was called Hasan Manzil in the Karnal bazaar. It is here that Papaji Vaddey and his family began living soon after Partition. Two servants had accompanied them. The Sikh driver, Khushiya Baba, was now the general fetcher and carrier, and the Hindu, Munshi Makand Lal, of 'To-let Sardar' fame, now managed the paperwork of the new allotments.

One day, Papaji was walking in the bazaar. As he walked, he was shocked by a jolt that felled him. Something thundered long over him and then there was silence. He opened his eyes to an octopus of wide mouths and eyes with many helping hands. 'Sardar Sahib!! *Theek ho?*'

The driver of the Ambassador that had run him over stopped the car and got out with visibly shaking knees. Did the crowd stop him or did he stop himself? I do not know. '*Oh, daffa ho!! Haramzada,*' said Papaji, and the driver lost no time in doing just that.

Acutely embarrassed that he was without his turban in public, Papaji marched on. Hearing the commotion, Khushiya fought through the crowd to reach his sardar. The patriarch of what used to be a family of fair-to-medium grandeur now stood vulnerable as a turbanless, small head.

Back in Rajkot, the crowd would have hauled the driver to the thana. That was less than a year ago. Less than a year ago, Sardar Bahadur was the Haneiry Magistrate at Rajkot, Pakistan.

'Khushiya!' Papaji was pale but composed, 'Let's go home. What a haramzada.'

At home, Papaji bathed and changed into a fresh churidar-kurta with a small headcloth instead of a turban. He put on the radio and, after a bit of twiddling, settled on Begum Akhtar's melodious power. He poured himself a whiskey and sat silently. Then, something prompted him to go back to the cupboard to take out the gutka (small prayer book) that had belonged to his wife.

*There is something here*, Papaji thought, perspective shaken by his near-death experience. Each member of his family had survived; they were embarking on a new life and they were hopeful and had humour. He had survived being run over by a car, for God's sake—what greater sign?

Whiskey in one hand, gutka in the other, he played on his gramophone a Begum Akhtar record while he read a prayer.

*Hamri karo haath key racha;*
*pooran hoi chit ki icchha,*
*Tav charnan man rahey hamara,*
*Apna jaan karo pratipara,*
*Hamrey dost sabhey tum ghavou,*
*Aap hath dai moh bachavo,*
*Sukhi bassey moro parivara.*
*Sevak sikhyau sabhay kartara,*
*Mo rachha nij kar dey kardiou,*
*Sab bairan ko aaj sanghariyo,*
*Pooran hoi hamari asa,*
*Tor bhajan ki rahey piyasa*

Give me your hand in protection; fulfil my heart's desire,
May my mind stay on meditating upon you,
Treat me as your own and help me,
You are my friend and accept my friends,

Protect me with the shelter of your hand,
May my family live in peace.
We are all servants to creation,
Protect my family as your own,
Let me defeat my enemies today,
Let my wish be fulfilled,
May I live praising your glory.

Papaji had found his metre. Since then, for the next thirty years
or so, till the day he died in 1975, Papaji read the Rehras Prayer
every evening while sipping a whiskey as Begum Akhtar sang in
the background.

Papaji liked fine things. His whisky, his music, his friends, a
fine garden. He was even a bit of an artist. He had tried to make
a film in Rajkot that Jindo remembers being shot in lamplight
in a jhuggi, but we don't know what happened to it.

Papaji recovered some form after Partition. He was more
than eighty years old when he played badminton with me. I
was six, maybe. I remember such moments of grown-ups playing
with me as rare pleasures. Otherwise, everyone seemed to live
in quiet auto-pilot mode, while I existed as in a negative of a
photo, waiting for the process to be positive. I knew it could
not happen in Karnal.

Do all new beginnings require stripping down? I guess they
do, given that the common phrase to describe the venture is 'a
clean slate'.

Papaji had an independent, busy life, because his pre-
Partition friend Sardar Butalia was also settled in Karnal and
a neighbour. Every morning, they would meet for coffee at
Gopinath restaurant, or at the canteens in the kutchehries, for
snatches of Punjab political gossip and crime stories around land.
Sometimes, they would see a movie together. They took turns
to buy tickets. They would have been repulsed at the modern
concept of 'going dutch'. Either paid, but the other would want

to quickly repay with another film and coffee, because neither wanted to die owing money. This life of leisure and comfort with death was not that of the nava-rajjiya (nouveau riche) but fresh deprivation that could not kill the habits of living well. It is this sensibility that protected from resigned submission to tight finance.

In a childhood of quiet elders who were too kind to let us see their unhappiness, small rituals stand out as moments of lasting connection. My lasting memory of Papaji is that of Rakhi, Rakhdee. I would tie one to Papaji and my Papa. Mama would post my rakhis to Tayaji, my nana, and various cousins.

I was expected to tie the first rakhi to Papaji. No one apart from me had free access to his bedroom. It would have been most inappropriate for the daughter-in-law, my grandmother, or the grand-daughter-in-law, my mother, to enter his room. Jindo avoided going there, unless he wanted to entertain himself by irritating him more than usual.

I would solemnly tie my rakhi on Papaji's wrist and then he would hug me and resume pottering around the room, shuffling about and seeming to forget that the custom required him to give me some money. I would sit on his bed, waiting for my just dues of a gift for the rakhi.

*Jao, beta. Ho gayee Rakhdee.*
*Papaji, paise?*
*Haan, acchha.*

Go, beta. The Rakhdee is done.
Papaji, some money?
Yes, okay.

And I would get a coin.

He spent his time reading the newspapers; cut out something, paste it somewhere, and then mix Ayurvedic medicine on a pair of finely-made scales. (I inherited them eventually, because I was the only one who knew about them, sitting on a shelf that I could reach by standing on a stool.) I heard the scales click, smelled the somewhat emphatic ittar that he got by mail order from Lucknow. I would sit there, feeling nothing but patient affection for this man, who was so busy doing nothing and so stylish in his triangular relationship with prayer, music and whiskey.

His ayurvedic tonics obviously worked because, till his last days, Papaji breakfasted on two eggs and fried liver on toast; mutton or chicken for dinner after two large whiskies, which he always made into interesting cocktails with ghastly smelling herbs or chooran.

At Papaji's last Rakhdee, I must have been about ten years old. I was playing in the verandah outside his room. I heard shuffling feet and looked up to see him. Frail but still lean, fresh in a white kurta pyjama and white turban, he smiled as he came to me, holding out his wrist. I quickly got up and tied my rakhi, and this time I got, without asking, the princely sum of ten rupees.

It might be my imagination, but I think we both felt deep love. Perhaps he felt the sadness of impermanence of any state. For me, Rajkot House was constancy, in contrast to the reality of Papaji.

*

Years later, I remembered Rakhi at Papaji's when I took my daughter to tie a rakhi to Jindo. 'My beautiful granddaughter,' Jindo said with pride.

Notwithstanding his humble spirituality, Jindo's relief was quite apparent that he did not have to learn his lessons afresh by dealing with ugly grandchildren.

I asked Jindo about his relationship with Papaji.

'He hated me,' Jindo laughed about his grandfather.

Every summer and winter solstice, grandfather and grandson had developed the following ritual exchange:

On the evening of the summer solstice, 21 June, Jindo would say, 'I think the day is shorter,' and Papaji would say, 'That's not the way it happens, you fool. You can't make it out in a day,' and Jindo would hide his grin in his beard.

On the evening of the winter solstice, 21 December, Jindo would say, 'I think the day is longer,' and Papaji would say, 'That's not the way it happens, you fool. You can't make it out in a day.'

And Jindo's shoulders would silently heave, happy that while they both were alive, this, at least, would never change, twice a year.

Jindo's cheek and drinking were enough reasons for Papaji to be driven to doting on his elder grandson, Tayaji. In him, he saw his too-soon departed, and perhaps that is why, particularly beloved son, Raghbir.

Papaji's health deteriorated steadily after a fall that broke his leg. He was more than ninety years old at the time. His meals were taken to his bed, and later, he had to be fed through a Ryle's nasal tube. Jindo asked the doctor whether he could serve Papaji his regular, two large whiskies, through the pipe. The good family doctor agreed.

Thus, till his last evening in this world, Papaji had two large whiskies that his irritating grandson poured into the feeding pipe fixed at his nose. If this was a moment of deep affection for Jindo, Papaji was sporting enough not to ruin the relationship by saying so. He died in his sleep.

I inherited Papaji's room and sundry junk, of which I kept the scales, and began my new empowered phase of privacy.

In the days following the death, the excitement of decorating my room overcame any grief. Old curtains were dyed a deep rust; drawers from the rotting desk were converted to a bookshelf; the walls cheered up with posters and comic strips; a small Tibetan rug in rust and deep blue given by my nana, by the bed. The old gramophone had stopped working and so became a console table.

Ganeve and I were supposed to share the room, but one day, we fought, and I threw her things out. I feel bad now. Our parents returned from somewhere to find Ganeve crying in the hallway, surrounded by her belongings.

Rather than scold or insist that we share a room, Jindo arranged for Ganeve's private space in the small staircase landing outside their bedroom. And then, later that year, he built for her ensuite rooms with a spectacular 360-degree view of the garden.

***

## 30. Rajkot House Karnal Was Still Rajkot House Gujranwala

The distance is a day's journey by car to the Wagah border, bristling with arms and goose-stepping soldiers. The tragedy of Tek Singh's metaphor of limbo in purgatory hangs heavy in the air. ('Toba Tek Singh', Sadat Hasan Manto.)

The life of the refugees was in contrast to the oorikey. In contrast to the refugees who had set up business or had a profession, zamindars like my family would never be able to match the economic class of the oorikey zamindars.

For our family, there was no money to even start building a house, but at least there was land to call their own. Eventually, brick by brick, was built Rajkot House Karnal.

By 1968 or so, we were in Tallania when Mama received Jindo's letter that I read over her shoulder, 'Bha picked a fight with me again.' Though relatively non-acrimonious, no partition can be without pain.

The land was divided into two lots by the farm manager, Chaudhari Deep Chand, who remained with Jindo at Bibiji's request. It was by the system of 'parchi pana', or drawing lots from two agreed lots, 'A' and 'B'. The younger drew first.

Bibiji settled money to Tayaji for his share in Rajkot House so that she and my father and all of us could have an intact roof over our heads. The partition between my father and uncle deeply affected my grandmother, making her a little distant from my uncle. Maybe Tayaji felt the distance, which is why I remember him saying that mothers always loved the 'nalayak' (unqualified) child. He was right, my father was nalayak compared to my uncle. But my father made one laugh and a lot is forgiven to someone with an original sense of humour.

Tayaji would diligently visit the farm from Delhi while Jindo, lolling in the verandah a few kilometres away, would say, 'Bha, have a look at my land as well and tell me about it on your way back.' And Tayaji would always do it.

Unlike Tayaji, Jindo was a popular member of the extended clan. He took pleasure in the delicious wickedness of family dynamics and saw more than most people gave him credit for. I loved my Tayaji. Notwithstanding his issues with my father, he maintained an impeccable avuncular manner for us, his nieces, and respectful formality with our mother.

The years passed. I never saw the brothers hug, though Jindo always said Sat Sri Akal to his older brother with folded hands and did a matha teko, a deep forward bend with folded hands and then a gesture to touch Tayaji's knees. And Tayaji would pat his brother on the back and say Sat Sri Akal.

That their mutual affection was deeper than such formal, tentative visibilities was apparent to me on a few occasions. For example, Tayaji arrived from Delhi when Jindo had his hernia operation. Even though the hospital was across the road from the house, Tayaji kept vigil in his car parked in the hospital driveway till the operation was pronounced as successful at three a.m.

Jindo, too, expressed his love for his brother indirectly. 'How is Bha?' he would ask when I visited Karnal.

'I have not met him in a long time, Papa.'

'You should meet him,' said with a reproachful smile, 'you should.'

'I will.'

Tayaji visited Jindo for the last time in Karnal sometime around 2008. 'Staying in bed is all very well,' he said, 'but at least tie up your beard. You were always elegant and are still good-looking'.

In 2013, Tayaji had a bad fall in the bathroom. 'No one recovers completely from a fall like that at his age,' said Jindo and extricated himself from his bed to travel to Delhi, lying in the back of his car to be carried upstairs to Bha's room for a cup of tea. He returned the same evening and that is the last time they met.

When we learned of Jindo's death at three a.m., we stopped at Tayaji's house on our way to Karnal. The front door was open, as is possible now only in the nicest part of the city. The dogs wagged their tails and thought nothing of us walking straight up to the bedroom.

As I woke up Tayiji, I was overcome with a fresh bout of tears. 'Tayiji, Papa has gone.'

She focused with a long effort of parting curtains of deep sleep and said, 'Gone where?'

'He has died,' I choked.

She then got out of bed suddenly, firm and focused, and walking to her husband's bed a few feet away, said, '*Hota hai.*'

'Yes,' I replied, crying.

Then she saw her sleeping husband was breathing and said, 'Oh it's YOUR Papa who has died,' with relief she was still too hazy to hide.

'Yes,' I said and could not stop a choked giggle.

By then, Tayaji woke up and got out of bed to dress without saying anything.

Ganeve and I returned to the van to go ahead to Karnal. First, there was silence and then I said, 'That was pretty funny,' and we both laughed in relief of togetherness at that hour.

A couple of hours later, Tayaji arrived: 'It was my turn.'

'It does not happen by turns,' cried my mother.

Tayaji died three years later.

*

Tayaji's daughter, my cousin, Tavleen Singh, and her son, Aatish Taseer, have described Karnal in their widely read works as being an ugly, sad concrete block. Notwithstanding their scathing comment about the lack of beauty of Rajkot House, let me describe for you the home I grew up in.

The house was open on four sides; lawn and garden in the front, sitting place on the western side, and vegetable garden on the back and eastern sides. Boundaries were marked by flower beds and mehndi hedges. The garden was Papaji's effort to distract himself and re-create a past grandeur. He would compete with the oorikey homeowners for the finest roses. There were fruit trees; one mango, shareefa, and plum. The most memorable, to become synonymous with the house, were the sweet limes, called just that; 'mitha' (sweet).

There was a soft, unspoken border between Papaji's east and

Bibiji's west-facing rooms. Both sides had generous verandahs framing parts of the garden. Papaji would spend winter afternoons under the dappled shade of an aloocha tree, tall and straight like him, branches clasping the sky in a wide embrace.

Bibiji's verandah overlooked a small lawn shaded by a magnificent harshingar tree. There was a bricked path bordered by sweet smelling mogra bushes, leading to the room that was the Darbar Sahib with the Guru Granth Sahib.

My parents' bedroom upstairs opened onto a bright, sunny verandah that was cosy in winter but an active furnace in the summer.

During the monsoon, mithas were prominent on our breakfast table. 'Have many,' Bibiji would advise, 'there is quinine in this. It protects from malaria.' We would suck the juice of the bitter flesh made pungent sweet with the skin.

I would fix a quarter sideways into my mouth to bare a green, demonic smile for the elders, accompanied with a growl to frighten Ganeve.

After Ganeve was born, I moved to Bibiji's room that was comfortably temperate, on the ground floor.

There was a large window through which peeked, without judging, a kindly harshingar tree. It watched my restless nights of bad dreams, prominent with snakes. Its shadow on a moonlit terrace would calm me back to sleep. The magic of the tree was packed in little coin-shaped fruit that, every dawn, showered a delicate, fragrant carpet of star-shaped white flowers with orange centres.

I understood abundance then; stunning in its powerful gentleness.

Mama would spread a 'khes' (spun sheet) under the tree, just at evening, so that I could sit among the flowers the next morning to drink the regulation glass of milk. What I never could do was sit under the tree when it rained the flowers. My nightly waking hours never caught that moment.

I learned to soak dupattas in an infusion of the flowers to release a sweet smelling, delicate dye of pale orange.

One trip to Karnal many years later, the harshingar tree was not there. Mama tried to explain its absence. But I did not want to know. It hurt too much. Since then, I have tried to grow harshingar in various pots on various terraces of modest apartments that I moved into at various times in my life at Delhi and it hurts even more to think of my grand old friend.

There was also a magnolia tree that rarely bloomed, but when it did, brought forth a generously proportioned flower the size of two large, wide handspans, holding waxy petals of a butter cool colour; like that of a cow's fresh milk. Its soft, citrus fragrance travelled across the garden. Indoors, the bloom sat in a silver bowl, its fragrance wafting into the walls and drapery. Nasturtiums and iris were delightful surprises in the garden, as if thrown by a broad casting hand to settle in unexpected places. The nargis had pride of place because they had come from Rajkot House Gujranwala. 'How did you manage that, considering you left your valuables there?' I asked.

'Over the years, before Partition, many bulbs had been taken from Rajkot House Gujranwala by Chacha Pritpal and Bha to plant in their various Army accommodations. After Partition, Papaji asked for them to be planted here.' I would often lie on the ground to contemplate the nargis as my blood relative from Rajkot Gujranwala.

After I read the Greek story about Narcissus, I was careful to place the fragrant nargis on the dressing tables in the house, so they could see themselves in the mirror. The original bulbs stopped blooming only about ten years ago and their progeny live in the garden now.

The process of cutting and arranging flowers indoors was one of beauty. On the dining table, or on Papaji's gramophone, now retired onto the verandah, were placed fresh flowers, their various-sized holders, a large jug of water, and all vases emptied and cleaned. Flowers for the house were carefully chosen. Every bit of the garden grew something that could be used in that ceremony of pruning and displaying. A dahlia flower and stem were to be matched with some foliage as a foil, but chrysanthemums in groups of maroon, yellow and white glowed on stems with their own leaves.

The charming, unruly sweet peas, with their heady smell, gathered in bushels of deep purple, hot pink, mauve, magenta interspersed with white and cream; bunches of calendulas to put in jam jars at the oddest places—a window in the stairway, or on top of the flush, or the bathroom window that opened onto the back garden.

In the fleeting spring, Darshan brought in branches of almond, peach, and pear blossom, while monsoons were fragrant with frangipani and small, leafy stems of mogra flowers, summers were coloured by the flamboyant zinnias.

Some flowers were so magnificent that they needed to be spoken to with reverence. A bush delivered one at a time so we would not be deflected by abundance and could truly savour each deep-red rose, painted over with a deeper red velvet to make it black. Each new arrival was taken indoors to sit in solitary splendour in a silver bowl, cushioned among its own stem of dark leaves.

I often wondered how the flowers felt as the chosen ones separated from their family. I would try and commune with them and tell them that they would be all right. After all, even I go to boarding school. But you are not going to die there, a solitary flower might tell me, sadly. In groups, though, they were of robust cheer indoors.

Many flowers fade by the end of the day if brought indoors but gleam proud and colourful for weeks in their garden beds, gathered in a boisterous, unruly mix of purple larkspur, pink balsam, and the antirrhinums in magenta, white, red, and yellow. Darshan showed me, 'See how they open their mouth to bark at you, bow-wow! It's called a dog flower.'

'Kutta phull,' said the maali, Khushiya Baba.

Khushiya hated the idea of cut flowers, claiming he could hear their pain even though Darshan's gleaming, ornate gardening scissors cut clean and sharp.

Khushiya had accompanied the family from Rajkot, Pakistan, where he had been a chauffeur and now that the family could not afford a car, worked the garden. He had a gentle, kind, Guru-Nanak face and loved me as much as he loved my father, whom he had taught to drive.

So much did Khushiya love Jindo that they suffered the same ailment of dislocation, except that Khushiya got to call it something unique to maalis: 'maalikholia' is how he pronounced it, and hence interpreted melancholia. He refused Jindo's medication, preferring a treatment of goat's milk sprayed straight on his head. So, when the boy came to graze his herd of goats and sheep in fields adjunct to Rajkot House, he would do two things—leave the lambs and kids for me to play with and, for a price, squirt Khushiya's head with milk from the heaviest udder among his charges.

At the end of the lawn, there were two kumquat bushes clustered close like siblings. They were just three feet high, and I have an early memory of being able to stand under them and look up at their oblong, small, citrus fruits, to be eaten whole with a sweet rind and sharp-tasting flesh. The bushes dried twenty years later, and the mandarin oranges planted in their stead are not even a close substitute.

Someday, while I was away at boarding school, the driveway was straightened and the roses transplanted and many bushes faded away. The black rose bush was gone, the magnolia tree dried up, and the harshingar cut. Eventually, the side and the back land was used for vegetables and it was never the same. After Papaji died, the focus on flowers lessened. A magnificent flower garden was no longer needed to assert to the world that all was well, because the household had come to terms with the dreary ordinariness of life in a small town. A large lawn was adequate to assert the status of being able to afford some unproductive space, and we began growing more vegetables on the compound. And so, the garden changed from a place of magic to a sweet, well-laid green.

As I grew older, though there were always fresh flowers in the house, they were never as grand as I remembered in my childhood.

If I remember my child's perspective, the garden's wild, carefree spirit that still gives me heightened colour and fragrance shows itself sometimes. *It is the child I left behind*, I think, as I sit cross-legged on the lawn that I had run across when it was flooded, ruining my brand-new expensive leather shoes made for the special needs of my feet.

The spirit of the garden, however, danced even for the most unimaginative during the monsoon. It began with the treetops playing with the easterly wind dressed in gossamer, reflecting the green of trees and grey-black of the clouds shot with a thread of silver lightning.

The red gulmohur, purple jacaranda, and golden chandeliers of amaltash that had burned in the white blaze now lit up the dark-skinned sky. A golden sunray dripped through, making one believe in a God. Then began the downpour of a generous, loving, joyous gift from the place without a beginning or end. Our garden was encircled by shimmering water channels.

After the dust-settling first rain, we were allowed to wander in the downpour to heal the itching red sores of summer sweat. Under the watchful eye of a grown-up, we explored each rain puddle sinking beneath our feet through soggy grass into delicious, brown gunk. Earthworms were plenty and to be imagined as snakes; the repulsiveness of which was joyfully expressed with a theatrical grimace.

The chiks, till then lowered over the verandahs against the afternoon heat, were now raised to watch the rainy show while eating hot pakodas dripping with chutney, washed down with a glass of steaming tea. I would lie on the takht in the verandah, heavy with sleep, swaddled into a bedsheet edged with roses embroidered by my nani, while my father lounged on a chair, feet up on a table.

This is the season when I saw him truly and deeply happy.

Monsoon nights were special because we were allowed to sit out late on the porch to catch those most beautiful things: fireflies. They flitted across the night as sequins that we managed to trap some in a glass that glowed on our bedsides. One night, my sleep was pierced by the golden haze that had freed itself from the glass. I let them out of the room, following the light, now here, now there, then very far away into the happy music of the monsoon nights made by frogs. Bibiji translated it for me:

*Meley jaana, meley jaana, croaks the big frog;*
*Kin, kin, kin, kin, ask the little ones;*
*Maaiin tu-maiin tu, he assures confidently.*

We will go to the fair; we will go to the fair croaks the big frog;
Who, who, who, who, ask the little ones;
You and me, you and me, he assures confidently.

The fan was now adequate to finally allow us a full night's sleep. We snuggled luxuriously under a cotton sheet with happy awareness of all being just fine.

Rain helped alleviate arid yearning for what cannot be. As the water collected in the potholed roads of the town, it nourished our souls and filled the craters formed by the death of loved ones and distance from home. The water smoothened the dry landscape, transforming uneven blocks of earth into a shimmering surface.

## 31. A Day in the Life

For its modern residents, Karnal is sometimes a transit place for better opportunities close to its either side: Delhi to the south and Chandigarh to the north. It is a transit town on the journey to an identity. I would not be surprised if each of its residents said they suffered a heavy heart, which they try to alleviate by trying to reach the history and mythology buried under its cement clusters for a sense of time past, which will make better the time future. The present is stagnant liminal.

A defining point at Rajkot House Karnal was the arrival of the Guru Granth Sahib. 'Did you have the book in your haveli at Mananwala?' I asked my mother.

'Yes, we had one in Gurmukhi and a small granthi in Hindi, which Buaji Ashram Waley gifted to you. On our way to India, my cousin Balbir carried on his head the Gurmukhi granthi to Nankana Sahib Gurudwara, the last stop at Pakistan.' They brought the Hindi granthi with them to India because they thought it would not be accorded the same respect as the one in Gurmukhi at Nankana Sahib.

'What happened to the Granth Sahib in Rajkot Gujranwala?' I asked.

'Their family was away at the time, as you know, so it must have been burned by the mob.'

I have the Hindi granthi with me now and it sits clad in silk that I open rarely, not so much to read as to meditate on its journey to me from a village in Pakistan.

Life in Rajkot House was a predictable routine. First was activity in the Darbar Sahib. Bibiji would set up the book by six a.m. for everyone to read. Her voice was not unmusical and her rhythm very sound. Next, Papaji Vaddey would read silently for about half an hour.

Jindo's entry into the prayer room was a delight because, like all of us, God, too, had to deal with his eccentric irreverence. '*Jo mangey thakur sey apne, soi soi devain,*' (Ask your God and you shall receive), his raucous singing from the Darbar Sahib resounded around the house and reached its destination of irritating Papaji to strike the ground with his walking stick and shout, '*Kis janwar ki awaaz hai?* This is no tariqa to pray.' (What animal's voice is this? This is no way to pray.)

But Jindo carried on, and every day, he demanded good things of God as an entitlement but expressed no bitterness when they did not come.

My mother was in charge of carefully wrapping the book in layers of silk for its night rest, even while daring to question whether it amounted to idol worship.

After prayer, we drifted to the dining room for breakfast. The seasonal fruit sat grandly on a centre tray surrounded by honey and jam jars and glistening white butter on a glass dish surrounded by floral china pots for coffee, milk, and tea. The eggs, toast, and parathas arrived hot from the kitchen. The table was cleared by nine a.m., and no one (including guests) risked asking to be served later.

By eleven a.m., the family sat on the verandah to read the

papers. I would turn up with my books and toys and play on the cool mirror floors. In winter, I would wander the garden to pull out moolis and gajar that were served with salt and pepper.

The household tasks were divided. Bibiji ruled with a fiery temper from a seat firmly supporting a matriarch's majesty. She would take accounts from the servants and order meals, though she never went into the kitchen. Bibiji did not know any cooking apart from making kada pershad on the monthly prayer occasion of Sangrand (the first day of the Indian solar calendar). Her other recipe was a marmalade of kumquat from the garden.

Darshan dealt with the dhobi and press-wallah. She did not drudge in the kitchen, preferring the pantry to practice the baking lessons she got from a friend.

Lunch was at one p.m. with a large lassi that brought a cloud of happy sleep. If one woke up by three p.m. and it was too early to call the cook, there was nothing to do but read. The sound of ice in glasses heralded four p.m. when the swing door from the pantry groaned open to a bearer with a tray of glasses of Rooh Afza dripping frost in summer and steaming tea in winter.

The groaning swing door was a constant sound of Rajkot House. It announced the movements between kitchen and dining room and also seemed to describe our life; it was happening, but groaning with the effort.

After our evening play in the garden, Ganeve and I had our bath at seven p.m.; dinner at seven-thirty p.m., served in small steel thalis, katoris, and glasses, and we were in bed by nine with a glass of hot milk, followed by the teeth-brushing and prayer ritual. *'Eha Khat chalo harr laha; agey basan suhela.'* (A night prayer for protection.)

The grown-ups ate later, and house guests livened things up. Invariably, talk would move to Pakistan, stories of summer holidays and fun events that were still funny, even in nostalgic remembrance. To us, the laughter seemed happy. We were too young to understand that we had a ghostly guest called Rajkot Pakistan, who had accompanied my family to this new place.

With each passing year, Bibiji owned Jindo more and more to fill her empty space, and Jindo dared not challenge the cloying over-possessiveness that would have embarrassed most young men. Jindo carried the burden of his mother's love bravely, partly from a reciprocal love that did not want to disappoint and also from fear.

The ownership was apparent to anyone. 'Where are you going?' if he got up for anything at all. The day was marked by mealtimes, and the time in between was weighted with large silences, sometimes broken by Jindo's humour when he was high on some drug. Bibiji was a despot who, though largely benevolent, could sometimes attack with speech as a broad, blunt weapon that hit hard on the head or below the belt. Ganeve and I were spared, but we cringed for those who were not. She used her knowledge of verse and chapter of the holy book to arm herself with the power of righteousness that, like all righteous people, was sometimes cruel in its assertion.

One argument in favour of Bibiji's control over Jindo was that she protected him from himself. But that is conjecture, for to conjure a Jindo without Bibiji is like imagining the earth without a moon. How would it be? We don't know, but certainly very different, and we don't know if for the better.

Bibiji shed the hauteur she projected to the world when she grandmothered my sister and me in a way she had not mothered her sons. Ganeve, too, by the time she was four years old, abandoned the upstairs cot to join me in Bibiji's room. Before beginning her four a.m. routine of bath and prayer, Bibiji would slip under our pillows small gifts of dried fruit wrapped in a handkerchief. The first thing we did when we woke was to eat our 'potli' with milk. These attentions were unusual for Bibiji, not known for tactile demonstrations of her love, which, for example, would have benefited Jindo as a child and during his year-long confinement at the sanatorium with tuberculosis.

## 32. A Birth

Fourteen years after Partition, in July 1961, my parents were received as a newly married couple in Rajkot House Karnal. I was born in the upstairs bedroom less than a year later, in May 1962. I grew up with Papaji Vaddey, Bibiji, Mama, and Jindo. My sister was born four years later.

I was born with clubbed feet, but no one allowed me to feel different, except that Jindo worried about my devaluation if they had a son after me. He probably also worried that he would not be able to charm a son the way he could his daughters.

In the first four years till my sister was born, I slept alongside my mother's bed in a cot designed by Jindo and carefully executed by the carpenter, Dhanbir Singh. It was made of fine, dark, glowing teak with slatted sides, three of which were fixed, while the fourth slid down to sit flush with my mother's bed. The fourth side could be raised and fixed with little brass latches to completely enclose the baby. It had a detachable base of a wooden frame that tightened the strips of canvas that made the bed. All of it folded easily to put away in a large trunk. I resurrected this cot my father had for me for my two children. Then, the cot moved to Ganeve for her two children and is now back in the trunk.

My memory of sleeping in the cot is also that of my bed-wetting days. I remember waking up with a heavy bladder. Too sleepy to wake my mother, I remember rolling onto her bed, scrambling over her and onto where Jindo slept to piss in relief, and then rolling back the same route to my dry and cosy cot haven.

But before I sank back into sleep, I would hear Jindo waking up Mama to say, 'She has wet my bed again,' and Mama would change the sheet. No one scolded me or worried because it was clear that the bed-wetting was not from lack of bladder control but simply that I was too lazy to ask to be taken to the pot. No one seemed to be in a hurry to discipline me, and that's always nice for a child.

I remember my sister being born in my parent's bedroom. Jindo paced outside, as all fathers in the world seem to do, and I ran alongside him.

'So, would you like a brother or sister?' I remember him asking me.

'I know people say it should be a brother, but I wish it is a sister for me to play with,' I said.

'I, too, want a girl,' said Jindo and we both paced side by side.

The nurse opened the door and said, 'It's a girl.'

We entered, and I remember a tiny, wailing fury attached to a long, grey, slimy pipe being washed in a plastic basin. *I thought they said girl*, I remember thinking. Rural life teaches you about the 'pipe'.

'Go out! Not yet, not yet,' said the harried 'lady doctor'.

Jindo and I stepped out again and then returned a while later, to see a baby fast asleep next to my mother. I felt many eyes and a heavy silence as I went close to her. I felt I had to do something and so reached out to touch the baby's cheek.

'Oh, don't touch,' said the doctor and nurse, 'you may scratch her!' I was relieved to step back.

After that, I remember the shock at the sight of my mother's naked breast. 'All is all right, but I don't like this,' I said. And my mother laughed and said, 'Alright.'

The birth of a second daughter to my father and a fifth granddaughter to my Bibiji was treated as cause for commiseration by the local women and rural relatives, but Bibiji flared imperiously against their clucking sorrow. 'Don't you dare say anything about my granddaughters. All are beloved and have brought their kismets that may well be better than many men.' And the women were intimidated enough to hold back any further stupid talk along such lines.

As to kismet, my Bibiji had, at the time my sister was born, settled a dispute with her brothers over a substantial inheritance that she became entitled to under the 1956 reforms of succession laws that gave her, as a sister, equal rights to them. Had they not been refugees, Bibiji might have given in to the custom of exclusive male heirs, but her straitened financial circumstances compelled her to assert her legal right to land. There was consternation among her entitled brothers and their families, but all had settled at my sister's birth.

An old grandaunt kissed my newborn sister, saying, 'Welcome, you have brought your khana-pani.' (Food and water.)

Jindo was a devoted father. 'Don't do that, or I will hit you,' he would say to us in mock seriousness. 'Go on, go on, hit us,' we teased, and he would tap our cheeks gently.

'He never picked up our children,' his cousins and aunts commented, watching him almost with envy as he carried Ganeve on his shoulder while I walked alongside, holding his hand.

No festival was celebrated at Rajkot House with a raucous show, but that did not mean there was no festive joy. I can imagine many Diwalis passing with sadness after 1947, but by the time I was four years old and walking, my father and mother stood on either side of me while I held my first phulljhari. They did this outside their room upstairs rather than downstairs, a cosy joy that they wanted away, even from Bibiji and Papaji. It was an invitation to the joy of normalcy but cautious, as if too much of a spectacle was vulgar for the deep, quiet happiness they actually yearned for.

For several years, till Ganeve became somewhat adequate company, I spent a lot of time with Jindo, including day trips to Delhi. I remember my first ride in an air-conditioned bus with him. I remember the safe comfort of him on the next seat and the deep, deep, sleep in the icy cool, cushioned interior, while the afternoon June sun melted the country outside.

I remember a visit to a kutchehry just across the road from our house. I remember the buzzing crowd. 'Chippy, wait here in the verandah outside. I just have to go into that courtroom, and I will be back. Okay? Don't move, okay? Not at all. *Theek hai?*'

I nodded seriously and did just that—I did not move. I have a memory of holding my hand on the verandah pillar in a particular way for a longish while, like in the game called Statue, hoping I would not get tired till he returned.

Just then, his reassuring largeness and booming voice returned, 'Chippy, you did not move?'

'You said not to,' and he laughed and carried me all the way home.

Courts and lawyers' visits were quite matter-of-course for me, now that I think of it. There was the big case that no one likes to talk of. It was a shoot-out fuelled by feudal arrogance and confusion, and perhaps anger at the new place they had moved to. Eventually, one granduncle was acquitted, and the other, who was my absolute favourite, was sentenced to life. But he was released for good behaviour and other such considerations after fourteen years. I believe this favourite granduncle of mine was too good a shot to have missed, and so he truly did not shoot to kill. He did not resent his brother's acquittal. 'He would never have been able to handle the pressure of jail,' he would say.

I remember accompanying my father on a jail visit to this granduncle. Jindo would hide two whiskey quarters on either side of his jacket front, and we would step across a small door within the large, spiked iron gate, above which was a very large board in Hindi.

'What does the sign mean, Papa?'

'I can't read Hindi,' he said. I was surprised, because I had not known it till then. I must have been about seven years old. *'Paap sey ghrina karo, paapi sey nahi,'* (Hate the sin, not the sinner), I read out to him.

On a parole visit, it was this granduncle who taught me cycling. Papaji Vaddey was angry at him about something during one of those visits and said something like, *'Jail ho aya, par akal bilqul nahi ayi.'* (He has been in jail but has still learned nothing.) My austere nana, there on a rare visit, made an equally rare, witty response, *'Jail gaya hai, Sardar Bahadur, boarding school nahi.'* (He went to jail, Sardar Bahadur, not to boarding school.)

This was also the time when I visited, with my father, a lady's home in Delhi. 'I will get you to meet a friend of mine,' he said. I remember her drawing room and being given a bowl of candy. I told my mother about the visit just as an extra bit of news of my day in Delhi. She clouded with a heavy sulk and Jindo looked very embarrassed, but nothing more was said.

My mother tried to scold me that she did not like that I visited the lady, but I remember being clear in my defence that I was not at fault as a mere child accompanying her father. My mother relented, but I sensed her distress without clearly knowing why.

Years later, I read a letter from a woman whose name was

Asha, or Kamala, or perhaps Rita. I found it in my mother's cupboard. There was nothing anywhere that particularly belonged to my father. He had no separate drawer or cupboard under lock and key. 'What do you mean by you are sorry?' I read. 'What do you mean by forgive you? I will never give you the satisfaction of having forgiven you.' Jindo, in one of his delusions, must have told her that he was going to visit Japan. 'I have heard of their miniature gardens; do see those,' she wrote.

I think my mother did not destroy the letter because of the last line. 'Go Jindo,' she said. 'I hope you learn to keep at least one woman happy.'

About a year before he died, my father asked me to get the number of the daughter of a famous lawyer who had acted for my uncles in their murder trial. I made no effort to get it, thinking he would forget, and so was uncomfortably surprised that he had managed to obtain it without my help.

He told me, 'Ring her up and tell her that you are my daughter and the message is that I stood before the firing squad and survived.'

'What a strange message,' I said. 'Do it yourself,' mortified at the thought of what the lady would say to me.

Jindo could be called a ladies' man, a dashing Casanova with several love interests, but his liking for women was not necessarily that of a 'male' as much as a deep affection for the way they were. He truly liked them. He hated accompanying all-male baraats, preferring the home comforts of staying back with the women. 'Senior lady,' Tayaji would scoff, and Jindo would laugh, 'You don't even have to make me senior because I am a man. I am the junior-most lady and quite happy to be so. It's bloody comfortable.'

What disappoints me, despite his comfort with women and the sense he gave us that he liked women, is that there was a complete conjugal incompatibility with my mother. She felt sorry but also irked that it was she who was sad at not being able to provide the 'companionship' he needed. My mother put up with him bravely, loyally, and honourably, and my father could not make her comfortable. His seeming progressiveness was for his daughters and not for his wife.

I, too, had a strange sense of what men could or could not do. Once, walking me to The Claridges hotel on a Delhi visit for waxing at the beauty parlour, Jindo said he would get his manicure and pedicure done while he waited for me. I said, 'Men don't get pedicures,' he said, 'Of course they do!' My mother had never visited a parlour except to get her hair done for her wedding.

I had the discomfort of his comfort with women when, at age eight or so, I complained of a pain in my breasts while I sat at the dining table. He lifted my dress to check and said to my mother, 'It's all right. She is just growing.'

Then, seeing my face, 'Sorry, Chippy. I did not mean to make you uncomfortable; I forgot that you are not that little any longer.'

Similarly, Ipsita, friend of cousin Kitten, had diarrhoea. She was on the pot and Jindo walked in with that wide-eyed, worried look that had become typical when anyone sneezed more than once. Ipsi did not misunderstand. She sat on the pot while Jindo, Kitten, Ganeve and I clucked around, feeding her glucose water right there, till Darshan cleared us out for the doctor.

# 33. Modern India

I was born in May 1962. A quick Internet search showed that the U.S. conducted its first nuclear test in the Pacific that month. In October began the month-long Indo-China war of 1962. I seem to have been well-cocooned in a separate baby peace, but the Indo-Pakistan war of 1965 did come close enough for me to remember even as a three-year-old.

We used to run out of the house at the sound of the siren to the trench in the back garden. Bibiji would call out to Papaji while rushing past his room, and his daily response was that he would die in his bed when his time was up.

I remember the ear-bursting, earth-shaking bellows. 'This bomb is very close, sleep, Chippy, sleep,' Mama would say.

The trench was furnished with durries and cushions for the grown-ups, and a small mattress for me. I think there was a separate trench for the servants, though I remember the cook, Bhola Singh, chatting to us from the edge of our trench.

The 1971 war is a very clear memory for me. I was in boarding school. We were ordered to keep under our beds a blanket, warm dressing gown, and a pair of socks. At the first wail of the siren, we were to dive under our beds, but a second one was a signal to quick-march outdoors, dressed in our woollies and socks.

At the end of term, I told Mama, 'It's great fun.'

'Don't say that,' she said. 'You have uncles from both sides of your family fighting at the front.'

'Front' always evoked laughter. In Punjabi, it is an active verb. '*Front ho gaya*' describes a person who is out in a no-holds-barred aggression. 'Watch it, oh, Sardar *front ho jayega*. Then what will you do?' It is difficult to handle a sardar who has *fronted.* This was in contrast to the ignominy of the 'bhagoda' or deserter.

The war continued into my vacations. The windows of Rajkot House were layered with newspapers to capture the light of one small candle in an inner room from which must not escape even a small glow to the night outside.

'Sing a song, Chippy,' the elders said, drinking tea among the exploding bombs. Tayiji and Kitten stayed with us while Tayaji was at the front. The older three children were probably at college.

We would sing the song of the '71 war sung to the tune of Lata Mangeshkar's song in the film 'Jagriti'.

*Aao bacchhon tumhe dikhayen jhanki Hindustan ki,*
*Iss mitti pe tilak karo,*
*Yeh dharti hai balidan ki,*
*Bandey matram, bandey matram.*

Come children, let us show you a glimpse of India,
Apply tilak on this soil,
It is the land of sacrifice,
Bandey Mataram, Bandey Mataram.

'No nationalist songs, please,' Tayiji said. We then had the fun song to the same tune:

*Aaoo bacchhon tumhe dikhain darhi Yahya Khan ki,*
*Is darhi mein bhari padi hain jooen Pakistan ki,*
*Bhutto besharam; andey-chai garam.*

Come children, let me show you Yahya Khan's beard;
This beard is full of the lice of Pakistan,
Shameless Bhutto; hot eggs and tea!

But it was not funny to any grown-up.

A particularly acceptable song to all was Nanak's:

*Kahe re ban khojan jayee,*
*Sarav nivasi sada alepa,*
*Tohi sang samayee,*

Where do you go to the jungles looking for me,
I forever reside within you.

We were in Delhi, sitting out on Tayaji and Tayaji's lawn, when my cousin Kitten called from the house: 'Ceasefire! Ceasefire!' and we all picked up the chant. We had won, but I felt bad about the photo of defeated General Niazi signing the treaty of Bangladesh, even when I felt happy for the victorious General Arora.

## 34. Nation and Newton's Laws

Life stories are influenced by separate experiences of governance, which can define individual personalities and family units.

The likes of our family, in the nodal point of transitioning society, steadily lost ground and found it difficult to survive into the next generation unless they managed to retain some family wealth from the socialist advent on the feudal ramparts. Our family was not of the class and wealth to be affected by the loss of privy purses, nationalisation of banks, and acquisitions of industry, but the land reform movement was a tectonic rumble in our lives. It was initiated by Vinobha Bhave, whom Jindo rudely called 'Uncle of the Nation' since the father's role had been bagged by Gandhi.

Jindo began to be restless. Long silent spells were broken by, 'I guess we can move to a cheaper place.' I thought the move would be exciting, because I had no idea what 'a cheaper place' could mean.

One afternoon in 1971, I was reading on a floor cushion while Jindo lay on his bed. Feeling his gaze, I looked up and saw tears flowing into his beard.

Shock. 'Mama, Mama, Papa is crying.'

Darshan was sitting in the verandah, embroidering a cushion cover. My sense of drama required that she throw down everything and rush to my father and so I was very irritated that she carefully tucked the needle into the cushion before going to Jindo.

I stood outside the doorway, heart in my mouth as if waiting for the doctor to emerge from the patient's room.

A while later, Darshan called me in. I lay down next to Jindo.

'What will you be when you grow up?' he asked.

'I don't know,' I said.

'You must do something. Don't be like us.'

'We have grown up with the call, *zameenan khus jaangiyan*,' (We will lose the land), said Darshan. 'It has finally happened. Thank God the government will leave us something. Otherwise, with our education, we would only be cleaning bartans in people's homes.'

Horror. The image of poverty became my permanent nightmare.

'Would it not have been simpler to sell the land during the rumour of the Land Ceiling Act rather than live in dread of it?' I asked Jindo years later.

'Sell? But I will be lost without land,' he said.

I understood what he meant. A distant uncle had recently visited our house, sombre with sorrow and regret. 'I have sold all the land I have. I have more money than ever, but I have never been so miserable. I saw the tractor and trolley laden with sugarcane parked outside your house, and I feel like crying.'

From Jindo and the prayers we were taught, we learned of

land as a living, generous being. He had avoided the intensive farming of the Green Revolution and would rest the land from time to time by growing nitrogen-rich dhaancha.

To not have a crop in those financially hard times required a commitment and patience, made possible by the local 'adhati' (moneylender), Choudhry Jog Dhian. I used to think he was the custodian of our money, and now I know, we were perpetually indebted to him.

Early morning calls: 'Choudhry Sahib, *paisey bhejo*.' The traditional bania would note it in his khata, and the money would arrive. I would sometimes visit him with Jindo. His skin was so dark that I fancied he merged into his room that had no sunlight and he saved on light bulbs. His gold earrings flashed his presence, and I would feel my way to the mattress and the gol takiya that he sat on. Sometimes, he sent us unforgettable neembu achars made by his wife.

My visits to the adhati were frequent enough for me to convert them into a role-playing game with Kitten.

Kitten would be Jindo. '*Choudhry-ji, kaise ho? Hamari fasal kaisi hai?*' (Choudhry-ji, how are you? How is our crop?)

'*Bahut achhi hai, Sardar Sahib; kitney paise logey?*' (It is very good, Sardar Sahib. How much money will you take?), I would say as the adhati.

The adhati ceased to be in our lives only fifty years later when Darshan took over running the farm, but a lot had to do with the fact that by that time, Ganeve and I were self-supporting.

When I went to scatter the ashes of Jindo's body on the fields on our farm, the barrenness that I remembered from my childhood days had become a continuous stretch of rich green.

Through his lethargy and disillusionment, Jindo maintained a love connection with land that was expressed with poetic simplicity. 'Never sell land, Chippy,' he told me. 'It is a lovely thing. It only gives, never takes.'

Over the decades after 1947, Jindo's grief about feeling exiled may have seemed less visible to an outsider, but for us, it had seeped into his inner being. His cynicism about governments and the intellectual mediocrity of stakeholders in power continued to be vocalised, albeit in a joking fashion. He was particularly amused by all politicians and had many jokes about pompous, pretentious government servants. Driving through Delhi, he would chuckle at name plates outside homes, the size and splendour of which called for scrutiny on the sources of income that all knew would never happen.

'They are the new aristocrats, Chippy,' he would say of the cash-rich trader, businessman, and industrialist, who resented the 'old-world elite'. Conversely, the old elite, resentful of their diminishing power, also never lost an opportunity to belittle the newly rich as nava-rajjiya, nouveau-riche. Yet, the Partitioned Punjabis developed a proclivity to display wealth not as an ostentatious statement but to mark the success of their struggle to regain, at least on the outside, what could not fill the wound within, as if material things were assertions of resilience and prosperity against odds. The joke of the five Ks of the modern Sikh can be understood then: kothi, kudi, kar, kash, kutta (house, woman, car, cash, dog).

A granduncle from a rich background in Pakistan was congratulated on purchasing a bicycle in India; he was beginning to accumulate wealth.

'Arrey, this is nothing. I have only made Bathu status.' Bathu was the village grocer.

Before we bought our first car, I have a bizarre memory of my father on a bicycle, on the handle of which was strung Darshan's brown leather 'ladies' handbag with a gold buckle. He had brought cash from the mandi.

The arrival of our tractor announced another layer of

prosperity for us. It was the Russian Belarus (that we pronounced bylarris). Jindo drove it to the Karnal Club with straight-faced casualness.

Papa, still with the memory of a good life and proud to be what was called a 'dandy', asked a cousin traveling abroad for a Rolex watch without, I am sure, knowing how expensive it would be. Only decades later, when Papa wanted to sell the watch, did we realise that the watch was a fake from 'Indo-China'. None of us resented the cousin when we found this out because it had kept Papa happy for decades, and the liquidity crisis had, in any case, passed. However, given his commitment to authenticity, Papa could not bear to wear the very good fake Rolex any longer and, by that age, had learned to be content with an HMT.

As to wisdom, Papa's favourite ditty used to be:

'Early to bed, early to rise;

Makes a man healthy and wise.'

The wealth was missing for him and he seemed to feel no bitterness about it. It was just the shock of the fall and then the sadness. But he woke up early and bathed and got back into bed.

I read *The Tao of Physics* in my early twenties, and spirituality and science managed to coexist for me. Later, when my husband died, I took succour from the conservation of mass theory: 'Matter cannot be created or destroyed but only changes its form.'

I saw Newton's Laws apply to politics and lives: the universe has a momentum that affects all, even without will. Thus, it can be slow or fast, but change is inevitable and nothing really stands still.

'That which has movement will carry on for a while after an external intervention to stop, and, conversely, that which is stationary will remain so till pushed by external force.'

On 25 June 1975, I woke to my mother's voice telling the

cleaning lady, Angoori, that the country was in a bad shape and so Indira Gandhi had declared Emergency. I did not understand the full implication till more than a decade later as a lawyer, but on that morning in 1975, it was just something different to wake up to.

By July, we were back in boarding school, closeted away from the political world, but the air was different in small ways. I was lunching at Kwality Restaurant with a relative who returned the cream as off, saying that they should be careful about these things in times of Emergency. Things seemed good. Restaurants were careful about standards, people were working, trains were on time.

By August, some news began filtering into school. A friend's college-going brother had been arrested for speaking against Mrs. Gandhi in a bus. Then, more serious news. Some friends from Calcutta with intense left-leaning families were disappearing. Dilip Simeon, son of the Doon School headmaster, Eric Simeon, had gone underground.

A family Emergency story is about my mother's cousin in Tallania, who, till then, had been distracted by heavy drinking from expressing his undoubtedly worthy intellect. He decided to invite jail time for an alcohol detox and to write the magnum opus simmering within him. Carrying an overnighter packed with a kurta pyjama and writing material, he made a provocative anti-government speech at the Tallania Mela but, unfortunately for him, Mrs. Gandhi lifted the Emergency a few days later, and my uncle was released from jail to return to alcoholic musings of the book that eventually died with him.

Jindo came to see me in school in those days. The papers reported the Supreme Court ruling in the A.D.M. Jabalpur case, whereby no citizen had the right to move the Supreme Court for violating their fundamental rights.

Jindo was stunned by the justice system, of which he had been a great admirer; the common-law idea of justice, equity, and good conscience. His favourite quote was the well-known, 'Let a hundred guilty go free rather than one innocent hang,' the principle that he had seen shielding his two uncles from the gallows in the Panipat shoot-out.

The A.D.M. Jabalpur ruling then seemed to have killed something in Jindo, and he reverted to a new outrageous delusion of being a monarchist, preferably the monarch. Alternatively, Jindo liked the idea of being like the Dalai Lama. He felt he had a special relationship with this self-exiled monarch with a moral force. Jindo also envied that even as an exile, the Dalai Lama seemed to count as one of the richest men in the world. I don't know how he came to that conclusion.

My father's private protest against Partition was that he would never vote. But he did vote in January 1977 for the Janata government as a reaction to the A.D.M. Jabalpur ruling by a weak judiciary.

In my teenage memory, the significance of the Janata government was George Fernandes throwing out Coca-Cola. It did not affect us children except for an important debate on the best substitute for our favourite drink. Ganeve and I carefully tasted the Coca-Cola substitutes of Campa-Cola, Thums Up, and Double Seven, and decided that Thums Up was the closest.

For me, Rajkot House was a wait within a womb. Till we were old enough to kick impatiently, it prepared us with its rich, loamy darkness, fertile with Jindo's imagination expressed in crazy words or palm upward gestures as if asking questions. He released his eccentricities into stories that, during the days of alcohol abuse, were lived as hallucinations.

An astrologer said, 'You have seen God.'

'Yes, I have,' says Jindo seriously. And no one had the courage to call him a fool because his confidence made one wonder, what if.

'How is the depression, Papa?'

'It comes and goes; the modern medicines are good.' His favourite drug, Dexedrine, had been banned as a prescription medication by then. To counter the drugs, and after he gave up alcohol, his continuing addictive habit drove him to drink water by the gallon. He would nurse a glass of water longer than he would have of whiskey.

*'Yaar, tu andar munji ugai hai?'* (Have you grown paddy inside?) his old drinking buddies would ask.

*

Access to good doctors firmly deflected my life away from suffering, my clubbed feet being a severe handicap.

My infant experience with needles and operations and plaster on my feet made me abnormally fearful of hospitals. I will still deliver any secret to avoid the horror of injections. During the polio eradication drive, I was vividly joyful over not facing another dreaded needle but a Parle-G glucose biscuit sprayed with the polio drops.

My annual nightmare was the T.A.B.C. vaccination and the nerve-wracking good cheer of the family doctor as he plunged the needle into our plump flesh. Jindo would present his bared arm for the first injection.

'It's all right, Chippy, Doctor Sahib is very good.' I would start crying from the moment of the feel of the cold antiseptic, the screams peaked just before the needle plunged, and then the shocked silence that it was not really as bad as I had thought was followed by the ouch at the needle pulling out and the joy of the reassuring press of the cotton patch. We were free for another year. The inevitable evening fever was helped by the special treat of a bar of Cadbury chocolate.

The smallpox vaccine was fearsome. It was a single, thick needle that was heated on a strange apparatus that the government person brought with him. The medicine was put on the needle and then scratched onto our inner wrist. For the next few weeks, there was a burning boil that changed colour, and we said, 'Oh my God, you really had a lot of smallpox germs in you.'

We all grew up with the famous triple-antigen scars on our thighs as three angry welts that softened over the years but never went away. I remember Darshan gossiping with a cousin that such-and-such young girl had triple antigen on her feet to avoid disfiguring her thighs. My cousin responded with a scornful, 'Unnnh! As if that would have been the only shortcoming in her beauty.'

I never found this type of thing funny since I was painfully awkward, certain in the knowledge that I was plain compared to my extraordinarily good-looking immediate and extended family.

## 35. Some Slides of Life at Rajkot House

I woke to Jindo's radio singing Vividh Bharati songs. Old Hindi songs still induce a deep melancholy in me, due to my misery of school mornings being serenaded by sad love songs.

Radio had settled into the air. A relative made it a medium of protest against the State. 'Oh, you know, Bhaji,' he told Jindo, 'when they announce on All India Radio that they are going off the air and good night, I keep it on. How dare they tell me when to go to bed?'

I remember our first gas cylinder. The man came to demonstrate and, watching her clumsy attempts to light the stove, asked, 'You don't cook, do you?' Mama laughed. 'None of the women in this house cook. Please teach Bhola Singh how to do it.' The mitti chullah was moved outdoors, next to the tandoor, and rarely used for seasonal sarson saag and kheer for the smoky flavour from a wood fire on which they cook, slow and rich.

Technology was manipulated by political leaders in a unique way. 'They have these dams for electricity,' said some leader of the Opposition in Punjab. 'But the water that comes to your fields is phoka, (dud) after the electricity has been taken out of it.'

Education helped another relative learn of the subterranean reserves of water, but the lesson was interpreted very differently. 'My tubewell seems always to strike on the banks of the underground river because it has not yielded water yet,' he told Jindo. Another relative was so happy to strike water that he refused a chance to move to Canada since he now had all he needed: a submersible pump that gushed abundant water on his fields.

I remember the arrival of the large, black telephone when I was about four. The number '253' was written in the centre of the dial by Jindo. It took me a while to overcome my fear of the disembodied voices it carried.

Because we were one of the few houses that had a telephone, many neighbours came to book a trunk call to speak to relatives abroad. 'Helloooo,' their shout would reach my room, and I listened with shameless interest to the details of the family and their nicknames. The operators would help communicate through a bad line. I thought of the operators as kind and concerned people who carefully delivered messages that connected families.

'He is saying such–and–such,' the operator would say.

'Please tell him so–and–so,' the speaker from Karnal would yell.

Radio and telephone were followed by the television in about the early seventies. We announced our new prosperity with a tall T.V. antenna on our rooftop, and the T.V. arrived as an honoured guest to sit in a prime place in our drawing room.

'What is it going to be, Bibiji?' I asked.

'Like a newspaper,' she said, 'but you will be able to see the persons telling the news.'

I imagined a series of magazine covers to accompany the radio sound of the news, and so, nothing prepared me for the shocking excitement of movement on a screen in my home. Even 'Krishi Darshan' was fascinating and we listened attentively to the advantages of a certain new fertiliser and how to manage a kitchen garden and what was best suited to grow for a particular season and the marvel of grafting orange and malta that formed kinnow.

To relatives and neighbours who came to watch, we would find ourselves saying quite frequently, 'I don't know why the reception is like this today,' embarrassed that our sky-scraping antenna should not seem a hoax. 'Must be from the back,' they would comfort us, and we would nod, grateful for their understanding.

The first film we saw on T.V. was 'Patita'. It was a strange story with a wicked woman (Lalita Pawar with one eyebrow raised) whose son pretended he was dead just so she would learn to be kind. He taught her tough lessons by speaking to her in a deep voice, resounding from the heavens. Having thus reduced her to a blithering penitent, he appeared at the end of the film. Where had he been all the while? In my child's memory, I think he had lived under the bed.

We were allowed to stay up late for 'Yes Minister' and 'Mind Your Language', and on Sunday mornings, we had breakfast in pyjamas to watch Captain Kirk travel to places where no man had been before.

But Louis Armstrong had already made that real. I remember his muffled voice and Bibiji saying, between verses of the prayer appropriate for that time of the day, '*Science di taraqqi vekho, aadmi Chund tey pahunch gaya.*' (Look at how science has advanced; man has reached the moon.)

The T.V., however, could not substitute for a cinema hall. The excitement began with the announcement of a new film on a rickshaw travelling the neighbourhood upon which sat a hoarding and a record player, blaring the film's songs. We would rush to the gate to see the actors on the film poster and hear the raucous music playing on a turntable, almost always at the wrong speed or with the needle jumping as the rickshaw lurched into yet another pothole.

Then, the decision to see a particular film on a particular day: me in a nice dress and shoes, Mama in a pleasant salwar-qameez, head elegantly covered with a chiffon dupatta, and Jindo always in smart casuals, even at home. It was only much later that he adopted the eccentric dress code of a house coat or a dressing gown, much like Oblomov.

The first movie I saw in the theatre was 'Ram Aur Shyam'. Later, Ganeve was old enough for her first visit to a cinema hall, but she hated the darkness and glaring screen and so was sent home mid-movie with the bearer, Balam Singh.

Eventually, Ganeve and I became good movie companions, addicted to our Coca-Cola during the intervals. We loved watching the ads together, particularly the one about Swastik Neem Sabun. The funny, fat, sad, dusty man who came morose and exhausted from the office and was transformed by his bucket bath in a dreary bathroom. The water did not do what the soap managed to do. 'Aaah' sung in breaks between one 'aaaah' and another, rising and falling discordant sounds that culminated in a (un)musical base chant; ah-ah-ah-Swastik Neem Sabun.

The man came into his own when he earnestly held aloft and lovingly looked at the soap he was advertising, till interrupted by his pretty, fair-skinned wife knocking on the door, *'Tauliya toh bahar reh gaya.'* (You left the towel outside!)

The nonplussed funny look at the audience collapsed Ganeve and me into holding each other through helpless laughter of shared slapstick humour. We promptly bought Swastik Neem Sabun.

Then, in later years, was the lovely Liril soap model, who shimmered in her bikini in sensual revelry of the feel of a mountain waterfall on bare skin. We then switched to Liril soap.

After the ads came the censor certificate. A witty cousin noted the tendency to read even that carefully and told us, 'Quickly see the number of reels so that we know we are getting our money's worth.'

Then the shudder of excitement as the film company logo dissolved to the title, emerging from the Technicolor clouds to lift us into another world.

We hid our faces in our mother's lap during the violent bits; we were scared together during mysterious films like 'Kohra' and 'Mahal' and the haunting song, 'Kahin deep jaley, kahin dil', resonated with the empty space that each person in Rajkot House yearned to fill.

The return to reality was always depressing.

Jindo's taste in films was popular extravaganza, particularly the grandeur of 'Pakeezah' and 'Mughal-e-Azam' and actors like Prithviraj Kapoor and Dilip Kumar. Anything else was ordinary, and something boring was 'art'.

In those days, Jindo was alert enough to want to be socially active and had even become a member of the local club where Dilip Kumar visited for the 'Ram and Shyam' film release. Jindo introduced himself to Dilip Kumar: 'I am Jitinder.'

'Yousuf,' said Dilip Kumar, shaking his hand.

Jindo then introduced us to him. 'This is Yousuf,' he said, and, 'this is Saira Bano, his wife. The others are actors, too.'

I knew Jindo was losing interest in life when he could not tell the difference between Rekha and Jaya Bachchan in 'Silsila'. Time passed. A little party here, a little gathering there, a magic show at the Rotary Club, where the magician produced cigarettes from the air and Jindo caught one.

'You smoke?' the magician asked, and Jindo nodded nonchalantly, though for a Sikh to smoke in public was as odd or offensive as a maulvi to admit to drinking.

Watching him, I was bold enough to get up to try and catch a conjured toffee, only for the magician to beat me to it and eat it himself, leaving me burning in embarrassment. The magician remains for me as a memory of a silly, crass, and ill-mannered man.

Then, even those little events stopped. Jindo had stopped drinking, so he did not feel like entertaining or going to dinner parties. Sometimes, he would have furtive excesses like going to Gopinath Restaurant and downing five shots of vodka at lunchtime because it would not smell. But Bibiji found out, and that stopped.

Then, he took to reading books that influenced my own literary interest, with easy access to a fast-growing collection of classic, popular, literary, historical, pulp, Russian, comedy, erotica.

For us, evenings were livened by the occasional treat of small toys from the balloon-wallah passing the house.

The fruit baba looked like Khushiya and carried on his head a huge basket, glistening with a variety of the season's fruit, of which bananas were my favourite and so I called him Kelian-Wallah Baba. Over the years, I saw the basket get smaller, and, just about ten years ago, I watched him pass our house holding a few bananas in his hand. I ran up to the gate and introduced my children. We bought the bananas, and that's the last I saw of him.

Childhood was easy in Karnal because foreign goods did not fuel hyper-status anxiety. The class that had access to them were too high for us to feel inferior to. The taste and smell of our bodies were of Socialist India products. We all washed our long hair with Helena Rubinstein Gleem Shampoo that smelt of guavas. We oiled it with a red Unani unguent called Benazir in a small, rectangular glass bottle. Our top layer was the sweetness of Johnson's Baby Powder and the baby lotion that we still use on our middle-aged skin, as does our mother on her eight-decade-old, increasingly fragile but only slightly wrinkled skin that drapes in gentle folds on high cheekbones.

A 'hadi soni' (paddy, wheat) biannual event was buying salwar-qameezes at the Bombay Silk store. Our arrival was greeted as if Christian Dior and his favourite dowager. Someone would be waiting to receive us into a brightly lit interior, smelling of strong incense and glowing with silk and satin and gold and silver brocades that were a bit off and too shiny in the harsh yellow and white light.

We sat in a private alcove, fingering and feasting on lengths of material—gardens of colourful or elegant pastels on fine voiles, or silks, or heavy cottons, depending on the season. The shop owner had a crooked mouth, and my grandmother called him 'Vinghey Mooh Wala'.

As the bill was being prepared is when he would produce something spectacular, and we would sit down again, cursing his trickery as we succumbed to buying more. Sometimes, he sent to Rajkot House yards of new lengths, much to Bibiji's irritation, because she felt obliged to buy something, as Vinghey Mooh Wala probably knew.

The bill was always paid later.

On one occasion, when we visited the shop, Vinghey Mooh's son was at the counter. He asked that we pay immediately, and my grandmother walked out in a huff. The most talented salesman followed swiftly to the house with bales of the material she had liked, apologising for the crass new generation.

Apart from such distractions, there was a dull, predictable routine of waiting for meals made interesting by Mama's baking, and evenings alleviated somewhat by going to the gurudwara at Model Town to listen to kirtan.

The only intense outdoor activity was long walks with my parents during which, sometimes, we would stop at a 'redi' (cart) for tikkas and fish cutlets and sometimes at Gopinath Restaurant for cheese pakoras and coffee. Gopinath catered at our weddings and the food was superb in simplicity and wholesome flavours, just as I remembered as a child.

Recently, I went after years to Bombay Silks. Vinghey Mooh Wala had died and the upstartish son had taken over. I said, as usual, that I was carrying no money, but the now mature man smiled and said, 'Of course.'

But the next generation took my mobile number, much to his father's embarrassment.

---

# 36. School

The individual journey is the road experienced by the traveller, unique in who she is and who she is moving to become.

Due to my clubbed feet, I began walking when I was about three years old, and so it seemed to me that my studies began from the moment I could walk.

My growing aches amalgamated with many other unexpressed anxieties, perhaps about not being able to keep up with other children when they ran, and perhaps I picked up Papa's sadness. But the ache never left, and I learned to live with it, and so it became a habit and then an addiction, where the absence of a shadow on any happiness gave me the anxiety of excess as if I did not deserve too much.

My cousins were all educated at Welham, and I was in awe of their confidence and English speaking. I believe I asked Papa when I was just a toddler that I, too, wanted to study at Welham. Perhaps remembering how he had gone to his mother crying because he wanted a good education like his older brother, he promised me he would indeed send me to Welham, though he could not afford it.

I began as a day scholar at the local co-educational convent school. I disliked the Karnal school. I remember thinking I would eventually go to Welham and felt I must tell the nuns the first day as full disclosure. Off I went, 'I am wearing a red ribbon today because Mama did not have a black one. Will wear the black ribbon tomorrow. Also, I will be going to Welham Girls in a year or so.' My father smiled with pride, and the nun smiled, too, and led me away to my class. I had never seen so many children.

I found comfort with one very tall girl called Amrit. I did not hate school. I was scared of it. I was scared of the size, the noise, and, most of all, the boys.

Every morning was a heavy heart speaking the same refrain like a chant for comfort. Every morning began with my telling my mother:

'*Aj school jana hai*?' (Do I have to go to school?)

'*Jee haan*,' (Yes, ji—my sister and I were always addressed with the respectful ji and aap, never tu.)

'*Jaldi ghanti vajjegi?*' (Will the end-of-school bell ring quickly?)

'*Jee, bachoo.*' (Yes, child.)

'*Amrit pass baithegi?*' (Will Amrit sit with me?) Her tall, reassuring presence calmed me.

'*Hmmm, Chippoo-ji. Kyun nahi baithegi?*' (Yes, Chippoo-ji, why won't she sit next to you?)

We were transported to school in cycle rickshaws that accommodated three children on the main seat, another three on a wooden bench placed in front of the seat and one or two children sat in the basket formed by the lowered sunshade hood of the rickshaw.

I still wonder at the wisdom of my father not sending me to school in the car and that I never thought of asking for it. The thought behind learning seems to have been a complete immersion in every experience of whatever life presented. However painful, however difficult, dive in! seems to have been the approach.

Early in the morning, Jindo walked in the driveway in a cotton salwar kurta, over which, in winter, he wore a dressing gown of dark blue-black with a thin broad check of light blue. While waiting for the rickshaw, I would walk alongside him, my school bag sitting on the verandah steps. The rickshaw would arrive, and the smell of my lunchbox, mixed with my misery, made me sick as I prepared to leave for another miserable day.

Other children on my rickshaw were all boys and all older than me. Anil, Sunil, Amarjit, and Narayanjit. On the first day, Jindo rearranged the seating so I could be in the middle of the main seat. The boys submitted to Jindo without question, but objected to the same arrangement on our return ride and the rickshaw-wallah, Radhu Ram, gave in to them. Sometimes, they would move me from the main seat the moment the rickshaw left our house. One day, they put me in the back basket, cheering as I smiled sheepishly. That is the day the rickshaw thinly avoided a speeding bus. Radhu Ram pulled me out of the basket and placed me in the front. 'Don't tell your father,' he said, and I never did.

In school, the boys, smelling my lonely misery, chanted '*Aj ghanti naio vajani*,' (Today the bell won't ring) terrifying me that if the bell did not ring, I would not be able to go home. One boy fought with me and mimicked my limp all over school much to my absolute, intense shame and mortification.

One day, the rickshaw did not turn up after a school play that I had acted in. I stood desolate with my schoolbag, clutching closely under my arm the shiny pink frock with a frilly flared underskirt cancan that I had worn for the play. It had three pink roses with faux pearl centres on the bodice and was a hand-me-down from Kitten.

My rickshaw companion boys made their own arrangements to go home that did not include me. I did not want to return to the classroom because I did not trust the efficiency or compassion of the nuns. Just then, Narayanjit walked to me with kindness in his eyes, 'I will walk you to your home.' The five kilometres seemed endless. He carried my schoolbag, and I carried the plastic bag with the frock. The cancan fell out. Neither of us noticed.

We reached the gate of Rajkot House, and Narayanjit clambered up the gate louvres to lift the latch. As it clanged, my family burst out of Rajkot House.

'What happened? We have been waiting.'

'*Main liaya ji*,' (I brought her), Narayanjit said proudly.

My four-year-old feet that had been walking for only about a year, were swollen and bleeding. Jindo carried me in and Darshan gave me a shikanji strong with sugar and black salt, and then I slept for two days. I would drift awake to find someone constantly massaging my feet. Since then, it has been the ultimate luxury and comfort for me to have someone stroking my feet while I sleep. I would often ask my mother to do it, and she would say, '*Ai hai*, Chippy, when I am dying, you will put your feet in my lap and say, "Just massage them one last time before you go."'

But poor Narayanjit—he was beaten by his father for running away with a girl, but became my special ally in school after that. Jindo, too, became very fond of him and always had a special kind word to say to him. Stories of the unruly but gallant Narayanjit always made him laugh, and the day he slapped a nun and ran away is the day Jindo became an absolute fan of Narayanjit.

It was also about this age that I remember being intensely groped by a servant, the shame of which only emerged later when I understood. It was a deeper cause of my sadness in boarding school that I went to at age six.

Boarding school was a fresh scooping of flesh after the incision of the first days at the local school. No one noticed the wound since there was no visible bleeding or tears. Everyone thought I was doing well as I filled my loneliness with activity that earned me the balm of approbation and accolades.

'You like school?' Jindo would ask, and I would nod silently because I knew my voice would dissolve in tears if I spoke, and that would upset him.

The drill was to walk towards the school dorms and not look back. Later, both Ganeve and I said the same thing to our children. 'Don't look back,' we called as our children toddled off into the world. The urge to look back was calmed by the certain knowledge that the parent was indeed looking on and that helped us to focus on forging ahead.

The first night in boarding school contracted my heart

to stone-heavy. My parents accompanied the matron to the dormitory. 'This is your bed,' Jindo said, 'don't get lost at night.' His concern was understandable. There were two rows of twenty beds each, a far cry from his own school residence of ensuite rooms and a servants' quarter.

'I won't forget my bed because I recognise my razai,' I told him, and he nodded as if it were he who had worried about losing his bed and was relieved by the tip of how to identify it.

After my parents left, I stayed back in the dorms, aching as my trunk with my name and number painted on it was opened to the smells of my toiletries and my mother's loving packing was unfolded by the matron and she complimented my mother's meticulous care. I glowed with pride for my very fine mother.

You could judge a girl's home from her luggage. The rich city children had foreign toothpaste that smelled like gum, silk-wrapped fancy rubber bands with little bonbons, and Disney pencil boxes for the classroom. My luggage was simple, unfrilled, small-rural town: Indian products and a bottle of mustard oil from the farm to protect from extreme winter dryness, my mother's big pound cake, and home-made marmalade for teatime on the first day of term.

Our mother knitted our sweaters and embroidered our bedsheets and nightwear that we wore with mixed feelings because home-made things were infra dig compared to mill-made or branded 'foreign' products. Our sweaters seemed too rugged next to the finer machine-made sweaters, which I thought was the height of fashion.

Mama's deep commitment to the finest and cleanest bed linen has defined us in a visceral way. When nothing else works, take a hot water bath and get into a clean bed cocooned in fine, sweet linen. I understood the value of that when crawling into my bed in boarding school and then suffered there, too, because

I discovered that I had become a bed-wetter but was too scared to tell anyone. I would wake up in a damp, smelly bed and cover it quickly before anyone saw it, and so it would be for a week till Sunday, which was the bedsheet change day. Thus, it was for me till I settled and stopped wetting my bed and settled into decent sleep after frenzied schooldays of being taught new things and learning to deal with girls of an ilk and class as new as the sums and English grammar that I was struggling with.

The night routine was typical, too. I watched the other girls and, like them, sat cross-legged on my bed with folded hands, eyes tight shut, and listened and moved my lips, pretending to know the words of the prayer that the girls sang while my mind pictured my parents at the dinner table, missing me as painfully as I missed them. But their pain, I imagined, was less than mine because they were home, and Ganeve was with them.

I worried about them and worried that they would die while I was away. My night prayer was that we all die together. Mama, Papa, Ganeve, Bibiji, Papaji and I.

A most memorable school moment was a surprise visit by Jindo. I was sitting in a music class, looking out of the window, thinking of home and what is unforgettable now is how my heart lifted at the sight, as if in a dream, of Jindo striding through the gates, tall and handsome. I ran out and hugged his knees. '"Chippy, Chippy, Chippy,"' and he lifted me with a swing of his arms to hold me close.

The teacher followed with a stern, sharp walk. 'No meeting the children without prior information and permission, sir.'

'I arrived this morning and need to return in a few hours,' Jindo smiled at the teacher. 'May I take her out for a while?'

'Well, just this once,' she said, and I was a little revolted by her simpering but canny enough to know that she would always like me a bit extra now that she had met Jindo.

We had lunch, the two of us. I could see he was impressed by my newly acquired proficiency with knife and fork. Fried fish with tartare sauce followed by Cassata Ice Cream for me, while he had a cona coffee.

Driving back to school, my heart tumbled around below my stomach as we took the last turn into the school gate. I could not cry because I worried that he would pull me out of school. The story was well known that he had once driven Bha's son Inder Vijay to the gates of Welham Boys School in Dehradun but returned to Karnal because Vijay had begun crying. Bibiji had to take her grandson to Dehradun the next day. I could not risk such paternal indulgence because I was quite sure, even at that age, that the only way to pull out of Karnal and tip into the world was to get the best education possible.

Jindo had done that for himself. It is he who had wept to go to a good school and yet lacked the stoic maturity to bear it at first. He was said to cry a lot when they left him there and, on one occasion, had to be dragged out from under the car.

*

School had various cultures and classes that those of us with functional social skills for survival learned to assimilate into friendships. I met girls with 'working' fathers and the occasional mother who was a social secretary at an embassy.

'What does your father do?' the girls asked.

'He is a farmer.'

Silence.

'He pulls the plough himself?'

'No; he has people to do that'.

'Ah,' the girls would say, relieved that I was not going to challenge a debate of kindness versus snobbery. And yet, it is I who felt sorry for them as they described their fathers' long working hours while I had the advantage of having everyone lounging at home through the day.

The reality of our cultural contrasts could be papered over with uniforms, study, and sport. I truly came into my own when I discovered a talent on stage. Then it was easy. I could be someone else and I was good at it.

I was good with the girls in school, but I did not meet them during the holidays. I could not really be like them. I did not swim in a club where boys and girls called out to each other comfortably; English movies were rare for me in a small town; I had no experience of Chinese restaurants (I still can't eat with chopsticks), and I had no familiarity with fancy Western food except cheese sandwiches and my mother's baking. I also dreaded someone asking me why I limped and suffered the paralysing shyness of the obviously alien.

My misery in school was heightened by the dreaded subject of Math. Mama tried her best, but my fear was deep. The bell that rang the Math period made me physically sick. I later learned that I had dyslexia with numbers; it is called dyscalculia.

The end of every school term was the same: 'How did you do in math?'

I would pull my mouth down and shake my head sideways.

'Failed?'

A nod.

'What marks?'

'Guess!'

'Thirty per cent,' said hopefully.

'Nope.'

'Twenty?'

'No.'

'Ten?'

'No.'

'Zero?'

'No.'

'Five?'

'Yes,' I would nod, embarrassed and miserable.

A pat on the cheek. 'Don't worry, when it comes to the crunch, you will pull through. Once, I got one out of 150 in Geography.'

Such acceptance, followed by a slap-up lunch at Kwality before leaving for Karnal, made it all vanish. The holidays had begun. I would really work hard and do better next term, I promised myself.

*

In contrast to still life in Karnal and incapacitating muteness in Delhi, I eventually grew well and quite cocky in school.

That is also when I processed the memory of the groping servant. I wanted to talk to my mother, which surprised me because I actually spent more time with my father. The movies had taught me shame; she may think it was my fault; she may think I am now stained. I saw a movie called 'Ram Teri Ganga Maili' and wept with a loudness quite disproportionate. I even dreaded that she would love me less, though I felt Jindo would protect me as he had my clubbed feet.

The thoughts weighed on me, and I became quite sad and depressed. When everyone else in class but me got their period, I felt it was because of that molesting. In the meantime, my voice was becoming deeper, and the memory of the abuse created irrational fears that I could not control—that something so bad had happened that it would prevent me from being a woman. About then, I had read in *The Illustrated Weekly of India* the story of a man who grew breasts and became a woman. If it was possible, and if it is reported in the papers, I thought it could happen. This meant I was turning into a boy and would have to be in Doon School and would have even more trouble because I would then be homosexual.

Then, one day, during a hot summer afternoon, I could bear it no longer and went to my mother in her upstairs cocoon and unburdened myself and wept as she held me close, saying nothing.

I felt lighter than ever before; no one else's sadness mattered. Jindo's depression was his own; everyone must bear their crosses. I was light and free.

And I went downstairs and sat with my family as I had not in a long while.

At seventeen, I got my period and was appointed school captain.

*

Here, I learned a lesson from Jindo that has cut deep.

It is Founder's Day. I am the school captain and am awarded the medal of 'Best Future Citizen' and also have the lead role in the school play. It is a peak of a type of life.

An unruly batch of senior girls comes to me and says that their parents should be given seating priority since it is their last year in school. I agree, and though it is not really my job, and I need to focus on the play I am acting in, I feel pressured to be seen as doing something. Emerging from backstage, I target a young couple sitting in the front—their simple attire proclaims small town, overawed by girls made confident by their posh parents.

'Please, sir and ma'am, these seats are for the seniors' parents,' and, without even waiting for me to complete the sentence, the couple quickly gets up to go to the last seat in the auditorium.

I find Jindo watching me. 'No, Chippy,' he says softly, just for me to hear, 'this is not right.'

'Papa, please, let me be. I know what I am doing,' and I buzz off to do some other nonsense authority work.

Later, from the stage, I noticed Jindo get up and call the couple to sit with them; my pride in him made more intense the shame I felt for my stupid, small self.

I then returned to being a child who is bad at Math but, for some reason, is head girl, and that's good, but no reason to become an insufferable prig. Jindo preferred irreverence. He loved me mimicking my teachers (and later, senior lawyers and judges).

Over the decades, I have lived with the awareness of not fitting in, for I know not what reason; surely not just a limp or a father who was depressed, but, yes, perhaps so. A wound heals but survives as a memory of pain that I pick at as a scab, and the body reacts with a plunging heart, the heaviness in the stomach, and tears that stay at the back of the eyes; for them to fall would be altogether too simple.

---

# 37. Some other Slides of Life at Rajkot House

The holidays at Rajkot House were a return to the safety of sameness. The furniture, unchanged from the time I was born, had been bought from a shop in Delhi called 'Araish', owned by a Delhi relative and Jindo's drinking buddy. Its clean, straight lines enhanced the glowing teak.

But some new purchases had begun. The advent of a coffee table and larger sofas to seat more people at a time. New tablecloths, a silver fruit tray; so rare were these new purchases that they stood out as almost gaudy against the fine and delicate fading of the old.

There was no money for Kashmiri and Persian carpets, but when I was about twelve years old, we bought an unassuming but cheerful one by O.C.M. from Ludhiana. We looked forward to it on cold winter evenings. Before the advent of the carpet, the floors were laid out with large, rough, thick, beige durries to protect against winter bite. After the grand arrival of the red O.C.M., the durries were not thrown away but simply used elsewhere and, eventually, with better things, went to line the servants' quarters.

Everything bought was of the finest quality as an investment for a lifetime. One would think that having lost it all, they would want to save money and buy less expensive things; after all, one never knew what could happen next. But it was a sense of shock, or maybe a resilience, to stay with the quality of a few rather than cheap quantity.

We were comfortable every day. Our razais were chenille, warm in colour and feel, lined with a bedsheet turned back to show an embroidered border. The bed linen, fine with long use, smelled of the sun. A good household always has a lot of bedding, my mother taught me. Her housekeeping was phenomenal. Pride in a job well done, laced with apprehension of reproach from her mother-in-law or any 'senior' lady and in competition with her sister-in-law, where she won hands down.

For beautiful things, Ganeve and I would look through Bibiji's cupboard.

It contained gifts from 'foreign-returned' relatives: a bottle of French perfume and a watch from Malaysia that was unique to us because she told us it did not have a battery but was activated by the rhythm of the pulse. She could often be seen shaking her arm vigorously, worried about her pulse being too subtle.

Her entire wardrobe consisted of about fifteen suits, all carefully wrapped in pink or white mulmul edged with gota, some

of which were sucha. One kurta of the finest cream-coloured
voile was edged with cut-worked flowers in many shades of blue.
I took that to wear at Delhi parties with a blue chemise under
it and a blue churidar pyjama. Bibiji wore lawn salwar-qameezes
with floral prints in old rose and light-green paisleys. The heavy
delicacy of a large white dupatta of Chamundi chiffon draped
well on the head and shoulders without slipping.

'These Rajkotia women may not have food in their kitchens
but will not compromise on chiffon dupattas,' the talk of local
Karnal women reached us on the relay, but we were quite proud
of that assessment.

At the bottom of Bibiji's cupboard was a Kashmiri silver
tea set finely worked with chinar leaves that had travelled with
her for that last holiday to the hills from home, to never return
because it became Pakistan while she was away.

Bibiji tried innovations for extra income: we grew grapes in
Rajkot House. Since no one had anticipated the problem with
the bees and the grapes were not sweet, the vines were cleared
after two years. The money from that last crop was just enough
for her to order a silver glass engraved with a bacchanalian border
of grape leaves interspersed with clusters of fruit. That was the
only silver glass for many years till the time Ganeve and I were
of marriageable age, and six glasses each, all similarly engraved,
were gifted to us by Bibiji.

We received with excitement some rare gifts from the foreign-
returned relatives. English soap and lotions, French perfume, and
Swiss chocolates were savoured and enjoyed with deep happiness.
My first pair of jeans were second-hand Texwood bought in
1979 because jeans were de rigeur.

To own a pair of jeans elevated you to a special place of
comfort and confidence. Match them with a cheese-cotton top
and Kolhapuri chappals, and you were in chic heaven made

popular by the Western hippies, who could be found wandering around Janpath with dreadlocked hair, generally dirty and unkempt, we thought. Jindo treated hippies as exotic animals that he pointed out as he would an elephant on the street.

Jindo found my need to own the second-hand jeans very funny, much to my embarrassment at being caught in my desperation to possess them. I snapped at his laughter, and he quickly drew away with an expression of such hurt that I have never forgotten.

Conversely, I was also embarrassed by Jindo's question to a blonde traveller in Shimla about how much his sleeping bag would cost. That he had no use for sleeping bags was beside the point. What mattered was that it was foreign goods. He may even have slept in it if the traveller had sold it to him. He may even have collected several sleeping bags to roll out for younger guests where they fancied. He may have got them for the servants and then been proud of how his staff was better treated than in any other household.

Jindo's one expensive indulgence was cameras. He had many wide-angled and long and short Nikon and Leica lenses that he used to capture happy moments as insurance against the inevitable depression later. When Jindo heard of the famous photographer Raghu Rai, he dismissed him with, 'He may be a great photographer, but I have better equipment.'

He would buy smuggled camera lenses from a shop in Chandni Chowk owned by a sardar called Lattoo. One day, Lattoo arrived to deliver a telephoto lens. Tayaji walked into the drawing room, where Lattoo and Jindo were sitting.

'Bha, meet Lattoo: the smuggler king.'

And Lattoo's modest smile thinly veiled his pride at the compliment, 'Oye, nahi, Sardar Sahib, I am nothing; you are very kind.'

We lived thus, on little money and an eccentric priority of expenses, and an abundance of trees that comforted as they grew thicker and shadier.

## 38. The Language of Darshan

Apart from having more money, the Rajkotias were English-speaking, in contrast to my maternal family that knew English, but refused to be anglicised. This dichotomy survived to my generation, and our relationship with English-speaking relatives and homes was riddled with complexes where we felt they were somehow better than us and were further irritated by their seeming agreement with our inferiority complex.

Darshan had been indoctrinated during the freedom struggle to feel revulsion for the English and their language. It is Buaji Ashram Waley who had to persuade her to at least learn to read and write it because 'the English are all over the world, and if you know their language, you will be able to know much more'.

My mother's reluctance with English marked her as very different in my father's family. But the good thing about this was that because of her, Punjabi remained our childhood language even while we read of English picnics with Enid Blyton and imagined the taste of ham and tongue sandwiches and the combination of boiled eggs and tomatoes and apple and cheese.

But at a deeper level, our anglicisation began with us calling our parents Mama and Papa rather than the customary Bapuji and Bibiji. The house began to change as boarding school further anglicised us. I met who we called the box-wallah children, who thrived in school and college, perceiving themselves (and we allowed it) as superior because of their English.

After an all-girls school, Ganeve and I went to an all-women college.

In college, the divides were three: the very rich, who wore brand new jeans and high heels and lipstick and came to college in a foreign car. Well-ensconced in their families, they stayed among their own class. Then there was handloom sari chic with a big bindi who spouted Marx and Sartre and Pablo Neruda through a whiskey and cigarette haze. They were generally the children of government servants posted abroad. The third group wore kurta pyjamas, rubber chappals, and jholas. The jhola-wallahs were committed activists who spent a lot of time on protest marches and street theatre, carrying the day's provisions in their cloth bags. They were usually the children of humbler homes who defined themselves around a political context, and many have gone on to become important leaders and influential intellectuals.

I was somewhere between the second and third but knew the first lot as well because of school. I was immersed in politics, buzzing in debate, theatre, and café talk over dosas, coffee and cigarettes.

The handloom sari was inexpensive, and we found our own place in college without the foreign stuff. Our only cosmetic was home-made kajal in a small enamel box with a silver 'suramchu' (applicator). For want of products to cover blemishes, we focused on good skin, ensured by a bottle of Safi drunk twice a year at the change of season. Makeup was not available except for Lakme lip colour and Max Factor. We bought one thing at a time.

Jindo watched with interest my friends from all these classes. He was charmed and charming and always remembered their names and stood up for them.

My comfort with 'the vernacular' fascinated my peers of classes 1 and 2, most of whom could 'understand' but not speak Punjabi, and class 3 was Hindi-speaking rather than Punjabi.

I felt sorry for them then, but now regret that my children 'understand but can't speak Punjabi'. At our home, Punjabi laced our English. In our first Punjabi lesson, we were taught:

*Punjabi da hazma bahut chunga hai;*
*Oh koi vee bhasha nu apney aap vich lappet lainda hai.*

Punjabi's digestion is very good; it wraps any language within itself.

A little cousin who grew up in Patna spoke Punjabi but also in a Bihari lilt, called to his Christian ayah when he wet his bed. '*Ree Rosie, ree, hum bheegan ray,*' (Oh, Rosie, I have wet myself), and faithful Rosie would lovingly change the sheets and pat him back to sleep.

Jindo's Punjabi was threaded with Persian that made even constipation sound poetic. 'I need some gulkand tonight. It is kabzkhushah.'

'How is your Mamaji?' I ask.
'*Makhdoom ull havas.*'
'What does that mean, Papa?'
'Without hosh or havaas.'
'Why are you so quiet, Papa?'.
'I feel that a powerful person has pronounced sentence on me. *Aboor dariaye shore.*'
'What does that mean?'
'I have been cast away beyond the salty waters.'

Jindo's memory was didactic. He remembered childhood verses and obscure poems that he may have read only once several years ago.

He told me a Persian couplet on ageing:

*Chira khamgashta migardand*
*Peeraney jahan deeda;*
*Bazerey khaak mein joyand*
*Ayyamaey javani raah.*

Why do you old and aged roam, searching the world with a bent back?
Beneath the dust, looking for the days of past youth.

'Ah that is lovely, Papa. Let me write it down.'

I kept it in my diary along with some other couplets that are less refined but as picturesque. He remembered a verse by Raja Surinder of Nalagarh.

*Shaikh botal sey hill gaya hota,*
*Nadaan kuch to mill gaya hota,*
*Sajda karney sey gar khuda milta,*
*Meri botal ko mil gaya hota.*

If one could find God by prostrating, my whiskey bottle would have
    found it.

A nursery rhyme we learned described King George's coronation darbar in 1903.

*Dilli dekhi,*
*Dilli waley dekhey,*
*Gorey dekhey,*
*Kaley dekhey,*
*Khaimon ka ik jungal dekha,*
*Uss jangal mein mangal dekha.*

We saw Delhi,
We saw the people of Delhi,
We saw the fair ones,
We saw the dark ones,
We saw a jungle of tents,
And the festivities in that jungle.

Then there was a fun Punjabi verse about the variety of Sardar beards.

*Koi dadian koi jhadian,*
*Koi la muahtey sadian,*

*Koi thindey kujjey keedian,*
*Koi kuttey pooch vatterian.*

There are some beards; Some bushes; Some beards shaped by fire;
Others so sparse, they are ants gathered on a spot of ghee; and then
    there are still others like dogs' tails.

Other Indians dealing with English was a source of fun for my
father, but the element of class snobbery cannot be ignored. He
learned from the best, and the 'others' learned more 'Indian
English'.

That's a complex problem for me, too, as I find my ear
placing the class and background of a person depending on how
they speak English. I can't be a snob about it because my dear
mother would clearly be the 'other' class.

The English-era Gazette mentions with great humour the
names of British officers as pronounced by the locals. For
example, Alexander Fraser was Alak Jullunder Sahib. Similarly,
Jindo taught us his childhood soldier's game with a sepoy in
the British Army. This is what he understood of the night
watchman's call:

*Haa hukam sadeha*
*Fraan Vijeeting araand*
*Aal jwaal.*

Halt! Who comes there?
Friend: visiting around.
All's well.

Language was a defining influence in our lives. An absence of
English crippled our mother's confidence; her innate strength
of character suffered a discomfited devaluation in anglicised
drawing rooms, where resentment bled into her aura, and I
watched her closely and hurt for her.

At home, however, we spoke Punjabi and bid goodbye to

English-speaking relatives (like Tayaji's family) with the same sense of relief as taking off high-heeled shoes after a strenuous party. I was torn between the contrast of my mother's family and that of Jindo, who was strongly influenced by his English-speaking older brother and Bhabhi.

Darshan's Hindi, too, however, was not as elegant as we thought it should be: it had such a strong Punjabi accent that Ganeve and I, schooled in Dehradun, Uttar Pradesh, fervently asked her to spare our ears the onslaught, and she would then revert to Punjabi with relief.

But the exquisite tonal variety and vocabulary of her Punjabi is something that we could never learn. The type where she will say '*ais gull tey chanan karo*' even without knowing the much-bandied English phrase of throwing light. She read Punjabi literature and would sometimes write me letters in Gurmukhi to help my school curriculum that had Punjabi as my third language. I still remember a letter from her that described the sound and colour of an early morning at Rajkot House, the talk of brilliant green and red parrots among the trees. She wrote of the puddings and cakes she would bake for me when I returned home.

Her cooking helped her positive persona; skill with uncompromising purity of ingredients. The care she poured into a rising cake alleviated the heaviness of her heart. Her puddings and casseroles and roasts became legendary, and her revenge was to silence all with flavours unfamiliar in the Punjabi kitchens of English-speaking homes.

She knit very English sweaters from patterns in the *Woman & Home* magazines that she used to subscribe to. Though uncomfortable with English, she made the effort to learn nursery rhymes from my cousin Kitten so she could teach us.

The English of my entire maternal family was limited to

the newspapers. Their reluctance to visit Delhi for important weddings or funerals was visible in their separate, silent groups, ever polite to whoever deigned to acknowledge them, while their impish minds created mischievous responses. For a start, they called themselves MBAs at Delhi: 'Marriage and Bhog Attendants'.

My Chottey Mamaji would say, 'We can't bear these functions; our mouths are tired, twisting to form English, and our ears ache trying to understand it. They even fart in English.' And Ganeve and I would rock with laughter while playing cards with him, sitting on a thin talai and khes spread on a manji at the courtyard of his house in Tallania.

My guilt about keeping a careful distance from them in Delhi, where I preferred being among the sophisticates, was exacerbated the day I read in my Hindi class the story of a government servant, who, embarrassed about his non-English-speaking mother, locked her up in a backroom while he entertained his English Babu boss. The old lady embroidered cushions to bide her time.

'The cushions in your sitting room are lovely,' said the boss, and the government servant began valuing his mother a little more.

The Hindi stories, though irritatingly preachy, touched a raw nerve, as did our Hindi teachers, whose raison d'être seemed to have been to denigrate English and the 'English-medium type'. I now call the rising Hindutva movement 'the revenge of the regular Hindi teacher'. I say ordinary Hindi teachers who ignored the liberal messages of writers in Hindi like Agyeya or even Munshi Premchand. In my childhood, as far as my family was concerned, the Jan-Sanghi of even the freedom movement had already acquired a pejorative meaning.

I would read Hindi stories to Jindo, who could not read

Hindi. Premchand's 'Idgah Mela' was a favourite about a little Muslim boy who spent his little bit of money to buy his grandmother a chimta to protect her hands from burning while she cooked his rotis. The other story was 'Pardah' of the Muslim home, which one day ripped to expose the starving, half-naked women in the house.

Papa once told a friend who commented that our house looked good and he must be making money, '*Sabdey pardey hundey nay yaar. Sabdey,*' (Everyone has a curtain. Everyone), said in a sad, philosophical tone.

As I read my Hindi lessons to my family, I remember their particular appreciation of the story of 'Bhola Nath ka Jeev', about a man's obsessive wait for his government pension. His soul escaped from Yama Devta's grip to attach to his pension files.

*

The sultry boredom at Karnal was relieved by rain, books, religion and music. Sikhism cannot be practised or experienced without music. Music was in the air, and many ragis in Punjab would be invited home to sing.

In school, I played the sitar and danced Kathak and impressed my Bengali guru with my intuitive ability (almost showing-off) to choose to go off-rhythm and yet enter the full circle of the metre at 'samm'.

'But that's nothing,' I said. 'No one in Punjab can go wrong with rhythm.' Punjabi is rhythmic, and music is in the smell of its soil that has birthed robust musicians singing strong, difficult taans of the Punjab Gharana, and more particularly, the Patiala Gharana.

Rhythm is beyond caste and class, and it is Punjab. Life played to a musical metre. Sometimes it was raucous and dreadful, as the besur jagratas in a park at night, or the mellow rhythm of the afternoon dholak of a Mata Kirtan in the neighbour's house, or the bhaiji reading the book, in the melody of a raga as prescribed, or the beautiful call to prayer from the mosque, but the undertow remained the collective silence between the different beats and various notes.

Jindo could not refuse me music lessons at home and borrowed five thousand rupees from the adhati to buy me a sitar.

My home music teacher developed a crusty pride to cover his just-competent musical ability. Once, his voice cracked while singing a taan, and I had to run to my room to laugh, where a visiting friend mimicked him within the teacher's hearing.

I returned to find a hurt guruji scathing about me thinking more of myself than I was. 'The only worthy person in the entire household is Sardar Sahib,' he said. I was bewildered by the intensity of his reaction till Jindo told me that he was the son of a 'lower Hindu caste' and must be carefully treated because he was finding new bearings. These were things not familiar to me as a Sikh though, of course, the Jatt and non-Jatt divide was there, where, however, both held their own with pride even while deriding the other.

In school, the music room sounds wafting over the campus calmed my aching heart. Theatre became my means to a more satisfactory world. Darshan worried that theatre would carry me out of the penumbra that they were comfortable with as 'respectable'. She was horrified when I played Draupadi; she with the five husbands.

So serious was she about her disapproval that she insisted (and Jindo did not argue) that now that I was done with school, they would no longer watch me perform on stage—but the theatre had become my safe place, where I could always be someone else. The place where I was completely alone in the bright lights and the applause just for me became addictive. The friendships formed standing in the wings, waiting for our cues, hearts in our mouths, were like no other. Uncaring of parental disapproval, I carried on my actor's life for decades.

Ganeve and I had many differences in perception with Darshan and were impatient with her quickness to judge all that was unfamiliar as somehow not 'right'. She was intuitively conservative in the same way Jindo was intuitively liberal.

We developed a complex relationship with our mother because we challenged each of her preconceived ideas, and though she responded gallantly, it always left a slight wound that made us guilty about our forays into freedom. Her wounds of responding to our modern ways of career and marriages of choice outside our community healed only in her old age, when her anxiety about us and the stresses of her relationship with Jindo had alleviated.

A deeper reason for our mother's unhappiness, however, was her lack of financial independence. Jindo managed the farm, but on behalf of his mother, and he could never say that it was solely 'his' even after partition with his brother. So, my mother could not really ask for money from Jindo because he had nothing as well.

She told me once of a journey with me to her village. I was five and wanted a coke. Her younger sister and brother-in-law were also travelling with us and, being the eldest in the group, our mother would have been expected to pay for everyone's drinks. She was carrying no money and so distracted me from the coke desire.

When we reached Tallania, her father, in general conversation, asked her, 'Bibaji, they (the Rajkotias) are well-off, so I expect you have no problem with money.' Darshan's stoic calm broke down. My nana then arranged to send her some pocket money every month.

My mother had considered leaving the marriage and getting a matron's job in a boarding school but gave up the idea because the principal said that I could not stay with her.

Darshan did not want to deprive us of the comforts of our paternal home and the joy of a benign and indulgent patriarch. She did not want to leave us at Rajkot House and away from a legacy that nothing she did or would inherit could match, even though it was all encumbered in debt at the time.

Over the years, Darshan carefully saved from the pocket money that she received from her father or from the housekeeping money to be able to gift each of us a sum of Rs 50,000 on our weddings.

I wept as she gave it to me, saying, 'It is not much, but at least the interest from it will buy you petrol for your car.'

Driving, for her, symbolised absolute freedom. She never learned to drive, though, had she asked, I doubt Jindo would have refused. Many years earlier, he had taught his brother's wife to drive.

Despite her conservative views on conforming to social mores of dress and deportment, Darshan so stressed inner freedom obtained from financial independence that she was almost militant in her insistence that Ganeve and I have careers.

Later in life, Darshan sometimes wanted to be without the dupatta on her head, but we were so used to it that we hated it when she was like that and said it made her look undressed. So, she never did.

Darshan was a traveller who carried her burdens with no help, the heaviest of which was Jindo's 'madness'. That's what she calls it, and she has not changed her mind to this day. He was mentally not well; he had delusions of grandeur; he suffered hallucinations that did not scare her but weighed and wearied her.

My interpretation of Jindo is sincere, but so is my mother's understanding of her husband.

Darshan was intensely conservative on sexual mores, which was defined by revulsion due to the violent sexual crimes during Partition and her proximity to domestic violence suffered by women who sheltered in her aunt's ashram. All this shaped her, and her marriage experience was not happy because of her sense of financial and cultural disempowerment and awareness that she was not a sexual or intellectual companion for my naturally liberal and experimental father. But she loved him and was proud of him. Towards the end of his life, my mother felt compassion for her husband when she said, 'He needed another type of woman to be his companion. I could not do it. I don't have it.'

Darshan began making small exits from the marital prison wardened by Bibiji and Jindo's benign guard. She learnt to reduce her persona to small and innocuous enough to earn the privilege of occasionally squeezing out between its social bars as her own person. A movie with a friend, a coffee, lunch. The kitty parties started then, and Bibiji was resentful and nervous about her daughter-in-law 'sprouting wings'. Darshan would grumble in her room, 'It's not that I want to dance at a nightclub,' which image, despite the tense times, made me grin, much to her further irritation.

Notwithstanding her quietness, a core characteristic of Darshan's personality is stubborn, dogged persistence. I, to buy peace, asked her to give up the idea of kitty parties, but Ganeve, all of ten at the time, had become Darshan's most passionate advocate and fought Jindo and her grandmother for her to go out more and have her own friends.

Darshan was not given to smiling and laughing too easily, though she was very tactile with the two of us. Our good-night ritual was a kiss on each cheek two times and a long hug. It was our way of reassuring her to be strong for us.

Given her views on women and sex and the power of individuality, Darshan preferred to admire my ability to be a widow and single mother rather than empathise with my inability to forge another significant relationship.

'I never wanted to be married,' she said. 'I wanted to work at the ashram and my dream was to have a room of my own where I would sit at my desk, writing a novel, occasionally looking out of the window to rest my eyes on a large, wide tree.'

She was not impressed when I told her about Virginia Woolf's 'A Room of One's Own'. 'Of course,' she said, 'it's so obvious that a woman needs a room of her own. I know that without reading this novel.'

There was never any pressure on Ganeve and me to marry. Jindo always used to say: you don't have to marry, just be an important socialite. 'Chippy will throw Delhi's best parties,' he would say. Marriage was a pain in the neck for both of them, and if you could do without it, then please do without it.

I had presumed that it was my mother who did not want me to marry again and so was acutely disappointed and shocked when my mother said recently that Jindo had wanted her to tell me not to marry again. 'Why did you not tell me earlier?' I asked.

'Because I know you hate to hear anything negative about your father.'

That Jindo did not want to become unpopular with me and so asked my mother to advise me on the wisdom of singleness did not surprise me. He was also a dissembler, albeit in a harmless sort of way, if he wanted something.

Not just Mama's needs and wants, but sometimes even ours got subsumed in his urgent need for instant gratification. For example, Ganeve and I would, at some expense and considerable labour, record popular music from our cousin's LPs onto the cheaper cassettes. Imagine my anguish, for there is no other word, to find that Jindo had recorded over The Rolling Stones, The Doors, Bob Dylan with Bhimsen Joshi, and country rock that he got from the radio.

'Sorry, I did not know,' he said, looking contrite in a way that I could not resist, and I said, 'All right, just be careful in the future.'

Ganeve, the brutal realist, said, 'Didi, don't buy into his story. Of course, he knew what he was doing.'

And Jindo was silent because he knew, as did I, that he was knowingly self-centred and was not going to change.

Slowly, Darshan and Jindo formed a functional equation. Then it became one of affection and towards the end. I like to think they had what is closest to love, whatever that means. They melded and could laugh together.

Though she is too shy to admit it, my mother was actually quite proud and drew great confidence from Jindo's 'purrsnallty'.

Once, she described that my father, Tayaji, and Tayiji were on a driving holiday and they ran out of petrol. So, Jindo walked to the nearest petrol station with a container. 'As he was walking back,' she said, 'I could make out from a far, far distance that it was he returning because he was so tall and handsome and not like any of the other men on the road.' Jindo was a trophy husband.

When my father died, Darshan said she missed him most when she returned home, and he, lying on his bed, would ask, 'So what's the news and gossip in town today?' She described her clever repartee to resist two of his bullying, fearsome cousins. Wit was not her instinctive talent, but proximity with Jindo had obviously developed some skill. Jindo smiled with great satisfaction and said, 'I am proud of you. You will manage well after me.'

Thus, as far as I am concerned, from the outside, despite

Darshan's early unhappiness and perhaps even anguish and loneliness, the marriage evolved to a good place and Jindo in his last years, admitted freely that Darshan had saved the marriage.

'Any other woman would have left me a long time ago.'

But the truth is that the central purpose of my mother staying in the marriage was her children, and any resolution with him was but a happy bonus.

<hr>

## 39. The Refugee Abroad

Around the late 1970s, a pernicious influence had begun to influence Sikh lives. The first photo was of a Sardar Jagjit Singh in chains, as a symbol of protest for a Punjab free from India. He named it Khalistan.

'What is Khalistan, Papa?'

'Some madness,' he said.

And then it grew. Khalistanis from Canayda, U.S., U.K.: The kinder experience of the Canada N.R.I.s was our Chachaji Devender, and I need to tell their story because under no circumstance must they think that I club them with my general (and, of course, too broad and here with considerable literary license) perception of 'N.R.I.s'.

From a Punjab village, he came to live with us at Rajkot House for vocational training at Karnal to prepare to go abroad. Chachaji Devender remembers the time with affection, and all of us loved his presence in the house. In the summer, he used to sleep on the verandah outside Bibiji's room. Jindo encouraged his truant episodes of late-night films, leaving a covered pillow to simulate his sleeping form should Bibiji check on him. Jindo would deal with Bibiji's scolding when she found out with a 'leave him, Bibiji. If he is not naughty at this age, when can he be?'

And she left him alone because, really, he was a genial, amiable man. He became very successful in Canada, and the subtext of our relationship with him shifted with no awkwardness from his status as a rural relative (read patronising, though no one wanted to be) to successful equality. In fact, his later visits could well have been an attitude of 'so, here I am now, and you remain a shabby thread of a disintegrating past'. But there was nothing but deep mutual affection, unlike with several other village relatives, who also stayed with us from time to time before moving abroad.

Chachaji achieved his aspirational goal when he told us, *'Main apney ghar di chaabi gorey nu dey ke aiayan haan.'* (I have left my house keys in the care of a white man.)

His sister Rani, our childhood playmate, was Darshan's ally in her early, lonely days in the unfamiliar ambience of a home she did not see any meaningful exit from.

I got a whiff of what a good marriage is from two incidents, one of which was seeing Chachaji Devender and his new bride on the morning after their wedding. I walked into their room to find them chatting like old friends, sitting in their razai. I understood something intuitively and hoped I would have it.

The other time I understood this as a deep instinct was watching my Chhotey Mamaji and his wife playing cards on their bed.

The newest N.R.I. in the family is the granddaughter of the chauffeur Daljit Singh, Simran, who is now studying in Canada. My nephews, Farid and Iqbal, were received at the Toronto airport by Chachaji Devender and Simran. Farid speaks Punjabi well. Things are changing, and the cause of embarrassment now is the absence of Punjabi rather than English.

# 40. Return to Pakistan

It was at the height of the Khalistan movement and Punjab militancy, around 1980, that we visited Pakistan at the invitation of Aitchison College. None of us had a passport. For some reason, Mama, Jindo, and Ganeve got theirs in Karnal, but I applied in Delhi.

I applied as a resident at Tayaji's house. Of the various required documents, one was a character certificate from a neighbour. He refused because, he said, though he knew me and the family, he could not vouch for my character. He had known our entire family for more than a decade. I knew his reservation was that we were practicing Sikhs and the Sikh separatist movement had picked up momentum.

Eventually, I managed a temporary document through a government connection of an uncle. We drove to the Wagah Border and walked across the no-man's-land, where stood a reception committee of tall, good-looking men in salwar-qameezes and blue safas.

The son of our host family guided us to his fancy foreign car that I can't remember the name of, having never seen one before.

The fields on the way to Lahore from Wagah seemed not as green as those in the Indian Punjab, and we saw no tractors or tube wells that had become ubiquitous on our side of the border. Yet, the home of our hosts exuded a wealth that we did not know in Rajkot House.

A beautiful lady greeted us and hugged my mother and us girls, saying, 'Khushamdeed, khushamdeed.' She did an elegant adaab for my father and led us to the guest suite of rooms with a cosy lounge, where she sat with us for a while.

She asked, 'My husband will be home for dinner. Is there something special you will eat?'

Jindo said, 'We will eat what you give us.'

She explained, 'Sometimes there are some prohibited non-vegetarian foods, as also the way the meat is cut...' and Jindo said he looked forward to their normal table.

There was visible relief on our hostess's face, and she said, '*Hum mey kya durian hain? Durian to governments ney banai hain.*' (What differences do we have? The only differences are created by our governments).

There was a deep quiet from my parents, and then they nodded and said, 'Yes, indeed.'

The next few days were a round of parties, where Jindo valiantly refused to drink to avoid the high probability of embarrassing us with excess since he would not know how to be moderate.

We saw the vast school grounds. We saw Jindo's room that was bigger than any we had stayed in. We saw his attached bathroom, across which was his valet's room. Jindo showed us a cluster of bushes along the main playing field, behind which was a cosy bench, where, he said, he would chat with other sedentary friends during games time. He told us that he had been a good rider and swimmer, but chose not to overdo it.

We went to the canteen, where Jindo called 'John', as he must have done as a boy, and a beaming, very elderly man hugged him and called him 'Jitty'. We all ate a cream custard that had been his favourite pudding, and we all approved of it as fine.

Then was the drive to Rajkot and Mananwala. As we neared Rajkot, Jindo looked for the malta orchard, but we lost our way in a jungle of housing colonies. I could feel Jindo's tension. The local residents directed us enthusiastically, first asking with affection, '*India sey?*'

We reached the fields around Rajkot, and Jindo stopped to ask for directions to the house. '*Tussi aithey hundey sau?*' (You used to be here?) they asked, and Jindo nodded because words were beginning to fail him.

'So-and-so hai?' Jindo asked about a few servants, and the person kept responding: '*Faut.*' (Dead.)

Finally, we reached Rajkot House, hidden in the remnants of the malta orchard. We drove into the porch and met a family of many tall men in salwar kurtas.

'Khushamdeed,' they said, 'Welcome home.'

And Jindo was absolutely quiet. They showed us around the house till we entered a bedroom and his tension broke into a flood of tears. 'This is the room I was born in.'

We went to the large drawing room, and the owner said, 'There is a man called Tallu who knows you,' and Jindo's face brightened, 'I would like to meet him.' Arrived a rustic man, whose mud-stained salwar kurta and deep brown, sunburnt skin proclaimed farm labour.

Jindo stood up and hugged him and they went to the verandah and talked quietly for a long time and no one thought of intruding.

They returned, and Jindo sat down on the sofa, while Tallu remained standing near it. 'You can sit next to your sardar,' said our host, and Tallu sat straight and stiff, and we knew he had never sat there before.

'So, how is the place where you live now?' the lady of the house asked my mother. 'It is in Karnal and we call it Rajkot House,' we said.

'Bechaari,' she said, clucking and looking at her daughter-in-law.

'We are not bechaara,' said Ganeve and I. 'We live in a very nice house'.

They smiled.

'Who is Amarjit?'

'My brother,' said Jindo.

'Ah,' they said, 'So, you are Jindo. The servants told us about you,' and they smiled.

'My father's samadhi is here in the orchard,' Jindo said, and they looked embarrassed.

'No matter. I understand,' he said.

I was surprised that a samadhi had been built for my grandfather, considering that Hindu and Sikh funeral rites are about dissipating the dead, leaving no room for worldly attachment to form.

We ate dried fruit with shikanji and were soon ready to leave.

Tallu enveloped us girls in a hug that smelt of the earth and musky sweat. Papa gave him 2,000 rupees, and Tallu then gave Ganeve and me 500 each. Then we wept and I said, 'Keep it; you are only giving back the gift,' and he smiled through his tears and said, 'You want more?' And we laughed, and this time, it was we who reached out to hug him.

Then we received a message that the people at the Chhoti Kothi (small house) also wanted to meet us because, after all, that house was ours as well.

So, we walked to the house of our great-grandfather's younger brother, who was called Babaji. We were received by an old lady and her daughter-in-law. There was a big picture of Khomeini on the wall.

We had another sherbet and some more dried fruit, and as we got up to leave, the old lady sent for a tilley waali jooti, brocade shoe.

'You are the daughter-in-law of this house, and I want you to have this small present,' she said. My mother accepted it with both hands and deep bow.

We turned to the door to leave, and the old lady said, 'I would like to see you wearing the jootis.' And my mother changed her shoes, and I picked up the old ones and was given a plastic bag to carry them in.

We left overwhelmed and drained from the tears that we did not know we had. We drove silently towards Mananwala, and my mother became more and more pensive while Jindo put on a brave smile of leaving it all behind yet again, knowing that after this time, he would never visit.

We reached Mananwala and went to Jindo's haveli that was his Bibiji's home. A man was waiting to meet us. He wore a turban tied in an attractive way; of one fold falling on the shoulder. My mother wept when she saw him, as did he. There was no hugging, but instead, a deep mutual bow, and he said, 'Bibaji, come and see your home.'

As we walked across to her part of the village, the munshi (that's what he had been) told her, 'We will go by the outer way to avoid the bazaar.'

But there was no point in the traditional respectable avoidance of a common market. The villagers had heard, and women surrounded and reached to hug my mother. I could see her getting restless with so much body contact.

We entered a huge courtyard with a dry fountain in the centre. 'Bapuji had renovated this house just a few months before Partition, and we had new furniture that had not even been unpacked,' said Darshan.

Each room in the haveli was packed with a family. In the niche built into the wall stood a cannon shell. My mother cried out, 'The cannon shell has never even been shifted!' and this struck deep. The cannon shell had been an intimate witness and remained untouched for forty years after Partition.

We returned to Jindo's side of the village. He was sitting with the zamindar, who was drinking a beer, though I noted with relief that there was no glass before Jindo.

'How was it?' asked Jindo, and my mother said, 'All right.'

Unthinkingly, they had played out the old ritual. She goes to her part of the village and he stays in his. It was unusual for a son-in-law to spend time in his wife's home. In all my years, I remember Jindo visiting Tallania no more than twice. The idea was not to burden the wife's family with formality and to allow her to be as carefree as she could possibly be in that twice-a-year break from the married state.

The next day was sports day and the Aitchison school parade. As the sons of our host family marched past, Ganeve and I cheered and called out their names in boisterous excitement while the boys smiled faintly under their uniform seriousness.

That evening, they said with surprised affection, 'You girls are so potty.' We were not decorous in the way they were used to girls being. After dinner, we young ones decided to play Scrabble, and both sets of parents came into our room as chaperones, which Ganeve and I thought was quite silly. Our host scoffed at the limited vocabulary of his sons compared to us 'clever girls'. We took the compliment as a matter of course. We were indeed very clever, good girls, and certainly better than most boys as far as excellence in anything sensible was concerned.

The next day, we left and we all hugged as you would a member of your family. Because it was early morning, Jindo was still wearing his 'thatha' that sets a Sikh beard for the day.

'Can I go like this, or will they think I am a terrorist?' and our host laughed and told my father he was safe.

My sister said she had seen some graffiti about Khalistan. We asked our hosts about Pakistan troubling India by fostering political unrest, not just in Kashmir but also by encouraging Khalistan. 'God knows what they do,' he said, 'it is disgusting,' and we agreed.

On the drive back to Wagah, we were silent again. We walked back across the border.

At the checkpoint, the Indian security officer asked how it had been across.

'Like going home,' said Jindo, and my mother, quick to speak for independent India, said, 'But now, India is home. We have spent a greater part of our lives here.'

'What do you do, Sardarji?' asked the officer at the border.

Jindo looked down at him benignly from his noble height and proudly said, 'I? I do nothing.'

Ganeve and I raised our eyes heavenward and comically rolled them around, but we were quite embarrassed at having a father who did nothing.

Daljit Singh, waiting on the other side, met us with his familiar, special smile.

It was dark by the time we entered Amritsar city. The roads were quiet. We stopped a lone elderly sardar. When Jindo put his head out of the window to call, as he did all strangers, 'Rai Sahib,' the sardar ran ahead as if being hunted. 'We only want directions,' called Jindo and the sardar, with palpable self-conscious relief, told us.

Jindo said with pity and sadness, 'Did you see the way he ran? He was worried we were terrorists.' And we were even more quiet.

Then we reached the house of our aunt, who was waiting with dinner followed by strong, sweet tea served in glasses. She did not say anything. None of us wanted to talk, and she understood.

The drive from Amritsar to Karnal was memorable for me because someone was singing 'Heer' on the car radio, and I saw my mother hold the handle above the car door, rest her face into her upraised arm, and cry as the singer sang, *'Doli chardian marian Heer cheekha: Mainu laeh challey, Babla, laeh challey; Mainu rakh ley, Babla, rakh ley; Mera aakhian kadi na modda saiin; Hun assi vaang musaafra beh challey.'* (Heer wailed while getting into her palki; They're taking me away, Babla, they are taking me away; Let me stay please, let me stay; You never refused me anything, and now you are sending me away as if I was a mere traveller.)

My father was sitting in front, and Ganeve was asleep, and I pretended I could not see her cry because I was repulsed by the intensity of the pain that I could not understand. We were together, we were going home, why should there be tears?

But I got it years later, listening to the same song on my iPod during my walk in Lodhi Garden. The singer sang: *'Aisa koi na milya jo gayan nun mod sakkey.'* (I never met anyone who can bring back those who have departed.)

## 41. The Separatist Movement

The Sikh separatist movement, fuelled by religious fundamentalism, was gathering a dangerous momentum, terrifying us ordinary, secular Sikh people.

We watched in silent fear and horror as Doordarshan T.V. interviewed howling Sikh men who had survived a bus attack by extremists. 'They took away my seventeen-year-old younger brother,' a man wept. The next morning, even the prosaic and practical Darshan said, 'I can't forget the way that man cried.'

Even though our family was intuitively secular and anti-fundamentalist, we felt defiled, disliked, hated and reviled as terrorists and perpetually vulnerable to a Hindu backlash outside Punjab. I mentioned this to a Muslim friend of a well-known Allahabad family. 'Welcome to our world,' he said.

Around this time, Ganeve and I began to be angry and defensive about Sikhi, and so we became more Sikh than ever before. 'Arrey, Sikhism is like Hinduism,' someone would say to us in Delhi.

'No, it's not,' I would say angrily. 'In any case, it's for me to decide on how close my religion is to Hinduism, not for you to appropriate us into your numbers.'

This was the time when we saw many a face glowing with a fervour of stupefied, self-righteous virtue that made for particularly irritating children as our playmates. One such girl, who rejoiced in the name of Sundari, was an overzealous daughter of the professor whose heart had beat faster near the kalgi at the British Museum. At the palki procession for Guru Gobind Singh's birthday, Sundari refused to accept pershad from a young man with a trimmed beard, and I was revolted by her excessive fervour and asked for a double helping of the pershad to appease the hurt that the young Sikh sewak clearly felt. My family agreed with me and understood moderation but would not call out the excess either, which I can understand now because of the courage it takes. Who all does one argue with in jingoistic, fervent times? The procession had been under heavy police security, and after it moved on and we all were walking home, I overheard one of the policemen mimicking the Sikh slogan of 'Raj Karega Khalsa'. I was embarrassed and explained as I walked with the policemen, 'Khalsa means pure. It only means let the upright and worthy rule.' 'Acchha ji,' the cop smiled and said a non-committal yes. But even I know it is likely that this was a convenient escape interpretation.

There is no doubt that 'Raj Karega Khalsa' was the war cry in the battle against the Mughal rule after Guru Gobind Singh. It was a call to sovereignty.

My cousin Tavleen, Tayaji's daughter, was an important newspaper journalist by then. She stopped in Karnal on her way to Punjab. Over tea, she said, 'This problem is here to stay,' in a strong angrezi accent that made me hide my smile and deflected from the seriousness of the prophecy of gloom.

The Punjab terrorist problem was eventually dealt with by an attack on the Golden Temple by the Indian Army in Operation Bluestar. On television, we saw soldiers stomping the inner sanctum. In our drawing room, we were relieved that it seemed over, even while something within ourselves felt trampled by the Army shoes.

The dreaded power backlash arrived when Prime Minister Indira Gandhi was gunned down by Sikh bodyguards as a reaction to Operation Blue Star.

I was at law school. Ishar Singh, a Sikh professor, walked in for the Constitutional Law class. We were hushed by his severe silence. 'Mrs. Gandhi was killed today,' he announced.

A split-second silence was broken by a raucous cheer from a student, who I had always found quite stupid. My heart dropped to my knees. How does he think of himself as separate from the country? How will he remain insulated from the damage this will do?

Ishar Singh sharply asked the stupid boy to shut up: 'This is a terrible thing that has happened for the entire country. We don't know who shot her, and they have taken her to an unknown destination.'

The class was dismissed, and on my way to the hostel, I stopped at a phone booth to call a friend.

'Any news?'

'She was shot by Sikh bodyguards.'

'Oh God,' I said, 'the backlash will be dreadful.'

'Well, of course it will. This is a terrible thing for the country, and you Sikhs again are thinking only about yourselves.'

My friendship was never the same after this careless clubbing of me with the killers.

By the time I reached my hostel, the news spread that rampaging mobs had frightened all transport and people off the roads.

I stood in a queue to call home. Till I obtained permission for an S.T.D. call, I decided to make a local call to Tayaji.

Virji, his son, picked up the phone. 'It's going to be all right,' he said, 'they have put Section 144.'

'Your faith in Section 144 is touching,' I said, already cynical and only a law student yet.

I finally managed to get permission for the call to Karnal. So calm Jindo and Mama seemed, and it was only when I had my own children that I understood how scared they must have been. I told Jindo what I had told Virji about his touching faith in Section 144. He laughed aloud. Then, silence.

'Papa,' I said, 'maybe if you cut your hair and shaved your beard, you will be fine. Just say I am not a Sikh any longer. What's the big deal?'

'Oh, I am just worried I won't be good-looking without a beard.' We laughed, and I hung up with that familiar heart that had gained even more in weight.

I knew that if he cut his hair and shaved his beard, he would never be the same, even if it grew back. It was the shame of submission, of giving in to the bully; that feeling was deeper than religion. It was about respect for the identity created by many things, of which religion was but one part, and it was about not being bullied into being a particular way or not being a particular way.

The riots raged across the country, and Rajkot House, too, was visited by the mob. Jindo was sitting on the verandah. 'Laoh-ji, they have arrived here,' he said as he put down the newspaper he had been reading but remained sitting.

My mother and grandmother ran into the house and locked

themselves. 'Jindo! Jindo, come into the house,' Bibiji shouted.

'Nahi, Bibiji, I am not going to run again. You exit from the back gate or stay indoors, whatever you think is right. I will wait. It may buy you time to save yourself.'

Is it abnormal to give up the flight instinct to survive? Was there a rush of flight adrenaline that he overcame by continuing to sit? I don't know. We never spoke about it.

For some inexplicable reason, the mob retreated. Perhaps the house was not on the hit list. Or was it that the house was known as God-fearing and milk and lassi from the farm was distributed to every passerby and kada pershad and tea served at the gate every puranmashi?

When the riots somewhat subsided, I escaped the Delhi University hostel to attend a peace march. As we walked past Gurudwara Sis Ganj, I saw Sikh priests standing at the gate, throwing flowers at the procession. Never before had I seen crying Sikhs.

I entered a Hindu household, and an old woman asked me why I was so anxious about Sikhs when so many Hindus had died in Punjab. 'Does it justify that Sikhs get killed here?' I asked.

She had no answer but remained unmoved. She did give me two torn dupattas. 'Sikh women wear them,' she said. We were at the beginning of the November cold.

The days of the riots were also the day the multinational Union Carbide leaked its poisonous gas in Bhopal. I could spare no thought to the dead thousands.

Life resumed after 1984. The Sikhs came back on the streets with their turbans, but many changed forever.

'Who is that absolutely beautiful man?' I wondered when classes resumed. It was a Sikh boy who had cut his hair and shaved his beard and embarked on a new life as a model.

Many Sikhs left the country. I knew the doctor at Safdarjung

Hospital who had been dangled upside down from a flyover till one of his Hindu patients saw him and pleaded with the crowd to let him go. They did, and he emigrated to the U.S.

A cousin had emigrated because he had been picked up by the police and beaten to force an admission that he was a terrorist.

After 1984, the relationship of the average Sikh with the police changed from comfortable presumption of innocence to presumed guilt.

While alienation and political polarisation raged across the country, over the years, I visited Pakistan again, this time as a visibly pregnant lawyer. Like before, it felt like home in the embrace of language.

I did not have to pay for a single thing I bought at Liberty Market.

'You are from India?' the shopkeepers asked.

'I am from here. Your language is what I have grown up with in India,' I answered, and they would take no money for my shopping.

Given my condition, I was offered a chair, and a shopkeeper brought me a large glass of fresh anar juice. A basket of fruit was later delivered to my hotel room.

That evening, I got a call from a Pakistani officer serving with the embassy in Delhi. 'What did you do today?'

'Are you calling because you are concerned about my well-being or because you want to know what I have been up to?'

'I am interested in your well-being, but believe me, they know what you are up to.'

That night, I slept fitfully with my television on, but only after I ate all the fruit in the basket.

How can I not be safe here? But I was not, I knew, and it had nothing to do with the people.

Then, in 2002, some kar sewaks in a train were killed at Godhra. Some say it was a scuffle over tea with some Muslims, but the bottom line is that the kar sewaks were burned in their train, and it was horrifying. This led to the reaction ('spontaneous' but sustained over days).

'What will happen, Papa?' I asked.

'I don't know.'

Then I asked the most shameful, selfish question that costs me to write, but I must, to be true: 'This is a goonda element, and they hit the poor? It happens among them—right?' Even then, I said it with shame. I also knew that it had not been true of the organised riots of 1984.

Jindo understood and did not judge the selfishness of my question. 'I don't know,' he said, 'I don't know any longer. They killed a Congress M.P. in his house.'

We were all silent.

I was scared because, for the first time, I felt Jindo was lacking in the power of reassurance.

The Gujarat pogrom, on the face of it, was no threat to him, but as a prayerful, humble man, he took the step of final withdrawal to a deep, separate, secluded place. It was not depression this time, but rather shock and disgust at humanity.

Jindo's pain could not be lessened by stories of other exiles and wanderers, yet it was better than most people who have had to move. His humility came from his constant pain. You are grateful for even the fleeting moment without it. He could not take his unformed, wounded self seriously. Closing to eighty, he collected the pain around him even while drawing away from its accumulated heaviness and struck the balance of stoic equanimity only in his eighties.

Yes, he suffered clinical depression, exacerbated by frank and open disappointment with the real world of human perversions that made happiness a fool's delusion.

Jindo hated that I got this overthinking habit from him. I told him, 'It is about fear. Fear of loss, fear of not being able to hold and grasp. It's not about inevitable death in old age—one has time to prepare for that—but what of dying children, murdered families? How do the murderers live with their own families after killing the children and husbands and wives of others?'

'It is evil, Papa. I fear evil. I weep when I read the newspapers. About communal riots and rape and politicians orchestrating these things: how can a person want something so badly that they will kill for it? Masses of people. Yet, I know I have to learn to find peace by persuading myself that I can choose the domain of gentle goodness, but just when I think I have a moment of peace, the newspaper drags me back to ugliness.'

'Well, it's not easy to be happy,' Jindo said with the wisdom of his eight decades. 'Frankly, you have to be thick-skinned and quite stupid to be entirely happy, and you are neither.'

And so, we, father and daughter, sat side by side. I cogitated about and agitated my misery, while he reached a bored calm.

I remember him telling me that 'gurbat' (poverty) bothered him the most. 'Long ago, I was at a park in Mysore,' he reminisced. 'A child picked up to eat a banana skin that I threw away. I gave her the banana and left, feeling...' and he shook his head, his face in a tight grimace.

'I know what you mean,' I said. 'Long ago, in the black and white Doordarshan days, I watched a report on a famine in Andhra Pradesh. A long, long queue of bedraggled, stunned people waiting for relief food. And I saw a bearded man looking over the shoulder of another man who was receiving the food in his bowl. I will never forget the longing, the relief, and the sheer desperation and poverty.'

Work helped calm my demons. 'I think I am better off

because I am very busy,' I told Jindo, 'but that is like treating the symptom. It distracts from asking the questions that will compel answers that one must deal with. So, perhaps, Papa, you are better off without distractions from dealing with the depression.'

Jindo nodded and smiled, and I saw and was content that my father had found, if not an understanding of peace, at least an inner place of shelter.

Over the years, Jindo's activity decreased. He slept through some days, sat quietly in company, and suffered such an incredible laziness that once, before visitors, he crawled across a carpet because he could not be bothered getting up from lounging on a floor cushion. We girls were mortified but could not help but giggle at his craziness.

Though he was not drinking any longer, he remained in a state of overwhelming exhaustion, some of which could be due to the strong medication. But the inner being was actively working on his personal journey of withdrawing beyond reach. It was a process that was drug-assisted to begin with, then prayer, and then finally, he found that space of quiet contemplation on his bed. He could not even be bothered to sit up in the lotus position but attained closure with his internal rebellion against norms. I joked that he had institutionalised laziness as a unique rebellion.

A life that was both rebellion and resignation is how we lived in Rajkot House Karnal.

## 42. Life Around Rajkot House

Life in Karnal was a comfortable bubble to wallow in and explore my discontent, but sometimes, it was like that large intake of breath that still feels that the lungs are not satisfied. We then looked to the town around us.

We did not expect much and still found it just on the lesser margin of adequate. Just adequate enough for us to be relieved to return home and enjoy it thoroughly for a while till the next need to step out for air.

Our forays outside Rajkot House were mostly within walking distance to two homes known as Mananwala House and Butalia House.

Mananwala House was large and lush and green with many cousins and aunts and we played many games, but there had to be a strict decorum in play that I found stifling and so preferred when the cousins came to our house.

The man of that house was Bibiji's younger brother and he was short, neat, and very funny and made us laugh a lot. His name was Sardar Kartar Singh Mann.

As you got to know him better, you would notice that his humour covered great anxiety. He was a lot like my father in that way. In fact, uncle and nephew had a rare bond.

Bapuji Chhotey, we called him, to differentiate from Bapuji Vaddey, who was my grandmother's older brother. To say Bapuji without reference to older or younger, we were talking of our maternal grandfather, who you have met earlier as Major Saab.

To give an example of Bapuji Chhotay's anxiety, he was nervous about missing train stops. There is the story of his pacing the train corridor so as not to miss the few-minute stop at Karnal; so hard and distracted was his pacing that he missed it anyway.

Bapuji Chhotey was a teetotaller and the story is that his father gave him his gudti (a baby's first sip) of a drop of whiskey on his baby lips with the words, 'May this be the only drink you have.' An important and life-shaping prayer that came true given that the stereotype of the hard-drinking sardar is not wrong.

He was great fun with a mild, malicious humour, an example of which is that he called a lawyer in Karnal, of particularly short and slight build, 'Pocket Vakeel,' with no thought to his own tiny size. There was another lawyer that uncle and nephew Jindo nicknamed Palkhiwala because he spoke with dreary pomposity about his work that in his mind was of national importance. Palkhiwala is what he became, and no one remembers his real name.

Everyone was fodder for Bapuji Chhotey's humour.

'I met so-and-so sardar who calls himself such-and-such "Calcutta" because that is where he is from.

'So, I went to him and said, "You are Calcutta?"' (Pronounced kal-kutta in Punjabi.)

'Yes,' said the sardar.

Laughter, while Kartar Singh Mann, poker-faced, repeats, 'So, how are you, Kalkutta Sahib?' and Calcutta would reply, grateful for the attention, 'I am well, thank you.'

And no one thought of turning the joke around to ask, 'I am Calcutta as well as you are Mann from Mananwala and Rajkotia from Rajkot and Patiala from Patiala.' There is also Lahori, Pishora, and Fareedi from Faridkot, but Kalkutta was unbeatable in drawing a good laugh. There was also a Sardar Jullunder, but it was never as funny as asking, 'You are Kalkutta?'

The connection of refugees with their lost land was visceral in a way that others who have difficulty understanding can become impatient. Seventy years after Partition, in this morning's paper, I read in the obituary section: 'Sad demise of Harbans Singh Sawhney of Kallar, Rawalpindi.'

The refugee yearns and aches for the irretrievably lost physical connect as one yearns for a dead beloved, carrying him in the heart as you deal with the physical day and waiting for the night to have them on the pillow with you. It is real and yet not like the love of Psyche for Cupid.

Bapuji Chhotey and my father decided to help found a Khalsa college. Neither religious nor political, both preferred to loll in their sunny lawns, eating moolis and gajars. For them, the college was just a diverting project with its fundraising meetings and conversations that made a nice change to their familial inactivity. After breakfast, they would go visiting to raise funds (ugrahi) and canvass—'kunvassing'—for votes on the managing committee.

There was no expectation to do anything beyond this fun stage. They had no aspirations to be on the board or something like that. I remember a nice photo of my father making a speech at the Khalsa College Founders' Day. I kept it for a long time because it felt good to have evidence of a father who was important enough to have given a speech. But I can't find it now.

Part of their fundraising plan was to invite the Maharaja Patiala, Yadavindra Singh, to the college, followed by tea at Mananwala House. The Maharaja arrived in a black Mercedes and emerged resplendent in a black sherwani, churidar pyjama, and a silver-headed cane.

He donated nothing. Even we children figured, and Ganeve said:

'*Ainna wadda raja.*' He was very, very tall.

'*Ainni waddi soti.*' The cane seemed very long.

'*Ainni lambi gaddi.*' His Murrsidees was the biggest, sleekest, and longest car we had ever seen.

'*Tey paisa kuchh na.*' But not even a little money

This became a legendary verse.

Down the other side of the road from Rajkot House lived the Butalias in what had been a courthouse in the British era.

The house was presided over by the Butalia daughter-in-law,

Rani. Born and brought up in Bombay, she was already married in Karnal when Darshan arrived as a bride. 'I met your mother at her wedding reception,' she told me, 'She was so beautiful and slim in a brocade churidar-pyjama-qameez and pencil-heeled shoes with a net top encrusted with diamantes.'

That sounds garish, but the shoes were actually very glamorous and just the sort I would have loved to wear if not for my clubbed feet. Ganeve has them now.

Rani and Darshan became close friends, and no one in Karnal talked of the one without the other. Their delicious guilty pleasure was coffee at Gopi Nath Restaurant between household errands.

Rani Aunty was a large persona in bright-coloured salwar-qameezes, with a loud voice and an honest laugh. Her Bombay upbringing gave her a cachet that quickly made her a Karnal socialite. She started the kitty party culture in Karnal and conducted home-cooking classes, where Darshan was a careful and diligent student who eventually surpassed her teacher.

Rani Aunty played cards every other day at the Karnal Club, and among the regulars was 'lady' doctor Mrs. Sher Singh, who spoke English while retaining robust Punjabi, wore saris, and remembered the birthdays of every child she delivered, including the two of us. We loved her, and even when I was much older, I only wanted to consult her.

Rani Aunty also ran a school and helped many, one of whom my mother felt guilty about because it was to assist a dullard student clear his law examination through some little bending of rules and sifarish.

'It will make his life and that of many generations after. He will make a good lawyer but just does not know how to do well in an exam,' Rani Aunty assured my mother.

Perhaps she was not wrong, but my mother was never

comfortable with relative morality. She had been brought up on Gandhian absolutes; her father had refused cancer medicine from the black market.

Rani Aunty's older son, Ninoo, inherited her good humour. 'So-and-so thinks she is as beautiful as Miss India,' said Ninoo. The name stuck, and no one now remembers the particular lady as anything but Miss India.

Miss India wore salwar kurtas in attractive floral prints, careful lipstick, and obviously dyed black hair, styled into a stiff bouffant. Her shoes, handbags, and handkerchief matched, and she wore diamond solitaires on her fingers and ears. She loved a good party, and when her father-in-law was hospitalised at age ninety-two, she began planning the bhog lunch that a life well-lived is sent off with.

'What would you like? Jalebis or dal halwa?'

'Don't be a miser,' I thought, 'why can't you have both?'

The old sardar recovered for another few years that were bound to be too long for Miss India, but the joke survived it all: 'Miss India was planning her father-in-law's wake, and he returned fitter than before, embarrassed about the mediocre, miserly lunch she had planned. Ha ha ha.'

*

The Civil Hospital and Police Lines were opposite us, and there was generally a buzz to watch from our rooftop terrace. The melancholy melody of the evening retreat bugle lingered and hung over dusk and in my heart until nightfall was brightened with electricity. My father and I both loved very well-lit homes. Some days, when he was very careful about the lights and switched off many lights and fans, were the days I knew the bill had arrived, and he was stressed about money. I still like all the lights, even though I know of the environmental issues. A poorly lit evening saddens me.

We had two picnic spots close by. One was a children's park with an artificial hillock that we thought was a long trek until, as a grown-up, I saw it was a mere gentle mound.

When the swings and slide were set up, it was momentous enough even for our parents to come with us, and my first ride on the slide was on Jindo's lap. A rare moment when he was in particularly good form.

We would sometimes carry a picnic to an English cemetery, the most famous occupant of which was the British Commander-in-Chief of the imperial troops, General Anson, who died here on his way to Delhi to curb the 1857 mutiny.

Sardar Mann Singh, too, would have ridden over this way to Delhi.

Outside Karnal was built an artificial lake called Uchana, then the name changed to Chakravarty after a Haryana governor, and now is Karan Lake. But the actual place of the myth of Karan is just a dirty little park called Karan Tal that squats in a cramped bazaar buzzing with floral cheenth in green, hot pink and red, freshly woven durries dyed in bright colours hanging to dry in the sun, and the air roiling with the smell of spices, gur, and achar.

*

Ganeve, Jindo, and I booklined our world for comfort. We would visit Delhi for our paperbacks from Janpath and many magazines. Papa was a member of a U.K. book society. Bibiji subscribed to some Punjabi magazines, and Mama subscribed to *Woman and Home,* the monthly arrival of which, rolled up in a broad paper band, was a highlight for me. I used to love opening it to the promising, attractive, floral, picturesque English world of cardigans, and coats and tea, gardens and china and silver tea sets. It contained everything that dusty, hot, small-town Karnal was not.

My sister and I wore unique bright jumpers that our mother knitted for us from the patterns in the magazine. One that I still remember and was worn by my sister after me, then both my children and then her two, was a bright yellow jumper that she knitted for us with a bright red apple pierced through by a red arrow.

It means something only if you know the story of William Tell, the Swiss marksman who shot an arrow through an apple placed on his son's head. We were the generation and the class that thrived on such stories. It connected us to the England of *Woman & Home* in a way that the Indian English daily newspaper did not.

Later opened the Pratap Public Library, which became a retreat. We were among its first members. It was set up by Mr. Bhatia, also from Pakistan, who resettled in Karnal. A Harvard graduate, he taught economics at Kurukshetra University. I was gratified that he spoke to me as an adult long before I thought of myself as one.

'Do you have students of the type you were when you were at Harvard?'

'No.'

I knew, without him saying, that he longed for a tower of books but was chained to his landholding, larger than anything he would ever be able to buy as a professor, too large to ignore, or delegate, or give up.

The first bookshop in Karnal was Readers Paradise, and its opening was an important event of cheer. We walked there almost every other evening for an ice cream and then to browse and almost always to buy something. Papa opened a running account with them.

The owners began well. I found my Enid Blytons, and then grew to Billy Bunter, Bessie Bunter, and Victoria Holt, Jean

Plaidy, Agatha Christie, P.G. Wodehouse, Daphne du Maurier, Taylor Caldwell, and A.J. Cronin. Of the romances of Mills and Boon, and Barbara Cartland, my favourites are still Georgette Heyer, which remain at hand for rainy afternoons.

I became the empathetic friend of Maugham's club-footed protagonist in *Of Human Bondage*. Graham Greene drew me, Sherlock Holmes excited me, and Douglas's *The Robe* transported me.

Then, I moved to classical interpretations of the Upanishads, which I understood more by intuition than intellect.

The shop even stocked erotica that I bought safely because the salesperson could not read English (or so I thought). I would carry the books in a brown package and stuff them under my mattress. Emmanuelle, Nancy Friday, Venus in India, and Pearl.

Over the years, the range and quality of choice narrowed as the shop began catering to popular tastes. The erotica is not there anymore. Eventually, it dwindled to a few pulpy paperbacks, with most of the shelf space taken up by foreign chocolates, cheap perfume, Chinese toys, greeting cards, pens, and lots of artificial flowers.

There were two cinema halls and walking distance from us was Ashoka Cinema that screened English movies every Sunday. That's where I saw 'Nicholas and Alexandra' and some war movies.

I could not understand everything because I could not follow the English accents.

The Sunday English movies at school were better because the Anglo-Indian Mr. Rick used to cycle down with his projector and then explain to us what we were about to see.

The opening of a new market near the club, unimaginatively called Club Market, tested and failed Karnal's bid for modernity by the barometer of gender equality. Two women set up an ice cream shop but were driven out by male hostility and sexual harassment. They complained to the local S.P., who caught the perpetrators and paraded them with blackened faces on a donkey, but that made them even more malicious to the women entrepreneurs, who eventually closed shop.

Not ready for the empowered modern woman, Karnal, however, did accept a spiritual 'Ma'. An ashram called Arpana, run by 'Ma', became influential for its fashionable visitors from Delhi. It boasted of an excellent hospital. Their shop in Club Market sold bedsheets, pillow covers, and towels embroidered by unhappy or content inmates, united in delicate and pretty floral designs.

Since some of the ashram inmates were foreigners, I managed to access their lending library, rich with books otherwise difficult to find. It was a wrench to return *Seven Years in Tibet, The Autobiography of the Von Trapp Family*, and T.H. White's *Once and Future King*.

The National Dairy Research Institute set up in the seventies, was of some interest to Jindo. We all went to look at the cows and buffaloes tethered in large pens enclosed with feeding troughs. We bought a Jersey cow for the house. She gave milk five times a day and even won a prize for beauty and fecundity.

A picturesque-looking man called Sadhu Singh arrived from the farm to look after her. He wore a tehmat and jootis and a turban with a fold cascading down his left shoulder. He walked around the compound and fought with the servants when he was not talking to the cow.

I was received with hospitality into the pen and fed the cow barsem leaves that she tugged at playfully, watching over me with bovine affection.

The best hiding place was to lie in the cool field of standing barsem. The problem was that no one wanted to look for me so far away, so I would have to sneak back into more accessible hiding places nearer to the house.

Reading, music, and playing pithoo on the lawn with the neighbours' children were actually only distractions from the underlying brooding of the town, which made Delhi particularly attractive.

Karnal did not even have the basics of what was considered essential by many: no curtain rings (though curtains and upholstery could be bought from Panipat, the textile hub of the North), no fresh coffee, and, for a long while, no books or children's clothes, but there was a small variety of suit prints and chiffon dupattas that my mother and grandmother wore and that we sisters began to wear as teenagers.

Delhi shopping was a big affair. A trip at the beginning of each vacation for a couple of dresses and my special bespoke shoes for my feet.

'A promise breaker is a shoemaker,' I warned my father once about something he had forgotten to do for me.

'I don't mind. I will make your shoes. They are bloody expensive!' he said.

Janpath, Cottage Industries; records from the music shop in Khan Market, books from the bookshop at the same market, and cheap paperbacks from the Janpath pavements.

Lunch at Volga with a live band or at a new five-star hotel. A final trip at the close of the vacations to pack for school essentials, and the constant awareness that it must be clear to every person on the streets of Delhi that we were not from there.

Our salwar-qameezes, tailored by Multani Durzee, Karnal Bazaar, contrasted heavily with the Western casuals of the Dilliwallahs. Delhi made me feel awkward, ugly, and lumbering. I remember, for that reason, excusing myself from accompanying some rustic Punjab relatives to Delhi, who stood out in their unfashionableness even more than I did. And so, I live with the guilt of having feigned sickness for fear of being seen with them by urban friends.

Jindo noticed but did not reproach me; he understood. 'I used to be self-conscious, too,' he said, though I found it hard to imagine Jindo ever being awkward. Jindo's classic elegance could not be faulted; pleated trousers in brown or beige with plain cotton shirts and, in winter, a carefully tailored jacket by Vaish Brothers in Connaught Place.

Eventually, since my limited means denied access to the trendy fashions of the day, I learned to dress differently. My mother thought it weird and hated it, but my father enjoyed it; I wore his shirts with tight pants. He taught me to wear his ties and cravats. A sharkskin jacket was altered by Ganeve for herself.

Mama dreaded Delhi because of the high expenditure, and Jindo loved it for precisely that reason. It made him happy to buy things for us, even though we should have and could have done without them, given the meagre farm income and perpetual debt.

Notwithstanding my complex relationship with Delhi, unpacking its purchases in Karnal was an exciting and satisfying experience. The smell of coffee beans spread as a rich brown silk on which I laid out my new clothes, books, sugared buns and chicken patties from Wenger's, chocolates and sweets from Empire Stores—toys, board games and the two L.P. records that I was allowed each year.

On Christmas, Papa would get us a box of Christmas crackers that we loved pulling open for the little toy inside. We had built a collection of these toys along with the ones that came with Binaca toothpaste. It was a common sight to see Ganeve and me, crouched over separate flower pots, building houses and zoos for our animals under the foliage.

The stereo player came to my room because it was off the drawing room and could be shared by all, but it also gave me the position of privilege. The first record I played was of kirtan by Bhai Darshan Singh that someone had gifted Bibiji.

'Ah! You want to play the kirtan first,' Bibiji said approvingly as the sound wafted out to the drawing room, where she sat. But my mother guessed, 'You want to test the player first, don't you? So, your own records are not damaged if there is anything wrong.' I denied it but secretly admired how my mother saw through me but did not judge me too badly anyhow. The kirtan was followed by the finest record I owned, 'The Greatest Hits of Cat Stevens'.

I actually did love the town of Karnal and my family, but as with all close family, I loved it the most when I was away; my love was biology and environment, but not the choice of friendship. I was cruel in my knowledge that it loved me more than I loved it but made no extra effort to forge a relationship. I fought its cloying possession when I was there and yearned for it when I was away.

Reaching Karnal was to sink into the familiar stillness with a relief that lasted for a day, two at the most. Then, after a deep, restful sleep, I wanted to live again, which, for me, happened with my life in Delhi.

The house and the town sat quiet, and every person in it was left to manage their individual selves. Separate worlds sat together in still silence. Ganeve and I read. Jindo thought. Darshan knitted or embroidered or read, and Bibiji prayed, looking out at the driveway for any visitors.

A visitor arriving was exciting. Relatives stopping by for lunch or dinner on their way between Punjab and Delhi. Darshan would take out our small silver collection, gathered slowly, spoon by spoon, over the years, to transform the table into something beautiful.

Tayaji's family were also frequent visitors from Delhi and often felt they could pull rank as older city-wallahs and give well-meaning advice. 'I don't like to show off,' said Tayiji once, with a clear look of irritation at Darshan's over-effort to please a guest. 'It's just a sign of respect for you and all guests,' said the provincial Dashan.

There was always talk of the garden, and Tayiji would advise on how to create a décor that was sophisticated and did not shout rural Punjabi wannabe city. Photos should not be on the wall but on tables in the room among the flower vases. The curtains need not be so stiff; who bought the upholstery?

The blue walls of the drawing room are too loud. 'It's plastic emulsion, the best paint there is, very expensive,' Jindo would say proudly.

'Chippy, it's very odd to wear a sweater under your short-sleeved shirt,' advised Kitten at my rustic effort to show off a new top.

Tayaji and her family were generally accompanied by their black Labrador, Chipper, who chased me with boisterous friendliness, but I was scared, and my screams awoke Tayiji from her siesta. She scolded me in English that I could not understand, except the words 'cream of society'.

For me, cream resonated as the swirling smooth white on Mama's culinary creations, and I did not see the sense of her telling me about it while scolding me about being scared of a dog. Later, I realised the lecture was about how the upper classes loved dogs.

Around the seventies, a common sight in Karnal was children swinging a small red cup to catch a little ball threaded to it. It announced that the child had visited the Asia Fair. We, too, visited the newly opened Pragati Maidan that opened us to a world. At the German Pavilion, Ganeve and I were gifted a bag with colour-pencils and books: our first direct foreign acquisitions.

# 43. Karnal Changing

Various British reports describe the principal families of Karnal; first, the Kunjpura family. About fifty years later, Nawab Liaqat Ali of Kunjpura would become the first president of Pakistan.

The *Chiefs of Punjab* treatise describes the Shamgarh family. The sardar of the family is mentioned as 'a well-behaved man, but he has unfortunately run into debt, and he and his brother do not live on good terms with the neighbours'. It was an old feudal family with many backstories of murder and intrigue.

We grew up aware that refugees like ourselves could never match the wealth of the Shamgarhs as an oorikey family. The Shamgarhs lived in a fort just outside Karnal. The current Sardar's daughter studied with me in college and described the pastoral charms of her home to the girls. 'Home-made milk, home-made eggs, everything home-made,' she would boast as we smirked, but she was not wrong; they had their own dairy and poultry farm.

They were not unfashionably provincial, either. Her grandmother drove a Fiat car, from which she stepped out in a pastel salwar-qameez with a matching handbag and shoes. I was quite fond of the old sardar, though he was said to have called Jindo a social parasite. Neither Jindo nor I believed it since the Shamgarhs were essentially of the same stock and lifestyle as our own.

The most recent conversation with the current Sardar ended on an amusing note: 'No one cares for history any longer, and achievement seems to be measured by the number of showrooms owned by a family. Thank God, we have none.'

Then there are the sardars of Sikri. The English Gazetteer reports that 'Tilok Singh, a twenty-three-year-old sardar had received the estate upon his father's death in a very embarrassed condition'. The later sardar, Atam Parkash, had attended

Aitchison Chiefs College, Lahore, with Jindo and they remained friends. In any case, they obviously managed the farms well over the years, as he educated four daughters at Welham and two sons at fine boarding schools as well.

The sardarni was a tall, handsome, English-speaking woman who managed the farm. Sardar preferred to listen to music and read and play with the children. He listened to Creedence Clearwater Revival, and I first heard 'Heard it Through the Grapevine' on a cassette that his daughter loaned me.

When we visited Sikri, we always took with us large quantities of Britannia bread because there was none to be had in their village.

Given the importance of Karnal to the British, it has two churches: one inside the bazaar and one in what must have been the cantonment area until the British moved the army camps to Ambala.

It says something about my limited life in Karnal that I visited one of the churches only in 2014. It is an attractive gothic-style building set on a vast ground. It seats about fifty. There is no resident chaplain. Hindu nationalism was on fresh, unprecedented rise, and several churches had been attacked all over the country. The caretaker of this one was too worried to speak to me.

The much-venerated Karan Tal was drained by the British to deal with the mosquito problem. They also forbade rice cultivation because canal water had been diverted to form a marshy field that was good for rice but created a malarial cloud over the town. Now, a marble plaque marks a Karan Tal revival project.

Then, of course, there is Kurukshetra.

On a recent visit, I took some pictures but could not capture—and nothing can describe—the untidy mess of trying to draw a myth into history.

There is a tree with the sign: 'Ancient Shiva Temple Witness of Foreign Invasions'. There is a modern marble structure with a stone inscribed, 'One who has not controlled one's mind and senses can have no intelligence, no power of concentration, and no peace, and how can there be happiness for one lacking peace of mind.'

This is where the Gita is said to have been expounded, but the aesthetic does not differ from that of the printed brochure that gives us this information.

A respectably old-looking (about seventy years) banyan tree bears a sign of a lurid yellow with the following inscription in red and blue, 'Immortal Banyan Tree: Witness of Celestial Song Bhagwad Gita'; the misspelling yet another slipshod mark in an inaesthetic environment.

We have to take off our shoes. My heels are asking to be lifted, which my lumbering, flat-footed walk cannot achieve, and so, toes curling squeamishly, I wade through mush. 'This place has been here a long time?' I ask the lady in charge of the shoes, sitting beside her on the pavement as I wipe my feet.

'*Arrey nahee*! It's brand new.' That is the most honest comment on the place.

Some people call themselves guides, but nothing about them makes you think they know anything other than the newly constructed stories passed off as mythology to make a point of Hindu greatness in ancient India.

For ten rupees, you can pick up a gaudy brochure with Krishna and Arjuna in layers of multihued garments, heavy crowns, and big jewels in the ears, chains clasping neck, arms, and waists that they want you to believe were traditional battle dress. The first page in Hindi says, 'To say, "I will go to Kurukshetra and stay there" washes all sins away.'

The obsession to wash is reduced to a travesty in this place of stagnant, smelly water.

There are 360 pilgrimage places in Kurukshetra, tells the author of the pamphlet, and the reader will look up in disbelief and look around and despair. There are only new buildings and new sarovars, like in an amateur attempt to 'make' antique furniture. The stagnant water of a huge sarovar has steps along which there are hundreds of beggars. People are cooking and sleeping, and some are washing clothes. It is an attempt to create the ghats of Banaras, but the construction is not complete, and there are no construction workers, just people who seem to be paid to sit there and look like pilgrims to an ancient land.

Outside, there are calendar art pictures of devis and devtas available for purchase. I buy a Shiva with a beard. The guidebook tells me that all the Sikh gurus visited here.

It does not tell the Sikh version that Guru Nanak came to visit during the Magh Mela and threw water towards his farm, saying that it should reach just as they expected that the water they were throwing would reach the sun and their ancestors. No one mentions that Guru Nanak cooked meat at the Magh Mela here.

The end of the book has two pages of sales advertisements for charms that claim to make you healthy and wealthy and happy, and also a magical ring and some other cures for joint pains, and impotence, and remedies for a 'vigorous' sex life.

When I visited this place as a child, it was quiet and cool, and we had a picnic lunch under the main tree. Later, I brought my children here to tell them the story of the Mahabharata.

There are many excavations around Kurukshetra for the ancient River Saraswati. Earlier thought to be a mythical river under the waters of the confluence of Ganga and Jamuna, it is now believed that there indeed was a great river that flowed through these areas till it dried up in the desert. There is a river called Sarusti that flows through Haryana, but whether it is Saraswati or not is debatable.

Jundla and talk of history sometimes could still pierce through Jindo's obvious disinterest. He spoke about the pottery he had dug up on the farm. He talked of the F.I.R. registered at Karnal in 1857 that a police officer had shown him.

Just as then, Karnal remains adjacent to modern-day power centres of violence and corruption in Delhi and Punjab, and it seems safer, but it is also the place that one leaves for opportunity in the big cities, and not many returns to retire here.

There are some famous Karnal persons:

Sardar Mann Singh travelled here with Colonel Hodson, as if to reconnaissance the place for his sixth-generation descendants who would arrive as refugees.

During the days of Colonel Hodson, Lola Montez spent a few years at Karnal when there were tiffany parties and balls at the club that stands to this day. She later became fashionable in European society.

There is a designer who now lives in Bombay but her linen sarees are woven with tree patterns that she remembers from the dairy farm where she grew up. And the most famous resident is Kalpana Chawla, the astronaut. An important hospital is named after her and it is a landmark.

---

## 44. Secret Undertow: A Death and a Marriage

In the stillness of the house and the focus on gurbani, my family lived in awareness of the unseen while I searched for signs of it. Irrationality and eccentricity are part of the mystery of the unseen, it seemed to me, and Rajkot House encouraged it.

I used to dream of snakes and sensed their presence, which I believe symbolised my lurking fear of I know not what. A baby cobra was found emerging from an eggshell under the bookcase in the hallway of Rajkot House. They searched for the mother under the rolled up durries, the linen cupboard, and the wood and wire dirty linen basket the size of a small cupboard, the store, the kitchen, everywhere, while Jindo and I sat on the bed, retching with disgust and shivering in revulsion.

They found nothing.

Jindo hated snakes but was fascinated by their mystery (Icchadhari Nag is a thing in Hindu mythology). He claimed to have read a newspaper report of a man on a bus to Shimla who turned into a snake. He had a friend called Budum, who said he was a snake-man. Budum even told Jindo about some powerful people like him. Someone in the Rockefeller family disappeared in the desert in America and left their clothes in the car. 'They were snake persons,' Budum said.

Jindo told me of the time he had closely pruned a sickening mango tree and a snake escaped from there. Later that evening, Budum arrived and said, 'So, you have thrown me out of the house?'

'A snake listens to a firstborn,' said Tayaji, the only time I heard him say something not rational. 'I saw one once,' said Tayaji, 'and said, "Snake!" and it held as if frozen long enough for me to take a photo before it slithered away.'

His son, my Virji, has a story of a cobra in his car. He drove to Karnal, did his errands and returned to the farm, got out of the car, and saw the cobra around the gear shift. When he told the story, I screamed, shivered, and rushed to the loo to vomit. I will never be rid of this.

Then there were the weird persons we met in Karnal. There was Kundan with the booming nonsensical monologue. He would be speaking in Mananwala House and we could hear him halfway to our house. His visits to Mananwala House were announced on the servants' grapevine.

'Kundan aaya,' and we would run to listen to Kundan holding forth as the grown-ups sat on cane chairs on the lawn and we giggled, sprawling on the grass.

Then there was the daughter of the Kamala family. She was not mad but crazily exuberant, which was most odd for a woman in those days. Once, she laughed so hard at one of Bibiji's jokes that she fell on the bed, crushing a box of sweets that Jindo had brought from Delhi. That's all I remember.

Then there was Papaji Vaddey's cousin; a picture book vagabond, he came to the house carrying his clothes in a bundle tied to the end of a stick that he held on his shoulder. He stayed in a room adjunct to the servants' block in Rajkot House. All was normal till he told Bibiji that a relative had just died in an ongoing war in some remote part of the world.

'How do you know?' Bibiji asked.

'It was announced on the radio,' he said and everyone would nod and say that was very sad, while he returned ponderously slow back to his room.

I went to his room one evening and heard him at the window, talking to himself, saying he had a gun that he would shoot everyone with. I ran back to tell Jindo.

'Poor thing,' Jindo said, 'don't tell Bibiji. She will get scared and he really can't have a gun. He is harmless.'

I would listen to his ramblings every evening outside his window, loving the excitement of the danger if caught. What if he really did have a gun?

He stayed a full year, till Bibiji said he could not really be here permanently. So, one day when he was out for a walk, his clothes were packed in a suitcase and his room locked. He did not seem surprised but simply took out his clothes from the suitcase, packed them in a large kurta that he tied to the end of his stick, and left the way he came, a picture book vagabond.

He walked across to Mananwala House and lived there, probably for another year.

Bibiji spent her life in close proximity to her belief that included the paranormal, of which she had many stories. Sikh prayer included accounts of past lives as well. Guru Gobind Singh described his previous life in Bachittar Natak:

*Ab main apni katha bakanu,*
*Hem Kunt parbat hai jahan,*
*Sapt sring sobhat hai tahan,*
*Sapt sring the nam kahava,*
*Pand raj jeha jog kamava,*
*Teh hum adhik tapasya sadhi,*
*Maha kaal kalika aradhi.*

Let me tell my story,
Where there is the mountain called Hem Kund,
Where the seven springs meet,
The seven springs earned that name,
Where the Pandava raja attained yogic powers;
There I, too, did penance.
meditating on timelessness

Two Sikh soldiers followed the account to what they thought was the closest description: A snow bound place above Joshimath that was called Hemkunt.

As they wandered the area, they met a yogi who asked, 'What are you looking for?'

'The place where Guru Gobind Singh is said to have meditated in a previous life.'

'Yes,' said the yogi, pointing to a flat rock from which could be viewed the valley. 'It is here.'

The soldiers walked towards it and then turned to the yogi, but he had disappeared. This place became the site for the Gurudwara known as Hemkunt Sahib.

Bibiji, too, visited Hemkunt and claimed that a bhaiji visited her the night before to give her pershad. 'Why did you not wake me up and share it with me?' I asked, but she avoided such simple questions.

She claims that later, when she actually walked up to Hemkunt, another bhaiji called out to her to give her pershad, and she recognised him as the man who had appeared in her dream.

Then another time, Bibiji claimed she was woken up by two nihangs guarding Rajkot House during an Akhand Path.

At sixteen, I witnessed the hypnotising delusion of faith. We were on our way to Hemkunt Sahib. We spent the night before the final ascent to the gurudwara at Gobind Ghat. Ganeve and I walked to a dhaba to have a cup of tea and saw a commotion around a flag post of the khanda sahib. People were looking up devoutly and some were weeping. One man was dancing with joy.

'What's happening?' we asked.

'Oh, don't you see,' said someone. There is the baaj (hawk) of Guru Gobind Singh.

When we looked befuddled and said we don't see, they looked at us with contempt. 'You are not a true believer or you would see,' they said. And my sister and I returned to our rooms to tell our mother, who looked tight-lipped and angry and sad at the same time.

As I grew older, I became less wide-eyed with Bibiji's accounts, but her last few days made me wonder.

My wedding was less than a month away and Bibiji began sinking. The doctors advised taking her to a hospital at Delhi. In the time we spent with her in the hospital room, we all heard her mention two names that were unfamiliar to us.

'They were her playmates, but they died in Pakistan,' said Jindo.

He leaned close to her bed and listened carefully. Jindo said, *'Eh tey ho kea aye ney,'* (she has been and come back), and I felt a surge of excitement. We deciphered her mumbling. One of those dead playmates seemed to have panicked upon seeing Bibiji and said, 'Oho Bibiji, there is no place here for you.'

And then the other, a man, said 'It does not matter. We will make the place.'

Then Bibiji mumbled, 'I took some karz (debt) and said I need to attend Chippy's wedding.'

'She has been there and has come back,' said Jindo again in a matter-of-fact way.

After she was discharged from the hospital, we decided that it was practical and less stressful for her to stay with Tayaji at Delhi till after the wedding. Bibiji was deeply unhappy away from Karnal and we were torn with the dilemma of having her with us and yet managing the wedding. Finally, Jindo and my mother agreed that they could not bear it and were going to have her back in her home and they trusted she would not die at an inopportune time.

Bibiji arrived at Rajkot House and looked visibly relieved and happy. The wedding drew closer. The Akhand Path to herald the beginning of the celebrations was over and she had the pershad. She saw my wedding lehenga and I said of the jewellery: 'Is it not beautiful Bibiji?'

'Of course, it is,' she said, 'it's all mine!' and everyone laughed. She also ate her favourite mithai, balooshahi.

Then, that evening, she began sinking again. We all gathered in her room. Mama, Ganeve, myself, and Bibiji's younger brother, Kartar Singh. The doctor arrived with an oxygen tank that she waved away. Just then, Devender Chachaji arrived from Canada and came up to her and said Sat Sri Akal and she smiled and whispered Sat Sri Akal. Mama got rotis made from the kitchen for her to touch, so they could be given away to passers-by on the road. The last daan.

Her eyes wandered the room, but Jindo had left it. I followed him. 'She is looking for you.'

'I can't bear it,' he said, but returned and stood at the bottom of her bed till she closed her eyes.

Then Jindo wept. 'Today, I have lost my father and my mother.'

An hour later, drying his tears, he said, 'Bibiji's was a life well lived, and there should be no delay for you Chippy, to start your new chapter. The wedding will carry on and tell Rakesh's family not to come to condole, because that is not how they should first enter our house.'

Perhaps my unnatural situation made me react quite oddly. After the initial weeping, I wanted to move on quickly, and since the whole family of cousins and my old playmates were there for the wedding, and thus also at Bibiji's death ceremony, I came up with the bizarre suggestion that we all play pithoo like we used to. We did. And no one said anything about its inappropriateness, and maybe it wasn't.

As my father had said, one chapter of a life well-lived is closed and a new one in your young life begins.

But I had that undertow of superstition. During my wedding mehendi, I accidentally threw off the mithai placed on my lap. 'Mama what to do?' I cried.

'Just put it right back,' she said.

Then, at the pheras, Rakesh's sehra, placed in my lap as another ritual to symbolise being the repository of the family 'honour', slipped to the ground as I stood up, but this time I quickly put it back, making no sound. My phulkari, which symbolises a bride, tore just as I was leaving the house in my doli.

During the wedding, Jindo would, every once in a while, withdraw from the buzzing activity.

My friend Abha said, 'Your father is walking around in the crowd as if it is someone else's wedding,' and I laughed and said, 'It is okay. That is how he is.'

I was proud when Jindo served dinner because the baarat was unacceptably late and proceeded to bed.

I woke him up from a sound sleep when the baarat finally arrived. His eyes bleared open, 'Ask Bha to receive them,' and he would have turned back to sleep had I not used my full body weight to pull him out of bed.

All the girls in our family, except for my cousin Pitty, married somewhat outside what was conventional for the times. I remember another ghastly relative, suggesting to our grandmother that the girls in our family were just too comfortable to want to leave for our married homes.

My father was, of course, was quite certain that he did not mind if I never married. You will work and supplement with what you inherit, which will make you independently comfortable. You will throw lovely parties and become an important socialite and people will say, 'What! You have not been invited to Chippy's party?'

My husband was a contrast to Jindo in height and build and he was as hardworking as Jindo's addiction to inactivity.

Four years later, Ganeve dropped the bombshell that she wanted to marry someone born into a Muslim family. Jindo had no real objection and Darshan had no choice but a sulky acquiescence because the girls and Jindo were together. She wanted the wedding in Delhi to avoid the scandal of a Sikh-Muslim marriage.

Jindo said the wedding would happen in Karnal to demonstrate family support. The ceremony was with verses from the Quran and prayers from the Guru Granth Sahib sung with special reference to Allah. *Avval Allah noor upaye kudrat key sab bandey.* (There is one great universal flame, all beings are of that.) The marriage was registered under the secular Special Marriage Act.

After Jindo's release from Bibiji's ownership, he and Darshan were free to travel a bit with Ganeve. I was too caught up in work and inherited Jindo's lazy resistance to break from the comfortable rut of my routine. Court, home, walk, conferences, reading and writing and sleeping at any window of opportunity. But my two children gave my parents much joy and I sent them to visit even without me.

Time passed. My life in Delhi became busier between children and work.

'Why don't you come here sometimes, Papa?' But Jindo did not want to. He hated leaving the comfort of the house and thrust himself deeper into the bed and sag of the sofa that he lay on as a change from the bed, when Mama insisted that he make some change, at least to where he sat.

In these years, the only way to draw Jindo from his separate space was to talk of the occult. Rakesh used to be amused by such talk till we shared an experience that he could not explain. Mama was brought to Delhi because of an overwhelming weakness caused by a bleeding ulcer. It was the only time she came to Delhi, lying in the backseat of the car while Jindo sat upright in front. The doctors advised immediate surgery. Rakesh and I were asked to go to Karnal to pick up her medical reports. We reached at night and were to leave at four the next morning to bring the records in time for the operation at eight a.m.

We decided to wake up at three a.m. We both awoke to the front door banging. I sprang out of bed and opened the door. There was no one. It was past three a.m. I called out to the cook, Heera, who said he had overslept as well. Who had banged on the door? He had not, and could not fathom who had. Even

Rakesh could not say anything when I claimed that Bibiji had woken us up, so we would reach Delhi in time with the records. When I told Jindo, he was not surprised.

Later, Mama's story was interesting. She said she dreamed that Bibiji was looking fearsome with her hair loose and trying to catch her. Mama said, 'I ran away, saying you can't catch me.' Mama said she was then sure that she was going to get well.

Then Rakesh died of a heart attack one October morning at three a.m. My parents arrived; My parents sat quietly in the hubbub, not intruding or directing, a couple silently grieving for their widowed daughter and a son in law who they loved dearly for his unassuming friendliness and openly declared love for me. Papa refused to see the body, saying he wanted to remember Rakesh alive. He just said that. That's all. No tears. My mother wept and said, 'What kind of old age will we have now?' and I remember being irritated that she seemed to have made it about herself. But yes, their presence first propped me up and later nourished me; I did not feel entirely bereft.

My mother even managed some humour when she said, 'You will be fine, you will have to work harder, I guess. Can't do any acting now,' and we both burst into quiet hysterical laughter in my bedroom. She meant my passion for theatre that Rakesh had supported in a way that my parents had not.

My father watched me closely for many months and would complain to Ganeve, 'You say she's handling it but why hasn't she started smiling?'

As to the others, there is no dearth of savage crude relatives, I thought when I heard later that one of Jindo's cousins had commented that it served us right for having a wedding so soon after a funeral, meaning my wedding two days after Bibiji's death.

There was a lot of unpleasant behavior on Rakesh's parents' part that made me want to leave after his death. My father agreed with me, but it is because of my mother that I stayed. It is she who said it would be kind of me to continue there because they were broken.

But later, I felt that the kindness was not appreciated, and they resented my continuing to stay at their house. My children were loved by them, but then the children began asking me whether the house was theirs and could they continue to stay there. That's when I decided to leave. If my children were insecure about living in that house, it means someone had told them, their home was not theirs.

Truth be told, I have still not felt grief because I was dealing with the stress of being a single parent and balancing my checkbook to get them the best education that I could, to be with them and make them happy and secure. I could not grieve. The grief of losing a father is for them to write about.

My father died, as is inevitable in old age, at eighty-five. He could have made it to his nineties, perhaps, but that's not the point. The point is that the loss of a parent in gentle transition is a blessing for them and us. My parents did not want to be a burden. They were not. They made me who I am. And it is because of them that I could negotiate a career and be a single parent. They made me believe I could do anything.

Truth be told, I believe that Rakesh would certainly have married again, because he would have felt the need to have someone look after the children. That is fine. I would not resent that, but just smile because, truly, as I saw in my own family and with Rakesh, a woman can actually do better on her own.

My grandmother was my hero and she had been widowed at the same age that I was. Sometimes, I felt that Rakesh was my grandfather reborn. He had the same characteristics. He was unusually short, brilliant but balanced, and hardworking and loving. He was so benign that he would be a boring character for a book, but he had a great sense of humor, and sometimes, would be funny like Rowan Atkinson and he made me laugh a lot.

Rakesh was unlike Jindo. Jindo was not a great husband at all because he did not make an effort for Darshan. He was a great father though, and changed himself for us to the extent he could, but no more. He was difficult even for us.

Jindo's father, my grandfather, was a good father to Jindo and he would remember him and talk about him. But Bibiji never did. I think she enjoyed being a matriarch and enjoyed her freedom of no accountability to a man.

There is a grief and loss that is life itself—the organic changes of losing loved ones in the natural course of events. Then there is the shock of losing a spouse too soon and then spending time recovering the balance of the boat that is rocked by losing the partner who was paddling with you.

And then there is the grief and loss of the parent who has lost a child. It is pure loss, and it has no stress: it has only heavy clouds and no sight of light. That's how I imagine it. My mother-in-law, after twenty-five years, still cries when she talks of her beloved son and despite the fact that I did not get on with her, my heart reaches out to her.

The shock of confronting death at thirty-six, as I had never done before, made me numb. I read many books and consulted many psychics, only yearning to know that there was a bigger picture. I found it somewhat comforting, but how and what that is, is another story. I can tentatively say, I do believe there is a bigger picture. But the post-traumatic stress disorder in me fears that I don't want this knowledge tested.

I would talk to Jindo about my interest in the occult. 'Have you met any mediums to connect with Rakesh?' he asked me.

I told him of Agnes, who said she sensed Rakesh's presence in the room along with Bibiji. 'He is here, with an old lady wearing a white dupatta, who says she is your grandmother.'

'Yes, my grandmother wore a white dupatta,' I said.

'She says she went through the same experience as you,' said Agnes.

'Yes, she, too, was widowed at about thirty-six,' I said.

'Rakesh says to concentrate on the work and the money will follow.'

'Yes, that is the kind of thing he would say,' I said.

'I am not very good with Indian names but is there someone called Veejay?'

'Yes. My cousin.'

'Your grandmother says he is going to have a setback but not to worry it will be fine.'

'What setback?' I asked.

'Can't say,' Agnes says. 'Setback is the message.'

I was irritated that even when visiting me in my grief, Bibiji would leave a message for her only and hence beloved grandson.

A few days later, I visited another medium, an Englishman visiting India. He made all kinds of hazy and predictable, general comments except for a precise description of my wedding.

But then, yet again, Bibiji was there with Rakesh, and then came the clincher. 'I am not very good with names but does Veejay mean anything to you?'

I gasped. 'Yes!'

'He will have a setback but all will be well.'

I left in a daze. Impossible that the two mediums would have met to discuss me and my problems and my visitors from the other world. Neither one of them had written my name down. It was not a formal system like a doctor's clinic, with files etc. Vijay did have a setback and he did get past it.

Then came another medium to the house, a Muslim man. He read the kalma and told me that Rakesh says he forgives me and has advised me not to drive. 'Forgive?' said I. 'Forgive? Who is he to forgive? I have to forgive him for leaving me stranded. And not to drive? I need to drive! I have to drop the children to school and I can't afford a driver. How can I not drive?'

A few days later, I knocked into a stationary car because I was harassed and miserable and lacking in focus.

Another time, I drove the children seriously and absolutely under the influence because I had drunk wine straight after a workout without eating. I awoke the next day, horror-struck at how vulnerable my sleeping babies had been with me at the wheel. I got myself a driver.

My friend Kadam told a story about Rakesh in the car while she drove my children somewhere and nearly ran into a truck. She says she felt Rakesh grab and turn the wheel in the opposite direction and heard him saying, 'Watch it! Those are my children in your car.'

Jindo believed all of that. He loved these stories, though Darshan worried that he would spiral back into hallucinations.

Tayaji, too, had a story. One morning, he announced that his older Mamaji had died because he saw him in a dream, walking up a mountain path. 'There was another man ahead of him; his face covered by a cloth,' said Tayaji.

Within a few hours, news reached us that Mamaji had died and his cook of fifty years had died a few hours before him.

'That's very stylish,' Jindo said, 'that the cook should go ahead to prepare his meal.'

Jindo seriously told us that Prince Charles was his chhotey Mamaji Jaswant Singh reborn and that Jindo was also somehow related to the House of Windsor. 'How come you are here, then?' I asked, 'and not in London, with the Queen?'

'I don't know. Hardship posting, I guess.'

Occult stories made life interesting; about the woman who died young and remembers being taken by two men to a place where there was another man, who said, 'No, not this one. You are mistaken.'

And the two men quickly returned but her body has already been cremated, so, she says, 'They locked me in a room.'

'That is clearly a womb,' Jindo said.

She was reborn in a nai's house. She would not settle and would keep crying for someplace where the train passed her house.

Finally, when she was about four years old, her parents took her to a village that matched her hazy description. She ran ahead and recognised her house, parents, and even pointed to the place where she had kept her embroidery scissors, which they said they could not find after she died.

'You met her?' I asked Jindo.

'Yes,' he said, 'she has been to this house and met Bibiji. She said the memory is fading, and she is happy, but sometimes regrets that she was born to a family of Nais when she should have been in a Jatt family.'

'Gosh! There are mistakes there, too?'

---

# 45. Now

Bapuji and Bibiji of Mananwala House are gone. Their son Zorawar died an untimely death, and now there is only his widow, Sonia, and Jamiat, their son. Sonia has quietly transformed the house to a new sophistication, and she is my new companion during my Karnal visits as if to replace my playmate cousins there. She and I go for long walks to N.D.R.I., and she tells me the current Punjab and Karnal stories that are unexpectedly racy. So-and-so and so-and-so are seeing each other. Such-and-such marriage is on the rocks; so-and-so has a child as a single father, but we are not sure whether she is adopted or his own. Have you been invited to such-and-such wedding? What are you wearing? I will go if you go. Come and see the new jewellery I have bought, though, of course, it's pointless to buy because nothing compares to what was old. Yes, such-and-such place is still good for phulkari embroideries. You should order it now for your children's weddings, they won't be available later.

The Butalia generation is gone. The grand old Butalia Sardar, Papaji Vaddey's coffee and movie friend, Mama's friend Rani Aunty and her genial, gentle husband Uncle Mohan are gone. Their sons have sold the house to a politician. A restaurant with depressing fluorescent lights on empty tables was opened on the property but did not do well because, I believe, the Butalia ghosts (particularly Rani Aunty) will not tolerate mediocre food in their house.

Jindo would sit up in his bed overlooking the garden wall behind which he watched the construction of a mammoth building. What was the old, grand police housing and offices, which identified our road as 'Police Lines', are being dismantled to build a hospital named after one of the most famous residents of Karnal, Kalpana Chawla, who died in a blaze in the outer skies.

The dust of the construction settles on the leaves of the trees in our garden. Traffic is difficult, and the building activity continues through the night, lit up by tube lights tied to high poles to shine on noisy cranes the size of a small house.

Big shady trees have been hacked, and the landscape is as if the pain and memory of Karan and the refugees are being excised to build over anew. Old residents around the area are inundated with displaced monkeys. Now, many trees are falling or dying around the city. The famed mango orchard along the main Mughal Canal is reduced to a page in a gazette, and even its memory is clouded by the smell of a sewage dump.

The dairy farm has some trees along the avenues; the Nilgai eat up the crops as their natural habitat is consumed by farming and construction. Our farm is troubled by Nilgai, too, but because of the uncomfortably close nomenclature to gai, we leave them alone, hoping something will be left for us to harvest.

## 46. The Final Giving Up

Jindo settled into a quiet, leisurely routine of reading and talking to us on the telephone. The walks in Karnal had long stopped, but when he went to Shimla for the summer months, he and my mother would walk up to the mall daily, have a coffee at the club there, buy bread and chocolate eclairs and pastries and patties if the grandchildren were with them and walk back by lunch.

Then, as they got older, they would stop to rest on a ledge on the roadside at a picturesque spot overlooking a deep blue-green grove of deodar trees.

Then they got older and began taking a bus back. I did not like the thought of them on a bus, but they had become frugal about small expenses. 'Papa, I am going to make enough money to buy you a Mercedes,' I said.

'How nice of you to say so,' he said, uncharacteristically formal. And then, 'As far as I am concerned, I have got it by your saying so.' And I had to be satisfied with that.

Jindo was sinking into the quicksand of his mind. He had become stubborn about not getting out of bed, and we learned to leave him alone. Any Good Samaritan who lectured him about the virtues of an active life was made to feel awkward for his pedestrian morality.

Jindo moved to the downstairs bedroom that had been mine after Papaji Vaddey. A large three-seater sofa and two single sofas were arranged alongside and around his king-sized bed. Darshan moved into a smaller room with a connecting door.

In Rajkot House, Jindo would sometimes come to eat at the dining table till even that minimal movement stopped. His meals were served in his room, where we would eat with him.

He loved company when it came but made no effort to seek out anyone. The people who visited were truly affectionate because no vested agenda could be served by meeting Jindo but for humour. He had no power, influence, or money to give away.

But how to explain Jindo's health to the world?

'How is your father?'

'Oh! Very well,' we would say to bewildered friends and family.

I started getting irritated by the questions and would say, 'As well as can be.'

Jindo was reading and watching the T.V. and receiving visitors and Darshan stayed healthy and well with the support of her lady friends, but a disturbing judginess about people was beginning to unnerve us.

Darshan answers a phone call. 'Oh,' says a meddling, inquisitive lady, 'how nice you are sitting next to your husband.'

She is irritated. 'I am always here,' she says.

She told me of the conversation, and I said, 'You don't have to tell anyone where you are. It's not their business, and we don't owe anyone an explanation.'

But Darshan suffered from the syndrome of most women, including myself. Anxiety to be right, to be good, not to be spoken about badly. To be super moms and as close to perfect at anything else. Perform, excel, but avoid risk: just the careful plodding of each step to be just so.

Around the same time, while Darshan and us girls were anxiously balancing our lives to deal with this man called Jindo, who we loved despite him being horrendously difficult, a self-righteous couple, concerned about the good behaviour of all, met me in Delhi and asked whether I had abandoned my parents. Too shocked by the blatant, ill-mannered intrusion of the question, I could not even say that it was none of their business.

Seething, I called up Jindo. 'You must be playing the victim and telling the world that you are lonely, Papa. Please remember it is your call that you don't want to move, and we are respecting it.'

'Never, never, never will I let down my family by complaining about them to the world at large. I have no complaint. I have lived to see your shaan (success) and that you live a lifestyle without any financial help from me. That cannot be said about many men, so why should I complain?'

I was quiet. Of course, he was right; maybe it was my guilt, maybe I should be in Karnal more often. The children and I had just spent two weeks in Europe and reached Shimla, where another self-righteous aunt, chin stretched long with disapproval, told us that being with old parents was more important than exotic holidays. Darshan, seeing me gather my wits to frame an acerbic response, silenced me with that one glance that has worked well with Ganeve and me since we were little.

Should an entire holiday be spent with old parents? Maybe, according to some, but we are glad we did not and I am prepared that my children will prefer to spend their holidays with their families that need not always include me. I did the same. I had not submitted to the stultifying boredom in Karnal during Bibiji's reign. We worked hard in Delhi and partied harder.

The parties became frenzied with a desire to make up for stagnant time in Karnal. I needed to encompass two extremes within myself. The quiet discontent of Karnal and the frenetic social activity of Delhi that, too, brought no peace.

Ganeve was more caring; the travelling that the parents did was with her. I found the contrast between home and my independent self too wide to manage, apart from my own laziness. I spent time torn between anguished boredom in Karnal for too long and yet unhappy about being away. Even after I got married and had children, as I write this, Karnal is my home.

I understood Jindo's anguish. He had spent more than three-fourths of his life in free India, but home was Rajkot Gujranwala, near Pakistan.

At least I had the base of Karnal to return to as and when I wanted, I persuaded myself.

My visits were becoming shorter as I worked the treadmill routine of work at Delhi. Sometimes, I would visit just for the day. Mama would say, 'Your father is asking for you. You must call every day.'

I did: every evening, Jindo, and every morning, my mother.

Conversations with him were still funny. 'What are you doing?'

'Shitting.' And then a loud laugh.

'But otherwise, it's nice hearing your voice. I love you.'

Mobile phones helped. I received a message from Jindo:

- How are you?

I felt a wave of emotion similar to the time of the surprise visit in boarding school.

- I am in court. Very nervous. Tough case, I messaged back.

- I will pray, Jindo messaged.

Then he got confused with the dictionary mode that would form its own words faster than Jindo's painstaking tapping.

He lost interest, and then his fingers lost their flexibility, and the boredom set in once again. 'Come and see me. I keep thinking of the things you used to do and say as a child,' he told me.

Once it was, 'I am feeling neglected.'

'Sorry, Papa, but I am really caught up.'

'Of course.'

Another time, 'I think I am going to die.'

'Don't be dramatic, Papa. Anyhow, please postpone death to a convenient date.' Laughter.

'I will come soon,' and then a quick visit to Karnal always ended with him saying as a ritual that I began to dread.

'*Jaldi aaya karo,*' do come and see me regularly.

'Of course, Papa,' but I knew I would not be able to visit as often as I should or even as often as I liked to. I missed them painfully, but extraction from Delhi was stressful because of work and sometimes a desire to do a different type of holiday, or simply the desperate need to stay in Delhi to do nothing for that one day in a frenetic week, to loll in bed, no bath, play the sitar, perhaps watch T.V., read a book.

The tide of ebbing visits changed with a phone call while I was in court. My mother had collapsed in the morning and was in hospital. I reached Rajkot House by three p.m.

'She is fine,' Daljit Singh told me on my cell phone as I drove into Karnal, 'you can have lunch at the house and then come to the hospital.' So I went to Rajkot House for a quick bite. The flavour of the dal and phulka and achar made intense with the relief that Mama was going to be all right was tinged with the guilt of not being able to hold my hunger till after visiting her.

After eating, I looked into Jindo's room. He was lying silently in bed, staring at the ceiling.

'Have you been to see her?' he asked first thing.

'Not yet. I just grabbed a bite before going because Daljit said she was okay, but I have not eaten since the morning.'

He smiles like he sees my weakness and is a little disappointed by my self-absorption but loves me too much to say anything.

But Darshan understood. The moment I walked into the hospital room, she asked, 'Have you eaten?' I felt my tears at the generosity of a mother who knows her daughter's weakness—not being able to fight hunger or sleep—like Jindo himself.

I returned from the hospital, 'I am sorry, Papa. I will never leave you alone for a long time like I have been doing. I realise the importance of visiting. I am sorry.'

'You don't have to be sorry,' said Papa, shy and sad and loving.

Ganeve and I were comfortable and confident in the knowledge that our father was in Daljit Singh's special care. From chauffeur to farm manager to all-encompassing caretaker of our lives, Daljit Singh symbolised all that was good, strong, reliable, and worthy in our lives. He had arrived when I was four, and we spent as much time under his watchful eye as with our parents.

Every day, he arrived on his bicycle to bathe and dress Jindo, instruct the servants, shop for fruit and vegetables (no one else had that eye), maintain the car, make renovations in the house, repair any machine, find any lost article, use a sewing machine to run up a new curtain, cook a kebab or a kheer or a vegetable or a meat curry for a special occasion, serve the guests, drive us somewhere, play with our children, as he had earlier with us. They loved him and called him Bha, and we loved how he called them 'ji'.

Then, one day, just six months before Jindo died, Daljit was hospitalised for sugar fluctuation. Jindo called him, 'Don't go without me, yaar.' Daljit laughed and said he would not. He died in May 2014.

Ganeve told me on the telephone. 'Where are you?' she asked.

'In court,' I said.

'Sit somewhere as I tell you.'

Minutes before dying, Daljit Singh took out a notebook with details of our farm and house: relevant telephone numbers and a list of routine chores divided into groups of daily, weekly, monthly, and annual tasks, and so on. He also handed over the key to his cupboard in Rajkot House. Jindo would need more than a cook; an establishment runs around him, and Daljit may have gone ahead to set that up and ensure that all was just so.

Daljit Singh's son came to work in his father's stead. The relationship now proceeded into the third generation, but a lot had changed. The son is computer savvy, and it is his daughter, Simran, who has gone to Canada for higher studies. She will probably have a better education than us.

Papa dealt with his loss by refusing to talk about Daljit Singh. Staff were the blood of the house; there may not have been enough money to travel and buy more clothes, but even a meagre income must feed and house them. They must be loyal, and that was possible only if they and their families were happy.

That is why Jindo would ask a new servant, '*Khush ho? Dil lag gaya?*'

It was about *dil*: life was measured by the response of the heart; the heart was good where there was barqat—open kitchens and generosity invited barqat, and so were good for the heart.

Daljit Singh's death hastened Jindo's withdrawal deeper into an inner world. He ate minimally and walked not at all. He prayed without any overt signs of doing so, met visitors with detached affection, and when someone wished him well, he said, in that case, they should pray that he dies soon and dies peacefully.

When I read about Mann Singh, I castigated Jindo for his grieving dislocation. Sardar Mann Singh must have stayed in one place for only a few decades.

'I am not uncomfortable with this, Papa,' I said, 'there is no dislocation because we carry our stories within us, and that is a much more practical way to travel—not bound to anything.'

We would be truly civilised if we had the right to build a continuous family through generations and time. And here, the law took away the right. We were displaced from our homes, security, and lacked tenure in our property, all by legal processes that we have to presume to be 'due' because it is by the government and all for the cause of the new country.

But the power structure remains the same. The politician behaves as horrendously as the old zamindar. An M.P. beat up a sixty-year-old Air India employee for not giving him business-class seating.

Ganeve and I raged and worried about such things over the years, but Jindo became quiet. He lay down. That is all.

His only lesson was, 'Don't lie; I have never lied. Even if they cut me to pieces, I will not lie.' But never could you call him boringly earnest in his truth. His crazy bent of mind made him unpredictable, like the joker in the pack, but for all that, he remained transparently straightforward.

'Such-and-such thing has happened,' someone would say.

'What rubbish! Who said?' another relative would say

'Jindo,' would be the reply.

'Oh, then I guess it must be true.' And that was final.

And since this is about Jindo's family, it is true that this is indeed a story of privilege—and a laziness that does not fight to stay relevant—but it is also a graceful acceptance of anonymity as the way to be truly free. I understood from him that 'if freedom is in being rooted to ancestral land, loss of ability to move is also to be unfree'.

With and through Jindo, I have seen the dusk of a type of life; the cloth shop owner bringing home yards of material, knowing Bibiji will buy something for his trouble; he is followed by the tailor with measuring tape and notebook. Sometimes, we visit the tailor, originally from Multan. He is overworked and tells us our order will take ten days, and we walk off in a huff only to return shortly because no one knows us the way he does. He fights us girls on the necklines as well. 'Masterji, make it wider and deeper,' we say. 'This is enough, Biba,' he says, and our mother looks at him gratefully.

One other tailor was a Sikh from Rajkot in Gujranwala. He was given our best orders to make, but we had to be patient with him because he had no sense of deadlines. A bottle of rum worked as an incentive only sometimes. Once he turned up a year after my order to check if my measurements had changed, but my muslin angarakha was worth the wait. I had never seen a cut or stitch like that Masterji had.

It was the time of a special relationship with the family doctor, whose visits to our house would extend to a very quick cup of coffee and a chat. He worked at the civil hospital that had many a story. Once, he said, a rustic man said, '*Daatar Sahib, ai tharmameter ghanta ho gaya kucchh main.*' (Doctor Sahib, I have had this thermometer in my armpit for over an hour). Doctor Sahib said, 'Really?' and reached for it to find a cloth-wrapped dattun, a neem stick used to clean teeth. Someone must have stolen the thermometer. Doctor sahib and my father's laughter resounded from the verandah.

We had open running accounts with every shop in the marketplace. Everyone knew that money owed would be paid. Servants got off their bicycles as we walked past. My car would not overtake Jindo's if we were, in later years, driving in a convoy. Our address was simply Rajkot House, Karnal.

It was a time of afternoon siestas, fresh, slow food, chatting over tea and pakoras, watching the rain from the verandah,

getting driving licences delivered at home and no savings—
because 'Rabb Rakha'—spending on lifestyle rather than the
acquisition of things.

One day, sitting with Papa, I felt an instinct to record those
times. So, I discovered a project: I would write about Karnal.
I would make my visits there creative. I would research at the
public library, sit with my laptop on the verandah with Jindo,
and we would discuss stories to write. He would teach me
Persian poetry. Maybe he could translate old revenue records.
Perhaps even the F.I.R., written in Persian, filed against the
'baaghis' (rebels) of 1857. But Jindo died two days later, and for
me, he merged into and became Karnal. My love, my grief, my
yearning, my heaviness, and the remedy to transcend it all, was
to write this book you hold.

I do not fight the gentle pain of nostalgia when it strikes deep
in my muscles and bones, because it connects to the essence I
share with my father.

Darshan lives in Karnal now. She is mobile in a way that she
could not be through her life. She enjoys her freedom, runs the
farm, spends time with her grandchildren, and travels. She enjoys
being an M.B.A. and deserves it. She talks to us every day and
visits us in Delhi. While Papa was alive and refusing to get out
of bed, she was constrained.

She plans our visits to Karnal, where she will serve dinner the
way it used to be at Gujranwala but has become Rajkot House,
Karnal. Chana dal and meat curry are central to the 'meeno'
(menu). There will be a pudding. She finds the energy for that
and it is still the highlight of the meal.

This last remnant of that life will eventually fade, and then
we, too, will go, but until then, life, that is also God, needs to
be lived bravely and as lightly as possible. To laugh as often
as possible is to understand that no one can take away inner

freedom and that, in the bigger picture, nothing really ends, even while nothing is permanent. Everything returns in cycles and spirals and changed forms, and that is the connected universality and those who fight and kill over religion are sorry fools, but I will try not to tell them that to their faces.

————

# Epilogue

Darshan died on 27 May 2020. It was during the Covid times. We wore masks during the funeral.

She, too, had been in good health. She was just eighty-five. Like with Jindo, here, too, I spoke to her at my usual time of seven p.m. Ganeve, a week before, had managed to secure a pass to visit her.

Here, too, we got an early morning call. Here, too, we left for Karnal at four a.m.

And we saw Mama on the bed that Jindo had lain in. She looked the young, beautiful bride who had arrived fifty-nine years earlier.

When we left the house for the funeral, the amaltash and jacaranda and gulmohur branches caressed the hearse as we passed under, showering their blossoms on her. Through the tears sogging up my mask, I remember thinking aloud: 'How beautiful.'

My mother's body did not have that aura of inner life I thought Papa's had. Her hand hung off the pyre like a delicate but very dead branch. Ganeve pointed to the hand and then gently and lovingly and carefully placed it by her side on the pyre as if on her bed. And for the second time that day, I said, now in my head, *how beautiful.*

The quarantine rules did not allow a gathering, but as the hearse drove through the streets, I saw people getting up and some bidding namaste. It was fitting and filled me with some peace because she should have been thronged by people paying respects. That's how well she was regarded. Karnal knew her personally, unlike the other members of my family, who were simply those who lived in that house. It is she who had done seva in the gurudwara, donated to charities, helped educate girls from poor families, and made marmalade and cakes for people's birthdays.

The death of this second parent marks the end of my childhood; the death of me as the child. How blessed that childhood stayed with me till I was fifty-eight.

Darshan had lost her mother, perhaps in her late thirties, and then her father when she was in her forties. She was the second of four and lost her youngest brother when she must have been in her sixties and then her older brother a few years later.

Mama lived a serious life, trying hard to cope with a family so different to hers and bringing us up as free and empowered but then struggling to understand that we were veering towards many things that she disapproved of ('fast girls'). That anxiety was exacerbated with our 'love marriages' outside the community, and to me, it seems she lived with bated breath all her life till she sighed with relief when her grandchildren were born.

She seemed to have finally stopped feeling bewildered by us and the new world and rejoiced that we seemed to have finally found our nests in a very predictable, traditional place. We had children and wanted to be 'good' mothers. When my daughter was born, I heard her laugh as I had never before.

She was a stupendous grandmother: generous, attentive, and indulgent. Our children know their grandmothers' cooking and baking as most children would know their mothers'. Her response to our children gathering around her, calling her Nani, was like watching a wilting plant revive under a cool sprinkler.

Our mother epitomised a Nani, and in her, I saw what I had

not seen when she was just Mama. She had grown into a gentle presence, finally at peace after surviving the turmoil of her earlier years with my father and her lonely struggle in the family she had been married into. After my father's passing, I saw her enjoy a freedom that I wish she could have had a bit longer.

'I only want to live till eighty-five; that's a good age,' she had said after he died. And though I laughed then, I knew that she had said eighty-five because of her husband, who she hated/loved, loved/hated and then settled into living with. That's how long he had lived.

My Tayiji arrived for the funeral and as her husband had wept for the death of his younger brother, saying it was his turn to die, my Tayiji blamed her brother-in-law, 'I know it's Jindo—he has sent for her,' and my mind whirled with wicked thoughts of patriarchy in the other world and a flash of dark humour that Tayaji had not sent for Tayiji, and what did that say about them.

My parents are gone. I am the elder and will leave, and that's how it should be. I am accepting of it as natural. I only pray that it stays that way. Because what one lives with is not fear of death but fear of that moment when everything changes, and you don't know when it will strike.

*Bagla karey kilo nadi kinare; Khelan khel aya baaj.* (The swan plays by the riverside; and the hawk pounces on it.)

*

The strangest thing happened after Mama died.

26 May was like any other day for us in quarantine times. We would occupy ourselves with our chores and books and thoughts, and in the evenings, the children and I would go to Ganeve and Yousuf in their flat downstairs for a drink and a movie. A kind friend had replenished our fast-depleting bar stock just the day before and so we all had that one extra thing to celebrate:

the absence of extreme rationing. So, when Ganeve and Yousuf came into my room at three-thirty a.m. on the 27th morning, I received the news with a very inconvenient hangover.

'Mama,' she said, and I sat up. I had spoken to my mother the night before, as usual. She was fine. She was going to eat dinner and then watch T.V.

She left just as she had lived, silently, with no inconvenience to anyone, and with her aesthetic dignity just as she had lived. I could imagine her knocking on heaven's door, wearing a beautiful floral light salwar-qameez and a generous flow of chiffon dupatta, framing her fine-boned face with delicate features in perfect balance.

We all reached Karnal, and the funeral was later that day. The few masked visitors were greeted by us, also masked, offering hand sanitisers before they came into the house.

After the funeral, we all gathered with a nourishing closeness in the house. We realised how hungry we were at the smell gliding out of the kitchen, which a relative took over until we got our bearings. The roti was hot, and the flavours of the pickle and subzi burst in our mouths as life-affirming. She went peacefully and lived a good, long life. Everyone must go, and this was surely the way we, too, would want to go when our time was up, we told each other. Who made this, someone asked. Sonya, we said as we reached for a second roti.

Now, let's have some tea, we thought as we gathered in the drawing room. So passed the day of the 27th and it flowed in the same way into the 28th. Sonya visited several times a day to oversee the kitchen. Then came the 29th, and we were better—a quiet, comfortable cheer. A parent's passing is inevitable. The going of the surviving parent is a deep tectonic shift. We were orphaned but were lucky we had each other and our own little families.

It was on the morning of the 29th that Ganeve noticed a duck flying just below the upper treeline level of the garden. How strange, she said, I have never seen a duck here. Yearning for continuity with my mother, I searched the internet for what a duck meant as an omen. I read that the dead send a sign of their presence with a bird.

We felt deep comfort and were happy for a while. In that glow, the children and I wandered into the garden, talking in little snippets of the colour of fresh green and the smell of grass, until we heard the cry that is universal as an anguished desperate call for help. Our entire bodies heard the call and we ran with every bone and muscle and skin and hair follicle towards it. In the house, we saw Ganeve standing over Yousuf lying on the floor.

The initial collective reach for life is water. Get water, throw it on his face, prop him to drink. Is he drinking? Is he swallowing? Call the doctor, no doctor will come fast enough, get him to hospital. Which is the closest hospital, where are the car keys? Call the driver—Sonya just left—call her.

Ganeve and Yousuf in one car with the cook and the driver and Sonya and I in the other arrived at Amritdhara Hospital; stretcher, emergency ward, glass partition at which we all stand: and then the curtain is drawn, and we still stand, looking at the curtain, willing it to part so we can see Yousuf. What are the chances of a second death in an already grieving household? It can't be; it's too improbable; even the wheel of life and fortune has probabilities.

I stepped away from the emergency ward and walked up and down and prayed as never before. It was a call from my being to whatever listens, if it listens. I did not want to miss the chance of a hearing in any forum.

Doctor comes: it's brain haemorrhage. The neurosurgeon has

arrived to drain the blood. Half an hour later, the procedure is done. He will live, but we don't know the extent of the damage. Go home, we are told.

We return and again reach the dining room. The children are waiting. We are given something to eat and then again, a cup of tea—strong, sweet tea—in a glass that we cradle for its warmth.

And I said, 'We saw a duck. Mama is protecting us. It will be fine.' Everyone was silent, and slowly, uncertainly, we went to bed even though it seemed too normal a thing to do. But we needed our energy. 'Conserve your energy; it's a long haul,' had been Yousuf's wise call over many a mountaineering expedition.

The next day, Ganeve was up at five-thirty a.m. and stepped onto the verandah. The duck flew low over the lawn. She told me later, 'It will be fine. Mama is reassuring us. She is not going to let anything happen to her son-in-law on her watch.'

Over the next two weeks, between thrice-a-day hospital visits to watch Yousuf inch himself out of his coma, the duck was seen a few times. With each passing day, as we became more cheerful, the duck became a blessed sight and made us smile. How ridiculous to have a duck in our landlocked small town of concrete expanding into urban mediocrity.

Yousuf arrived home after about three weeks. Daily physiotherapy, music, and a close family circle had him doing absolutely well. The day he walked in the garden by himself and broke into a light trot with the joy of freedom was when I returned to Delhi.

Two days later, my sister posted a message and some videos and photos on the family group titled 'Good Times at Rajkot House'. 'The battakh (duck) family was wandering the compound, the chicks following the mother's footsteps closely in a straight, orderly line. Sometimes, the line would stop for the last chick to catch up, who seemed a little slow. Sometimes, the father would be there, but mostly, he was on treetops, "watching out for snakes," our gardener said. A few days later, they were seen no more.'

My relationship with Rajkot House is fifty-eight years old. I have never seen a family of ducks there, and no one I know who lived there has ever seen one.

The duck family is a sign of healing by family love, I said.

A picture that Ganeve had posted she had titled, 'Battakh family.'

In those days, I had also been talking to a psychic healer. I spoke to your mother; yes, I said, trying to look normal and straight-faced. It's difficult. I believe; I don't know, and I don't think my belief is irrational. What did my mother say? I asked the psychic. 'She says she got into the car to go to the hospital (it's true she had walked to it), and she lay on the backseat and put her head on the caregiver's lap. She closed her eyes, and she saw her mother. 'I did not feel like opening my eyes again,' my mother told the psychic. That sounds just fine. I felt at peace. Her mother had died fifty years ago. That's how a parent is. Always like yesterday: just so close, even if beyond reach.

As I looked through her things, my protected halo of childhood that I had left in Karnal seeped into me and dissolved, making me complete.

Memories. Like pieces of music that I can't grasp. I just watch them float by: the comfort of the rough Harris tweed of my father's jacket. My mother's perfume, pink and beige floral, lightly reaching for me. My husband's white shirt with the barrister's collar, so proud and just so. All of us harmoniously together at a tea table in a café where plays the music of my memories.

I felt strangely healed then.

As I finish this book, I think of that last conversation when my father had wondered aloud what he had really done, and when, sensing that his final days were upon us, I had ached for him and for myself and had held him tightly and said, 'You are our link with the here before and actually you have shaped the link to the hereafter and the link is worthy and strong. We love you, Papa, and thank God for the experience of our love for you and yours for us.'

Now, sitting in my home cum office in the city, I reach for a decent (not too expensive, though Jindo would have preferred that it was) full-bodied red wine and know that the life he lived deserves that he now sits on a takht under a fruit tree beside a fast-flowing clear stream. The God within him, and outside, and all-encompassing and all pervasive, which is the entire creation as it is. It manifests in the causality of space and time, causing it to constantly become while being: that expanse is naturally benevolent, and Jindo is part of it, and managing to make it laugh. And Darshan is where she wants to be. Somewhere unexpected that is entirely, freely, her own.

# Acknowledgements

I name the following people as more than just friends. They are my energisers, who were parental in their unconditional affection towards me.

Thank you:

Ganeve Rajkotia, Pradip Krishen, Sonal Narain, Javed Gaya, Michael Dwyer, Nivedita Menon, Chatty, Kitten, Upasana Garnaik, Akhil Sibal, Aruna Ghosh, Sunil Mehra, Shalini Krishen, Philip Oldenberg, and Binoo John.

Each member of my office, who is like family to me, and who supported and enabled me to have the time to write this book.

Meru Gokhale, for her invaluable suggestions and superb editing to make this a better book; Ravi Singh, my publisher; Pragya Singh, for her very careful line editing; and Jasjit Purewal, for the title.

I am grateful to Rajeev Gupta for the lovely, evocative cover.

Most of all, thanks to Shreiya Maheshwari for her belief in my book, which gave me so much confidence, her patient attention to detail, and her dealing with many unearthly-hour WhatsApp messages as I remembered this story.

This is an account of history as received and memory as recovered. Many may think otherwise, but it is true for me and what I remember of my home and family.

# WEAVING WATER

*An autobiography*

## Ajeet Cour

### Translated by Masooma Ali and Meenu Minocha

The literary journey of this powerful voice in Punjabi Literature extends our understanding of home, moving beyond its physical boundaries to a quest for identity and belonging. *Weaving Water* is the English translation of Ajeet Cour's Sahitya Akademi Award-winning autobiography; the heartwarming and candid story of a life beset by tragedy, yet carrying a message of courage, hope and happiness.

Growing up in pre-Partition Lahore, Ajeet Cour spent a childhood wrapped in warm and enticing experiences despite her disciplinarian father. From such a beginning, her life moves on to a first true love that is lost on account of a misunderstanding; a violent, bitter marriage that leaves her with two young children to raise; the death of a beloved child, and the loss of love once again, when at last she seems to have found it. Tragedy always seems to follow her, but Ajeet Cour's story is still one of courage, hope and a sort of happiness, as she finds her eventual refuge in herself.

Ajeet Cour was born in 1934 in Lahore, migrating to Delhi in 1947. She began writing short stories as a teenager and is now the author of over twenty books, including novels, novellas, short stories, biographical sketches and translations. In 2006, she was awarded the Padma Shri for her writing and contributions to social uplift.